Bibliotheca Indo-Buddhica Series No. 93

Suttanta Pitaka

MAJJHIMA NIKAYA
Medium Length Discourses of the Buddha

TWENTY-FIVE SUTTAS FROM UPARIPAṆṆĀSA

Sri Satguru Publications
A Division of
Indian Books Centre
Delhi – India

Published by :

SRI SATGURU PUBLICATIONS
Indological and Oriental Publishers

A Division of

Indian Books Centre
40/5,Shakti Nagar,
Delhi-110007
(India)

ISBN-81-7030-294-3

Edition ; Delhi 1991

Published with the Arrangements of'Burma Pital
Association,Rangoon,Burma.'

Printed at:
D. K. Fine Art Press, Delhi.

PRINTED IN INDIA

Namo tassa bhagavato arahato sammāsambuddhassa

Veneration to the Exalted One, the

Homage-Worthy, the Perfectly

Self-Enlightened

******

The Buddha is an Arahat and he is worthy of the highest veneration. All beings including devas and brahmās venerate the Buddha because the Buddha is the Supreme One, who has extinguished all defilements, who has become perfectly self-enlightened through realization of the Four Ariya Truths, and who is endowed with the six great qualities of glory, namely, *Issariya* (supremacy), *Dhamma* (Knowledge of the Path to Nibbāna), *Yasa* (fame and following), *Sirī* (noble splendour of appearance), *Kāma* (power of accomplishment) and *Payatta* (diligent mindfulness).

Publisher's Note :
To reduce the cost of production of the book,the lost of the donors is not included in the present edition.

INTRODUCTION

The Pāḷi Texts which embody the teachings of the Buddha can be classified in two ways, either as Piṭakas or as Nikāyas. When they are classified as Piṭakas they are divided into three categories which are known as the three Piṭakas or Baskets. The three Piṭakas are the Vinaya, the Suttanta and the Abhidhamma. All these three deal with Morality (Sīla), Concentration (Samādhi) and Knowledge (Paññā). However, the Vinaya Piṭaka, which prescribes the Rules of Conduct for bhikkhus and bhikkhunīs, is concerned mainly with the observance of precepts of morality (Sīla), the Abhidhamma is concerned mainly with the study leading to Knowledge (Paññā) and the Suttanta is concerned mainly with development of Concentration. The Suttas or discourses comprise exhortations relating to observance of precepts, explanations and expositions of the dhamma leading to liberation from Saṁsāra, the round of rebirths. They are stated simply and clearly to suit the occasion and the intellectual level of the audience.

The Suttanta Piṭaka consists of five Nikāyas or Collections, viz., Dīgha Nikāya or Collection of long discourses; Majjhima Nikāya or Collection of medium length discourses; Saṁyutta Nikāya or Collection of groups of shorter discourses, connected or related in subject matter or in persons concerned; Aṅguttara Nikāya or Collection of numerically-graduated divisions and Khuddaka Nikāya or Collection of miscellaneous treatises.

When the Pāḷi Texts as a whole are classified into Nikāyas, the five books of Vinaya and the seven books of Abhidhamma are also included in the Khuddaka Nikāya.

The Majjhima Nikāya has three divisions viz., Mūlapaṇṇāsa, Majjhimapaṇṇāsa and Uparipaṇṇāsa, each paṇṇāsa containing roughly fifty suttas. To be exact, Mūlapāṇnasa has fifty, Majjhimapaṇṇāsa has fifty and Uparipaṇṇāsa has fifty two suttas, -- thus bringing the total to one hundred and fifty-two suttas. Each of the three paṇṇāsas has five subdivisions called vaggas. The vaggas from Uparipaṇṇāsa are Devadaha vagga, Anupada vagga, Suññata vagga, Vibhaṅga vagga and Saḷāyatana vagga.

The Myanmar Piṭaka Association has already published two books from Majjhima Nikāya, the first book containing twenty-five suttas from Mūlapaṇṇāsa and the second book containing twenty-five suttas from Majjhimapaṇṇāsa. The present book is a collection of twenty-five suttas from Uparipaṇṇāsa. We have chosen five suttas from Devadaha vagga, five from Anupada vagga, three from Suññata vagga, six from Vibhaṅga vagga, and six from Saḷāyatana vagga. All these suttas were translated by U Nyi Nyi. Preliminary editing of the translation was done by Daw Mya Tin with the assistance of U Tin Nwe and U Tin Wa, under the guidance of Sayagyi U Kyaw Htut and Sayagyi U Aye Naing, the chief doctrinal consultant and doctrinal consultant respectively of the Myanmar Piṭaka Association. The final editing was done by the Editorial Committee of the Association, with U Shwe Mra as chairman.

The numbering of paragraphs of the suttas is the same as that in the Paḷi text as approved by the Sixth International Buddhist Synod held at Yangon. Thus there is a gap in paragraph numbers between the suttas if they happen to be not consecutive. When the translation of the whole Paṇṇāsa is published the numbering will be consecutive.

The Twenty-five Suttas from Uparipaṇṇāsa

Many of the discourses in this collection are on the physical and mental aggregates which are the objects of Clinging, the sense-bases and the primary elements, with a view to eradicating the concept, 'My self; mine and I.' The Buddha also expounded extensively the Eight Constituents of the Ariya Path, freedom from defilements and faults, the most beneficial way of making offerings, and the importance of forbearance which eradicates ill will. In the Acchariya-Abbhuta Sutta the Buddha said to the

Venerable Ānanda, "Ānanda, let the marvellous and extraordinary phenomena concerning the Tathāgata be made evident to the fullest extent," and the Venerable Ānanda complied, giving the facts about the conception and the birth of the Buddha. The discourse on the Venerable Bākula also mentioned the marvellous and extraordinary facts concerning the Venerable Bākula, who was free from sickness throughout his life and who realized parinibbāna while sitting in the midst of a gathering of bhikkhus by meditating on the element of heat (tejodhātu), causing flames to arise from his body and consume his body leaving only relics.

The discourses in this collection, with the exception of a few, were given by the Buddha. Among the exceptions are the Gopaka Moggallāna Sutta given by the Venerable Ānanda to the brahmin Gopaka Moggallāna, the Anāthapiṇḍikovāda Sutta given by the Venerable Sāriputta to Anāthapiṇḍika on his death-bed, and the Nandakovāda Sutta which contains Nandaka's exhortation to five hundred bhikkhunīs headed by Mahāpajāpati Gotamī. Most of the discourses in this collection were given on the Buddha's own initiative in the form of straightforward exhortations or in the form of questions and answers, but some were given in reply to questions.

Discourses Given on the Buddha's Own Initiative

Bahudhātuka Sutta, Ānāpānassati Sutta, Kāyagatāsati Sutta, Bhaddekaratta Sutta, Dakkhinā Vibhaṅga Sutta, Devadūta Sutta, Mahācattārīsaka Sutta and Indriyabhāvanā Sutta may be cited as examples. In Bahudhātuka Sutta, the Buddha exhorted the bhikkhus to be wise and to have foresight, as all fears, dangers and troubles arise on account of the foolish and not on account of the wise. Here, the Buddha defined a wise person as one who is skilled in understanding the Elements, the sense-bases, the Theory of Cause and Effect (Paṭicca samuppāda), and in understanding the possible and the impossible. In Ānāpānassati Sutta and Kāyagatāsati Sutta, the Buddha taught the bhikkhus the methods of cultivating mindfulness and the advantages and benefits accruing from such practice. In Bhaddekaratta Sutta the exhortation was to contemplate the presently arising physical and mental phenomena, to meditate ardently and diligently by day and by night and to make the effort this very day, for one may die tomorrow.

In Dakkhiṇā Vibhaṅga Sutta, the Buddha showed the most beneficial way of making offerings. Once, while the Buddha was residing at the Nigrodhārāma monastery in Kapilavatthu in the country of the Sakyans, Pajāpati Gotamī brought a new pair of robes spun and woven by herself for the Buddha and entreated him to accept her offering of the robes. But the Buddha instructed her to offer the robes to the Order of bhikkhus, for by offering them to the Order she would have venerated both the Buddha and the Order. Pajāpati Gotamī offered the robes three times to the Buddha and he gave her the same reply three times. By this the Buddha showed her that an offering made to the Order is of greater merit than that made to an individual. It was also shown in this sutta that the offering is most beneficial and pure when both the donor and the recipient are endowed with morality. There would accrue a lesser degree of merit where either the donor or the recipient is lacking in purity. In the case of the seven categories of offerings made to the Order, the one made to the Order containing both bhikkhus and bhikkhunīs headed by the Buddha is the noblest. In the case of offerings made to individuals, the noblest offering is one that is made to the Buddha; next comes the offering made to a paccekabuddha; then comes the offering made to an arahat, and so on and so forth, down to the common worldling without morality. The lowest in the scale of such kind of offering, as far as merit is concerned, is that given to animals.

In Devadūta Sutta, the discourse on the messengers of death, the Buddha spoke about the destination of beings on death and dissolution of their bodies; how they arise in good or bad destinations according to their own kamma-actions, how the evil-doers have to undergo terrible sufferings in niraya. These evil-doers have not heeded the warning of the messengers of Death, such as rebirth, old age, sickness. And being unmindful they have committed evil and failed to do good deeds in their life-time. In this sutta, the Buddha spoke at length on the miseries of niraya.

The Buddha did so not solely to frighten beings with the sufferings of niraya, but primarily for beings to take heed to the warnings of the messengers of death. He did so out of his great compassion for all beings and solicitude for their welfare and to wean them away from acts of evil-doing.

In Mahācattārīsaka Sutta, the Buddha expounded the Faultless Right Concentration (Ariya Sammāsamādhi) and also gave a methodical explanation of the Ariya Path of Eight Constituents, stressing the importance of Right Concentration and Right View. Of the Eight Constituents, Right Concentration (Ariya Sammāsamādhi) arises together with the seven other constituents as its cause and its accompaniments. Of these seven factors, Right View which leads the way is always accompanied by Right Effort and Right Mindfulness. Right View, Right Effort and Right Mindfulness go together and one cannot be on the Ariya Path without Right View, Right Effort and Right Mindfulness. These three factors always lead to and accompany Right Thinking, Right Speech, Right Action and Right Livelihood. A sekha, one who has attained the first magga and is still undergoing training to attain arahatship, is endowed with these eight factors.

Further, the Buddha explained that in one who has thus established the Ariya Path of Eight Constituents, there can arise Right Knowledge, sammāñāṇa, and in one who has Right Knowledge there arises Right Liberation, sammāvimutti, which means attainment of Arahattaphala. Thus, an arahat is endowed with ten factors.

These ten factors give rise to ten meritorious factors, thus making twenty factors. Each of these twenty factors obliterates its opposite. For example, Right View obliterates Wrong View and its resultant demeritorious factor. And then it goes on culminating in Right liberation which obliterates Wrong liberation and its resultant demeritorious factor. This enumeration comes to a total of forty factors.

The discourse therefore comprises forty factors, twenty meritorious and twenty demeritorious. Hence the name Mahācattārīsaka Sutta, the discourse on Forty Factors.

Indriyabhāvanā Sutta is about the Cultivation of sense-faculties. Once the Buddha asked Uttara, a pupil of the brahmin Pārāsiviya, how the brahmin taught the cultivation of sense-faculties to his pupils. When Uttara replied that his teacher taught them that visible objects should not be looked at with the eye, sounds should not be listened to with the ear, in cultivating the sense--faculties, the Buddha countered by saying that, in that case, the blind and the deaf would have (without doing anything) cultivated the sense-faculties. The Buddha also pointed out that the feelings of pleasure, displeasure, and neither pleasure nor displeasure that arise on contact of sense organs with sense-objects are conditioned, gross, and causally produced; but that the equanimity of vipassanā insight is serene and sublime. Giving an example for each sense-object, the Buddha also pointed out how, for one who practises vipassanā meditation, these feelings pass away in an instant and equanimity of insight remains firm. The bhikkhu then becomes weary of, ashamed of and disgusted with pleasure or displeasure or neither pleasure nor displeasure that has arisen in him. In fact, he has become a sekha, i.e., one who is still in the process of practising the Teaching, not yet having attained Arahatta Fruition. When he has completed the cultivation of the sense--faculties he becomes an arahat.

Discourses Given in Reply to Questions

Sunakkhatta Sutta, Gaṇaka Moggallāna Sutta, Mahāpuṇṇama Sutta, Cūḷakamma Vibhaṅga Sutta, and Gopaka Moggallāna Sutta, may be cited as examples of discourses given in reply to questions. In Sunakkhatta Sutta, Sunakkhatta the Licchavī prince asked the Buddha whether all those bhikkhus who claimed to have attained arahatship really had attained arahatship or not. The Buddha replied that among those bhikkhus some had indeed attained arahatship. There were also some who sincerely but mistakenly thought they had attained arahatship. Such bhikkhus are those who have attained jhāna, and who may remain for a long time without defilements arising in them and so might think that they have no more defilements in them and that they have become arahats. There were also some who falsely and deliberately claimed such attainment with a view to gaining prestige and material benefits. The imposters, who falsely and deliberately claimed the attainment of magga and phala, have committed a grievous offence entailing loss of status as a member of the Saṁgha.

In Chabbisodhana Sutta also the Buddha spoke on the same subject of bhikkhus claiming attainment of arahatship. The Buddha told the bhikkhus neither to accept nor reject the claim but to put questions to such a bhikkhu. In this sutta the Buddha mentioned six ways of testing a bhikkhu who claimed to have attained arahatship. If all his answers were found to be correct and appropriate, the bhikkhus should rejoice and acclaim thus: "Our meeting with such an excellent fellow-bhikkhu is great, good fortune." By means of these questions and answers the Buddha indirectly pointed out the practice leading to the attainment of arahatship.

In Gaṇaka Moggallāna Sutta, the brāhmin Gaṇaka Moggallāna asked the Buddha whether it was possible to prescribe the stages of training, performance and practice in the Buddha's Teaching just as there are steps in the staircase of the pinnacled monastery of Visākhā, just as there are successive stages in the study of the Vedas, in the art of archery and in the study of mathematics. In reply, the Buddha explained to Gaṇaka Moggallāna the successive stages in the training of a bhikkhu. Initially, the bhikkhu is required to be endowed with morality, that is, to observe restraint according to the fundamental instructions on conduct and attitude, to adhere to right behaviour and lawful resort in going round for alms-food, and to see danger even in the slightest faults. The bhikkhu is required to follow, step by step, other instructions such as, guarding the door of sense-faculties, eating in moderation and with proper reflection, and practising vigilance. After this he should cultivate mindfulness and clear comprehension, etc. The ultimate goal of the training of a bhikkhu is Nibbāna. In this connexion, the Buddha has said, "Brahmin, I am a Tathāgata who only shows the way."

Mahāpuṇṇama Sutta was given by the Buddha in reply to the questions asked by a bhikkhu at the Pubbārāma monastery on a full moon night. The questions were about the aggregates which are the objects of Clinging, about the wrong view of Sakkāya, i.e. the illusion of Self. In this discourse the Buddha explained that all khandha aggregates are impermanent, painful and changeable and thus cannot be considered as atta; and that it is not proper to consider what is impermanent, painful and subject to change as 'This is mine, this is I, this is my Self.'

In Cūḷakammavibhaṅga Sutta we find the Buddha's exposition on the force of Kamma. This discourse was given in reply to the question of Subha, son of Todeyya. Young Subha asked the Buddha why among human beings, although all are human beings alike, some are inferior and some are superior, some have short lives and some have long lives, some are sickly and some are healthy, some are ugly and some are beautiful, some are insignificant and some are influential, some are poor and some are rich, some are of inferior lineage and some are of superior lineage, and some are ignorant and some are wise. The Buddha's reply is that beings have kamma (act or deed) as their possession, kamma as their inheritance, kamma as their cause, kamma as their relative, kamma as their refuge. This brief answer was not fully understood by young Subha. So the Buddha gave him a more detailed explanation, dealing with each of his fourteen questions.

Gopaka Moggallāna Sutta is another example of a discourse given in answer to a question. Once, after the passing away of the Buddha, Gopaka Moggallāna asked the Venerable Ānanda, "Is there any single bhikkhu who also is just as fully and completely endowed with Sabbaññuta ñāṇa as the Honourable Gotama was?" The answer was, "There is not." Then the brahmin Vassakāra, Chief Minister of Māgadha, arrived on the scene and on learning about the conversation between the Venerable Ānanda and Gopaka Moggallāna, asked the Venerable Ānanda thus: "Is there a bhikkhu now who will be your refuge, nominated by the revered Gotama before he passed away, or chosen by the community of bhikkhus and elected by senior bhikkhus?" The answer again was, "There is not." Now, the brahmin Vassakāra wanted to know why, in the absence of such a refuge, there was unity and concord among the bhikkhus. To this, the Venerable Ānanda replied, "Brāhmin, it is not that we have no refuge, we do have a refuge. Brāhmin, the Teaching is our refuge." The Venerable Ānanda then explained how the Buddha had prescribed the Pātimokkha, the fundamental precepts for bhikkhus. To the further question whether there was a bhikkhu who could be respected and esteemed the Venerable Ānanda replied that the Buddha had expounded the ten attributes fostering respect for a bhikkhu. And that a bhikkhu who has these ten attributes was indeed respected and venerated by bhikkhus.

The Buddha used to conclude some of his important discourses such as Āneñjasappāya Sutta and Indriyabhāvanā Sutta in this book with these words: "Ānanda, what a compassionate teacher, who has the welfare of his disciples at heart, should do out of compassion, that I have done for you. ... Ānanda, meditate! Do not be unmindful. Do not be remorseful later! This is our instruction to you all." The Buddha's message is quite clear. It is meant not only for the Venerable Ānanda, but for all his disciples and followers.

The above examples of the Buddha's teaching contained in the discourses included in this book are enough, we hope, to indicate to the reader how the Buddha showed the way to those who went astray; how he held up a lamp in the darkness for those with eyes to see; and how he revealed the dhamma to many, in various ways, each according to the stage of his knowledge and comprehension.

May the Buddha's Teaching shine forth like the radiant sun.

The Editorial Committee
Myanmar Pitaka Association,
Visākhā Hall,
Kabā-Aye Pagoda Estate,
Yangon.

28th July 1988.

The fullmoon of Wazo 1350 ME.

MYANMAR PIṬAKA ASSOCIATION

EDITORIAL COMMITTEE

Doctrinal Adviṣer	.....	Sayadaw U Kumāra, B.A., Dhammācariya (Siromaṇi, Vaṭaṁasakā).
Chairman	.....	U Shwe Mra, B.A., I.C.S. Retd., Former Special Adviṣer, Public Administṛation Diviṣion, E.S.A., United Nations Secretariat.
Members	.....	U Nyun, B.A.,I.C.S. Retd., Former Executive Secretary, United Nations Economic Commiṣṣion for Asia and the Far East; Former Vice-President, World Fellowship of Buddhists.
	.....	U Myint Too, B.Sc., B.L., Barriṣter-at-law, Vice-President, All Myanmar Buddhist Association.
Member and Honorary Chief Editor	.....	Daw Mya Tin, M.A., Former Head of Geography Department, Institute of Education, Yangon.
Chief Doctrinal Consultant	.....	U Kyaw Htut, Dhammācariya; Former Editor-in-chief of the Board for Burmeṣe Tranṣlation of the Sixth Ṣynod Pāḷi Textṣ.
Doctrinal Consultant	.....	U Aye Naing, Dhammācariya, B.A.
Add. Chief Editor	.....	U Myo Min, M.A., B.L., Former Profeṣṣor of Engliṣh, Yangon Univerṣity.
Editors	.....	U Hla Maung, B.A., B.L. U Tin Ụ, B.A., B.L.
Editor and Secretary	.....	U Tin Nwe; B.Sc.

CONTENTS

Page

(iii) Suññata Vagga

(iv) Vibhaṅga Vagga

Page

(v) Saḷāyatana Vagga

Namo tassa bhagavato arahato sammāsambuddhassa

(i) DEVADAHA VAGGA

5. Sunakkhatta Sutta
6. Āneñjasappāya Sutta
7. Gaṇaka Moggallāna Sutta
8. Gopaka Moggallāna Sutta
9. Mahāpuṇṇama Sutta

5. SUNAKKHATTA SUTTA

Discourse to Sunakkhatta

55. Thus have I heard:

Once the Bhagavā was residing at the pinnacled monastery in the Mahāvana Wood near Vesālī. On that occasion, many bhikkhus in the presence of the Bhagavā were claiming the attainment of Arahatship, saying 'Rebirth is ended. The Noble Practice of Purity has been accomplished. What is to be done (for the attainment of Magga Insight) has been done. Nothing else remains to be done (for such attainment). We know this'. Sunakkhatta of the Licchavīs heard that many bhikkhus in the presence of the Bhagavā claimed the attainment of Arahatship, saying 'Rebirth is ended. The Noble Practice of Purity has been accomplished. What is to be done (for the attainment of Magga Insight) has been done. Nothing else remains to be done (for such attainment). We know this'.

Sunakkhatta of the Licchavīs then approached the Bhagavā, made obeisance to the Bhagavā, seated himself at an appropriate place and said to the Bhagavā: "Venerable Sir, I have heard that many bhikkhus in the presence of the Bhagavā claimed the attainment of the Arahatship, saying 'Rebirth is ended. The Noble Practice of Purity has been accomplished. What is to be done (for the attainment of Magga Insight) has been done. Nothing else remains to be done (for such attainment). We know this'. Venerable Sir, have the bhikkhus who in the presence of the Bhagavā were claiming the attainment of the Arahatship been speaking the truth, or have some of them been saying so without attainment in their belief[1] that they have really attained Arahatship?"

---

1. **belief:** *adhimāna*: adhimāna is generally translated as undue estimate of oneself or overconfidence. According to the Commentary, here it means a sincere but mistaken belief that they have really attained Arahatship.

56. Sunakkhatta, of those who in my presence were claiming the attainment of Arahatship, saying 'Rebirth is ended. The Noble Practice of Purity has been accomplished. What is to be done (for the attainment of Magga Insight) has been done. Nothing else remains to be done (for the attainment of Magga Insight). We know this', there are some who have been speaking the truth while others have been saying so without attainment, in their belief that they have really attained Arahatship. Sunakkhatta, of these two kinds of bhikkhus, those who have really attained Arahatship have been talking truly just as they have said. Regarding those who have been talking in the belief that they have really attained Arahatship, it occurred to the Tathāgata to teach them the truth. Sunakkhatta, although it so occurred to the Tathāgata, there are some empty men[2] who repeatedly formulate questions,[3] approach the Tathāgata and put these questions to him. (Therefore) Sunakkhatta, even my (initial) desire to teach them the truth has disappeared.

"Venerable Sir! This is the time for the Bhagavā, this is the time for the Sugata[4] to expound the dhamma. Hearing it from the Bhagavā the bhikkhus will bear it in mind."

"Sunakkhatta, if that be so, listen and pay good attention. I shall speak."

"Yes, Venerable Sir," replied Sunakkhatta of the Licchavīs to the Bhagavā. And the Bhagavā said this:

57. Sunakkhatta, there are these five (kinds of) sense-pleasure. And what are the five? They are: visible object cognizable by eye-consciousness, desirable, delightful, pleasing, alluring, accompanied by sensual passion, and enticing; sound cognizable by ear-consciousness, ... p ...; smell cognizable by nose-consciousness, ... p ...; taste cognizable by tongue-consciousness, ... p ...; physical contact cognizable by body-consciousness,

---

2. **empty men:** *moghapurisa*: these are the foolish people who have no chance of attaining Magga and Phala.

3. **formulate questions:** This refers to the formulating of questions by some low-minded bhikkhus to get knowledge about Arahatship so that they may be able to falsely claim such attainment, with a view to gaining material benefits.

4. *Sugata*: He who speaks only what is beneficial and true.

desirable, delightful, pleasing, alluring, accompanied by sensual passion and enticing. Sunakkhatta, these are the five sense-pleasures.

58. Sunakkhatta, it is possible that in this world there might be some person whose mind is inclined towards sense-pleasures (lokāmisa).[5] Sunakkhatta, such a person takes interest only in words relating to sense--pleasures, repeatedly thinks and reflects on thoughts relating to sense-pleasures, associates with persons who talk about such things, and takes delight in words relating to sense-pleasures. He does not listen, pay attention to, or try to understand words relating to the state of imperturbability[6]; neither does he associate with persons who talk about such things and takes no delight in words relating to the state of imperturbability.

Suppose, Sunakkhatta, there were a man who, for example, has for long been away from his village or market-town. He might meet another man who had recently left that village or market-town. The first man might ask that man whether there was peace, prosperity and freedom from sickness in that village or market-town and the second man might tell the first man about the peace, prosperity and freedom from sickness of that village or market-town.

Sunakkhatta, what do you think of this? Would the first man listen, pay attention to and try to understand the words of the other man? Would he associate

---

5. **Sense-pleasures:** *lokāmisa*: The five sense-pleasures are known by three different names. They are (i) vattāmisa, so called because the five sense-pleasures tend to prolong the round of existences; (ii) kāmāmisa, so called because the five sense-pleasures are desired and delighted in with craving; and (iii) lokāmisa, so called because the five sense-pleasures are generally enjoyed by sentient beings.

6. **state of imperturbability:** *āneñja samāpatti*: The four arūpa samāpattis are generally known as āneñja samāpattis. But here in this sutta, the term 'āneñja' also applies to the four rūpa jhānas and to the first and the second arūpa jhānas only. The third and the fourth arūpa jhānas are specifically mentioned by their respective names, ākiñcaññāyatana jhāna and nevasaññānāsaññāyatana jhāna.

The jhānas, being free from the arising of defilements, are imperturbable and are marked by tranquillity and steadiness of mind. Hence they are called āneñja samāpatti.

with that person and take delight in words relating to his village or market-town? "Venerable Sir, he would."

Sunakkhatta, it is possible that in the same way, in this world, there might be some person whose mind is inclined towards sense-pleasures (lokāmisa). Sunakkhatta, such a person takes interest in words relating to sense-pleasures, repeatedly thinks and reflects on thoughts relating to sense-pleasures, associates with persons who talk about such things and takes delight in words relating to sense-pleasures. He does not listen, pay attention to, or try to understand words relating to the state of imperturbability, neither does he associate with persons who talk about such things and takes no delight in words relating to the state of imperturbability.

Such a person should be known as one who is detached from the state of imperturbability but whose mind is inclined towards sense-pleasures (lokāmisa).

59. Sunakkhatta, it is possible that in this world, there might be some person who has attained the state of imperturbability. Sunakkhatta, such a person takes interest only in words relating to the state of imperturbability, repeatedly thinks and reflects on thoughts relating to the state of imperturbability, associates with persons who talk about such things, and takes delight in words relating to the state of imperturbability. He does not listen, pay attention to, or try to understand words relating to sense-pleasures (lokāmisa); neither does he associate with persons who talk about such things and takes no delight in words relating to sense-pleasures (lokāmisa).

Sunakkhatta, just as a withered leaf that has dropped from the twig cannot be green and fresh again, so also, Sunakkhatta, the person who has attained the state of imperturbability is detached from the fetter of sense-pleasures.

Such a person should be known as one who is detached from the fetter of sense-pleasures (lokāmisa) but whose mind is inclined towards the state of imperturbability.

60. Sunakkhatta, it is possible that in this world, there might be some person who has attained the jhāna

of Nothingness (ākiñcaññāyatana). Sunakkhatta, such a person takes interest only in words relating to the jhāna of Nothingness, repeatedly thinks and reflects on thoughts relating to the jhāna of Nothingness, associates with persons who talk about such things and takes delight in words relating to the jhāna of Nothingness. He does not listen, pay attention to, or try to understand words relating to the state of imperturbability; neither does he associate with persons who talk about such things and takes no delight in words relating to the state of imperturbability.

Sunakkhatta, just as a slab of rock splintered into two cannot become whole again, so also, Sunakkhatta, the person who has attained the jhāna of Nothingness, is detached from the fetter of the state of imperturbability. Such a person should be known as one who is detached from the fetter of the state of imperturbability but whose mind is inclined towards the jhāna of Nothingness (ākiñcaññāyatana).

61. Sunakkhatta, it is possible that in this world, there might be some person who has attained the jhāna of Neither Consciousness nor Non-Consciousness[7]. Sunakkhatta, such a person takes interest only in words relating to the jhāna of Neither Consciousness nor Non-Consciousness, repeatedly thinks and reflects on thoughts relating to the jhāna of Neither Consciousness nor Non-Consciousness, associates with persons who talk about such things and takes delight in words relating to the jhāna of Neither Consciousness nor Non-Consciousness. He does not listen, pay attention to, or try to understand words relating to the jhāna of Nothingness; neither does he associate with persons who talk about such things and takes no delight in words relating to the jhāna of Nothingness.

"Sunakkhatta, if, for example, a man has eaten some delicious food and has vomited it. Sunakkhatta, what do you think of this? Would he have any desire to eat again the food he has vomited?" "No, Venerable

---

7. **Neither Consciousness nor Non-Consciousness:** *nevasaññānāsaññā.* Lit., Neither Perception nor Non-Perception. In this case the word saññā is used because it is regarded as the leading factor in Consciousness.

Sir, he would not". "Why is that so?" "Because the food vomited is regarded as detestable."

Sunakkhatta, so also the person who has attained the jhāna of Neither Consciousness nor Non-Consciousness has cut off[8] the fetter binding him to the jhāna of Nothingness. Such a person should be known as one who is detached from the fetter binding him to the jhāna of Nothingness, but whose mind is inclined towards the jhāna of Neither Consciousness nor Non-Consciousness.

62. Sunakkhatta, it is possible that in this world, there might be some person whose mind is well inclined towards Nibbāna. Sunakkhatta, such a person takes interest only in words relating to Nibbāna, repeatedly thinks and reflects on thoughts relating to Nibbāna and associates with persons who talk about such things, and takes delight in words relating to Nibbāna. He does not listen, pay attention to, or try to understand words relating to the jhāna of Neither Consciousness nor Non-Consciousness; neither does he associate with persons who talk about such things and takes no delight in words relating to the jhāna of Neither Consciousness nor Non-Consciousness.

Sunakkhatta, just as a palm-tree that has been cut off from the neck cannot grow again, so also, Sunakkhatta, a person whose mind is inclined towards Nibbāna has entirely cut off the fetter binding him to the ihāna of Neither Consciousness nor Non-Consciousness. It has been made like the palm-tree stump (which will not grow again), has been rendered incapable of coming into being again and has been made impossible to arise in the future.

Such a person should be known as one who is detached from the fetter binding him to the jhāna of Neither Consciousness nor Non-Consciousness but whose mind is inclined towards Nibbāna.

63. Sunakkhatta, it is possible that in this Teaching, there might occur to some bhikkhu thus, 'The Samana Buddha has taught that Craving is (like)

---

8. **cut off:** *vante*: lit., vomited.

an arrow. Ignorance is (like) poison, it is aggravated through desire, Craving, and ill will. I have extracted the arrow of craving and have removed the poison of ignorance. I have a mind that is well inclined towards Nibbāna.' In thinking thus, he might be wrong. He might seek sense-objects unbefitting one whose mind is well inclined towards Nibbāna. With his eye, he might seek to see improper sights. With his ear, he might seek to hear improper sounds. With his nose, he might seek to smell improper odours. With his tongue, he might seek to taste improper tastes. With his body, he might seek to experience improper touch. With his mind, he might seek to entertain improper thoughts. The mind of that bhikkhu who thus seeks with his eye to see improper sights, with his ear to hear improper sounds, with his nose to smell improper odours, with his tongue to taste improper tastes, with his body to experience improper touch, and with his mind to entertain improper thoughts, would be spoilt by attachment. That bhikkhu with his mind spoilt by attachment would encounter death or suffering that is near-death.

Sunakkhatta, suppose a man were shot with a thickly poisoned arrow. Then his friends, companions, relatives and kinsmen might bring in a surgeon who could take out the arrow. The surgeon who could take out the arrow might operate on the opening of the wound with a knife and might search for the arrow-barb with a probe. He might then extract the arrow-barb and might remove such poison as remains. The surgeon knowing that there remains no poison in the wound, might say to the man thus, 'O man, I have extracted your arrow-barb and removed such poison as remains. There is (now) no possible harm for you. Take what food is suitable. Do not take food that is unsuitable, thereby causing your wound to suppurate. From time to time wash your wound with astringent solution and apply medicament to the opening of your wound. Do not let the opening of your wound become septic by neglecting to clean it and to apply medicament to it. Do not go about in the sun or wind and let the opening of your wound get infected with dirt. O man, you should constantly take care of your wound and let it heal properly.

It might occur thus to that man, 'The arrow-barb

has been removed from me, such poison as remains has been removed, there is now no possible harm for me'. He might take food that is not suitable and by his taking food that is not suitable his wound might suppurate. He might not clean his wound from time to time, he might not apply medicament to the opening of his wound from time to time. By his not cleaning his wound from time to time and by not applying medicament to the opening of his wound from time to time it might become septic. He might go about in the sun and wind and by his going about in the sun and wind the opening of his wound might get infected with dirt. By his not constantly taking care of the wound, it would not heal properly. Because the man does what he should not, the wound might become septic although it has previously been cleansed of poison. Because of these two reasons – (the man doing what he should not do and the opening of the wound getting septic), – the wound is aggravated. Because the wound becomes aggravated, that man would encounter death or suffering that is near-death.

Sunakkhatta, in the same way, it is possible that in this Teaching, it might occur to some bhikkhu thus, 'The Samaṇa Buddha has taught that Craving is (like) an arrow. Ignorance is (like) poison, it is aggravated through craving and ill will. I have extracted that arrow of craving and have removed the poison of ignorance. I have a mind that is well inclined towards Nibbāna.' In thinking thus, he might be wrong. He might seek sense-objects unbefitting one whose mind is well inclined towards Nibbāna. With his eye, he might seek to see improper sights. With his ear, he might seek to hear improper sounds. With his nose, he might seek to smell improper odours. With his tongue, he might seek to taste improper tastes. With his body, he might seek to experience improper touch. With his mind, he might seek to entertain improper thoughts. The mind of that bhikkhu who thus seeks with his eye to see improper sights, with his ear to hear improper sounds, with his nose to smell improper odours, with his tongue to taste improper tastes, with his body to experience improper touch, with his mind to entertain improper thoughts, would be spoilt by attachment. That bhikkhu, with his mind spoilt by attachment, would encounter death or suffering that is near-death. Sunakkhatta, in this

Teaching, leaving the Order of bhikkhus means death. Sunakkhatta, commission of a sullied, grievous offence means suffering that is near-death.

64. Sunakkhatta, it is possible that in this Teaching, it might occur to some bhikkhu whose mind is well inclined towards Nibbāna, thus, 'The Samaṇa Buddha has taught that craving is (like) an arrow. Ignorance is (like) poison, it is aggravated through Craving and ill will. I have extracted the arrow of craving and removed the poison of ignorance. I have a mind that is well inclined towards Nibbāna.' That bhikkhu would not seek sense-objects that are unbefitting one whose mind is well inclined towards Nibbāna. With his eye, he would not seek to see improper sights. With his ear, he would not seek to hear improper sounds. With his nose, he would not seek to smell improper odours. With his tongue, he would not seek to taste improper tastes. With his body, he would not seek to experience improper touch. With his mind, he would not seek to enteitain improper thoughts. The mind of that bhikkhu who does not seek with his eye to see improper sights, with his ear to hear improper sounds, with his nose to smell improper odours, with his tongue to taste improper tastes, with his body to experience improper touch, and with his mind to entertain improper thoughts, would not be spoilt by attachment. That bhikkhu, with his mind unspoilt by attachment, would not encounter death or suffering that is near-death.

Sunakkhatta, suppose a man were shot with a thickly poisoned arrow. Then his friends, companions, relatives and kinsmen might bring in a surgeon who could take out the arrow. That surgeon who could take out the arrow might operate on the opening of the wound with a knife and might search for the arrow-barb with a probe. He might then extract the arrow-barb and might remove such poison as remains. The surgeon who knows that no poison remains might say to the man thus, 'O man, I have extracted your arrow-barb from you and removed such poison as remains. There is now no possible harm for you. Take what food is suitable. Do not take food that is unsuitable, thereby causing your wound to suppurate. From time to time wash your wound with astringent solution and apply medicament to the opening of your wound. Do not let the opening of your wound become septic by neglecting to wash the wound and to apply medicament to its opening. Do not go about in the sun or wind and let the opening of your wound become infected with dirt. O man, you should constantly take care of your wound and let it heal properly.'

It might occur to that man thus, 'The arrow--barb has been removed from me, such poison as remains has been removed, there is now no possible harm for me'. He would take food that is suitable and by his taking only food that is suitable his wound would not suppurate. He would clean his wound from time to time, he would apply medicament to the opening of his wound from time to time. By his cleaning his wound from time to time and by his applying medicament to its opening from time to time, the opening of his wound would not become septic. He would not go about in the sun and wind and by his not going about in the sun and wind, the opening of his wound would not get infected with dirt. Because of constant care of the wound, it would heal properly. Because of doing what he should do, the wound has been cleansed of all poison without any remainder. Because of these two reasons, (the man doing what he should do and the wound being cleansed of all poison without any remainder,) the wound would gain new skin and would be healed. Because his wound has healed with new skin forming, he would not encounter death or suffering that is near-death.

Sunakkhatta, in the same way, it is possible that in this Teaching, it might occur to some bhikkhu whose mind is well inclined towards Nibbāna, thus, 'Samaṇa Buddha has taught that craving is (like) an arrow. Ignorance is (like) poison, it is aggravated through craving and ill will. I have extracted the arrow of craving and removed the poison of ignorance. I have a mind that is well inclined towards Nibbāna.' That bhikkhu would not seek sense-objects that are unbefitting one whose mind is well inclined towards Nibbāna. With his eye, he would not seek to see improper sights. With his ear, he would not seek to hear improper sounds. With his nose, he would not seek to smell improper odours. With his tongue, he would not seek to taste improper tastes. With his body, he would not seek to experience improper touch. With his mind, he would not seek to entertain improper thoughts. The mind of that bhikkhu who does not seek with his eye to see improper sights, with his ear to hear improper sounds, with his nose to smell improper odours, with his tongue to taste improper tastes, with his body to experience improper touch and with his mind to entertain improper thoughts, would not be spoilt by attachment. That bhikkhu, with his mind unspoilt by attachment, would not encounter death or suffering that is near-death.

65. Sunakkhatta, I have given the said example by way of illustration. In the said example, the following is the meaning. Sunakkhatta, the wound stands for the six internal sense-bases.[9] Sunakkhatta, poison stands for ignorance. Sunakkhatta, arrow stands for Craving. Sunakkhatta, probe stands for mindfulness. Sunakkhatta, knife stands for the pure vipassanā insight. Sunakkhatta, the surgeon who takes out the arrow stands for the Tathāgata who is worthy of special veneration and who is truly self-enlightened.

Sunakkhatta, that bhikkhu keeps watch over contact with the six sense-bases, and knowing that defilements[10] are the root cause of suffering, is free from defilements and realizes Nibbāna, which is free from defilements. There will be no possibility (for him) to become attached physically or mentally to sensual pleasures.

"Sunakkhatta, suppose there were a drinking bowl filled with beverage that is good in colour, scent and flavour, but is mixed with poison. Then, there might come along a man who wishes to live and not to die, who wishes to be happy and is averse to suffering. Sunakkhatta, what do you think of this? Knowing that if he were to drink this beverage he would meet with death or suffering that is near-death, would he drink that beverage?" "Venerable Sir, he would not."

---

9. **the six internal sense-bases:** *ajjhatikāyatana*: The eye, the ear, the nose, the tongue, the body and the mind are the internal sense-bases.

10. **defilements:** In the Pāḷi Text the term *'upadhi'* is used. Upadhi is a basis or cause or condition. The four upadhis are Khandhas, Kāma, Kilesa and Kamma. Here Kilesa Upadhi is meant.

Sunakkhatta, in the same way, that bhikkhu keeps watch over contact with the six sense-bases, and knowing that defilements are the cause of suffering, is free from defilements and realizes Nibbāna which is free from defilements. There will be no possibility (for him) to become attached physically or mentally to sensual pleasures.

"Sunakkhatta, suppose there were a snake with instant and deadly poison. There might come along a man who wishes to live, and not to die, who wishes to be happy and is averse to suffering. Sunakkhatta, what do you think of this? Knowing that if he were bitten by this snake with instant and deadly poison, he would meet with death or suffering that is near-death, would he dare to touch that snake with either his hand or his toe?" "Venerable Sir, he would not dare."

Sunakkhatta, in the same way, that bhikkhu keeps watch over contact with the six sense-bases, and knowing that defilements are the root cause of suffering, is free from defilements and realizes Nibbāna, which is free from defilements. There will be no possibility (for him) to become attached physically or mentally to sensual pleasures.

Thus spoke the Bhagavā. Delighted, Sunakkhatta of the Licchavīs rejoiced in what the Bhagavā had said.

End of the Sunakkhatta Sutta, the fifth in this vagga.

6. ĀNEÑJASAPPĀYA SUTTA

Discourse on the Attainment of Imperturbability

66. Thus have I heard:

Once the Bhagavā was residing at the market-town called Kammāsadhamma in the country of the Kurus. There the Bhagavā addressed the bhikkhus, saying, "O bhikkhus" and they replied to him, "Venerable Sir." The Bhagavā said:

Bhikkhus, sense-pleasures[1] are impermanent, empty,[2] deceptive and transient. Bhikkhus, they are illusory; they make the foolish say what is untrue.[3] Whether they are sense-pleasures of the present existence or sense-pleasures of the next existence, whether they are perceptions of sense-pleasures of the present existence or perceptions of sense-pleasures of the next existence, both sense-pleasures and perceptions of sense-pleasures are Māra's domain, Māra's realm, Māra's seed bed, Mara's pasture. These sense-pleasures are conducive to covetousness, ill will and disparagement of others, arising out of an eviland demeritorious mind. These bring about danger to the ariya disciple practising in this Teaching.

Bhikkhus, concerning this matter, the ariya disciple reflects thus, 'Whether they are sense-pleasures

---

1. **sense-pleasures:** *kāmā*: The objects of desire such as visible objects, sound, smell, taste and physical contact are called vatthukāma, while craving for such objects is called kilesakāma. Both are meant here.

2. **empty:** The sense-pleasures are empty because they are devoid of permanence, stability and substance.

3. **what is untrue:** Being deceived by sense-pleasures the foolish say: "This is my son, my daughter, my wife, my gold, my silver and my possessions." Such a statement is not true as these objects of desire, in reality and in the final analysis, do not belong to anyone.

of the present existence or sense-pleasures of the next existence, whether they are perceptions of sense--pleasures of the present existence or perceptions of sense-pleasures of the next existence, both sense--pleasures and perceptions of sense-pleasures are Māra's domain, Māra's realm, Māra's seed bed, Māra's pasture. These sense-pleasures are conducive to covetousness, ill will or disparagement of others, arising out of an evil and demeritorious mind. These bring about danger to the ariya disciple practising in this Teaching. It would be well if I could abide with a jhāna mind transcending the world of sense-pleasures, with a mind extensive and lofty. In me who abide with a jhāna mind transcending the world of sense-pleasures, with a mind extensive and lofty, there cannot arise covetousness, ill will and disparagement of others, arising out of an evil and demeritorious mind. By getting rid of these, there will arise in me a consciousness that is not inferior, and that is incomparable and well developed'. Practising thus and continually abiding in that practice, the mind of the ariya disciple becomes lucid because of its concentration on the object of meditation. When his mind is lucid thus, he abides, in this very life, in the state of imperturbability (of the fourth jhāna) or he may even attain Arahatship. (Even if he fails to attain Arahatship,) on the death and dissolution of his body, it is possible that the resultant consciousness of that bhikkhu would become imperturbable (arising in the realm which corresponds with the jhāna he has attained). Bhikkhus, this is said to be the first practice that is appropriate to the attainment of the state of imperturbability (of the fourth jhāna).

67. Again, bhikkhus, the ariya disciple reflects thus, 'There are sense-pleasures of the present existence, sense-pleasures of the next existence, perceptions of sense-pleasures of the present existence, perceptions of sense-pleasures of the next existence, and all forms of matter, namely, the four primary elements (mahābhūta) and the material properties which are dependent on these four primary elements. (All these are impermanent).' Practising thus and continually abiding in that practice, the mind of the ariya disciple becomes lucid because of its concentration on the object of meditation. When his mind is lucid thus, he abides, in this very life, in the state of imperturbability (of the jhāna of the infinity of space), or he may even attain

Arahatship. (Even if he fails to attain Arahatship,) on the death and dissolution of his body, it is possible that the resultant consciousness of that bhikkhu would become imperturbable (arising in the realm which corresponds with the jhāna he has attained). Bhikkhus, this is said to be the second practice that is appropriate to the attainment of the state of imperturbability.

Again, bhikkhus, the ariya disciple reflects thus, 'There are sense-pleasures of the present existence, sense-pleasures of the next existence, perceptions of sense-pleasures of the present existence, perceptions of sense-pleasures of the next existence, matter (rūpa) in the present existence, matter in the next existence, perceptions of matter in the present existence, perceptions of matter in the next existence. Both (sense--pleasures and matter) are impermanent. It is not proper to take delight in what is impermanent. It is not proper to speak about them with joy. It is not proper to get absorbed in them.' Practising thus and continually abiding in that practice, the mind of the ariya disciple becomes lucid because of its concentration on the object of meditation. When his mind is lucid thus, he abides, in this very life, in the state of imperturbability (of jhāna of the infinity of consciousness), or he may even attain Arahatship. (Even if he fails to attain Arahatship,) on the death and dissolution of his body, it is possible that the resultant consciousness of that bhikkhu would become imperturbable (arising in the realm which corresponds with the jhāna he has attained). Bhikkhus, this is said to be the third practice that is appropriate to the attainment of the state of imperturbability.

68. Again, bhikkhus, the ariya disciple reflects thus, 'There are sense-pleasures of the present existence, sense-pleasures of the next existence, perceptions of sense-pleasures of the present existence, perceptions of sense-pleasures of the next existence, matter (rūpa) in the present existence, matter in the next existence, perceptions of matter in the present existence, perceptions of matter in the next existence, perception of the state of imperturbability and all other perceptions. The jhāna of Nothingness (ākiñcaññāyatana jhāna), where all these perceptions are rendered extinct leaving no remainder, is calm and sublime.' Practising thus and

continually abiding in that practice the mind of the ariya disciple becomes lucid because of its concentration on the object of meditation. When his mind is lucid thus, he abides, in this very life, in the jhāna of Nothingness, or he may even attain Arahatship. (Even if he fails to attain Arahatship,) on the death and dissolution of his body, it is possible that the resultant consciousness of that bhikkhu would attain to a state of Nothingness (arising in the realm which corresponds with the jhāna he has attained). Bhikkhus, this is said to be the first practice that is appropriate to the attainment of the jhāna of Nothingness.

69. Again, bhikkhus, the ariya disciple, having gone to a forest, or to the foot of a tree or to a solitary secluded place reflects thus, 'This (complex of the five khandhas) is void of atta, Self, Soul or of what belongs to atta, (as possession, property).' Practising thus and continually abiding in that practice, the mind of the ariya disciple becomes lucid because of its concentration on the object of meditation. When his mind is lucid thus, he abides, in this very life, in the jhāna of Nothingness, or he may even attain Arahatship. (Even if he fails to attain Arahatship,) on the death and dissolution of his body, it is possible that the resultant consciousness of that bhikkhu would attain to the state of Nothingness (arising in the realm which corresponds with the jhāna he has attained). Bhikkhus, this is said to be the second practice that is appropriate to the attainment of the jhāna of Nothingness.

70. Again, bhikkhus, the ariya disciple reflects thus, 'There is no 'I' (Self) anywhere. There is no 'I' (Self) anywhere for anyone to worry about. There is not another Self anywhere. There is not another Self anywhere for me to worry about.' Practising thus and continually abiding in that practice the mind of that ariya disciple becomes lucid because of its concentration on the object of meditation. When his mind is lucid thus, he abides, in this very life, in the jhāna of Nothingness, or he may even attain Arahatship. (Even if he fails to attain Arahatship,) on the death and dissolution of his body, it is possible that the resultant consciousness of that bhikkhu would attain to the state of Nothingness (arising in the realm which corresponds with the jhāna he has attained). Bhikkhus, this is said

to be the third practice appropriate to the attainment of the jhāna of Nothingness.

Again, bhikkhus, the ariya disciple reflects thus, 'There are sense-pleasures of the present existence, sense-pleasures of the next existence, perceptions of sense-pleasures of the present existence, perceptions of sense-pleasures of the next existence, matter (rūpa) in the present existence, matter in the next existence, perceptions of matter in the present existence, perceptions of matter in the next existence, perception of the state of imperturbability, perception of the jhāna of Nothingness and all (other) perceptions. The jhāna of Neither Consciousness nor Non-Consciousness, where perceptions are rendered extinct leaving no remainder, is calm and sublime.' Practising thus and continually abiding in that practice, the mind of the ariya disciple becomes lucid because of its concentration on the object of meditation. When his mind is lucid thus, he abides, in this very life, in the jhāna of Neither Consciousness nor Non-Consciousness, or he may even attain Arahatship. (Even if he fails to attain Arahatship,) on the death and dissolution of his body, it is possible that the resultant consciousness of that bhikkhu would attain to the state of Neither Consciousness nor Non-Consciousness (arising in the realm which corresponds with the jhāna he has attained). Bhikkhus, this is said to be the practice appropriate to the attainment of the jhāna of Neither Consciousness nor Non-Consciousness.

71. When this had been said, Venerable Ānanda asked the Bhagavā thus: "Venerable Sir, in this Teaching, a bhikkhu practises thus, 'If there had been no kamma-action (performed by me in the past), there would be for me no resultant effect (in the form of fivefold khandha aggregates of existence). If there were no kamma-action (performed by me in this life), there would be for me (in the future) no resultant effect (in the form of fivefold khandha aggregates of existence). I renounce the fivefold khandha that exists and that has manifested itself.' Thus he gains equanimity.[4] Venerable Sir, will that bhikkhu realize parinibbāna, or will he not?" "Ānanda, in such a case, some bhikkhu will realize parinibbāna, some other bhikkhu will not."

4. **equanimity:** here means vipassanā insight.

"Venerable Sir, in that case, what are the causes, what are the conditions for some bhikkhu realizing parinibbāna, and some other bhikkhu not realizing it?"

Ānanda, in this Teaching, a bhikkhu practises thus, 'If there had been no kamma-action (performed by me in the past), there would be for me no resultant effect (in the form of fivefold khandha). If there were no kamma-action (performed by me in this life), there would be for me (in the future) no resultant effect (in the form of fivefold khandha). I renounce the fivefold khandha that exists and that has manifested itself.' Thus he gains equanimity. That bhikkhu takes delight in that equanimity, speaks about it with joy, and gets absorbed in it. The consciousness of that bhikkhu, who takes delight in that equanimity, speaks about it with joy and gets absorbed in it, is dependent on that equanimity and clings to it. Ānanda, the bhikkhu who has clinging cannot realize parinibbāna. "Venerable Sir, if that bhikkhu clings, to what does he cling?" "Ānanda, he clings to the jhāna of Neither Consciousness nor Non-Consciousness". "Venerable Sir, if that bhikkhu clings to it, does he not cling to what is the most sublime of the objects of Clinging?" "Ānanda, you are right. That bhikkhu clings to what is the most sublime of the objects of Clinging. This jhāna of Neither Consciousness nor Non-Consciousness is the most sublime object of Clinging."

72. Ānanda, in this Teaching, a bhikkhu practises thus, 'If there had been no kamma-action (performed by me in the past), there would be for me no resultant effect (in the form of fivefold khandha). If there were no kamma-action (performed by me in this life), there would be for me (in the future) no resultant effect (in the form of fivefold khandha). I renounce the five-fold khandha that exists and that has manifested itself.' Thus he gains equanimity. That bhikkhu does not take delight in that equanimity, does not speak about it with joy, and does not get absorbed in it. The consciousness of that bhikkhu who does not take delight in that equanimity, does not speak about it with joy and does not get absorbed in it, is not dependent on that equanimity and does not cling to it. Ānanda, the bhikkhu who does not cling to it realizes parinibbāna.

73. "Marvellous, Venerable Sir! Unprecendented, Venerable Sir! You have taught us, Venerable Sir, deliverance from the whirlpool[5] through successive attainments (of the jhāna). Venerable Sir, what is the most sublime liberation?" Ānanda, in this Teaching, the ariya disciple reflects thus, 'Sense-pleasures of the present existence, sense-pleasures of the next existence, perceptions of sense-pleasures of the present existence, perceptions of sense-pleasures of the next existence, matter in the present existence, matter in the next existence, perceptions of matter in the present existence, perceptions of matter in the next existence, perception of the state of imperturbability, perception of the jhāna of Nothingness, perception of the jhāna of neither Consciousness nor Non-Consciousness, all these phenomena constitute the three forms of existence[6] in saṁsāra (round of existences). Deliverance of the mind through not clinging to them is deathless Nibbāna.

Ānanda, I have expounded the practices appropriate to the attainment of the state of imperturbability, to the attainment of the jhāna of Nothingness, to the attainment of the jhāna of neither Consciousness nor Non-Consciousness. I have expounded the deliverance from the whirlpools through successive attainments (of the jhānas). I have expounded the most sublime liberation. Ānanda, what a compassionate teacher, who has the welfare of his disciples at heart should do out of compassion, that I have done for you. Ānanda! There are the places at the foot of trees. There are the secluded places. Ānanda! Meditate! Do not be unmindful. Do not be remorseful later! This is our instruction to you all.

---

5. **whirlpool:** *ogha*: Ogha means whirlpool or flood that has the capacity of whirling and sucking in victims falling into it. There are four kinds of Ogha which have the capacity of whirling and sucking in victims in the flood or whirlpool of saṁsāra, the round of rebirths. The four oghas are (i) kāmogha, (ii) bhavogha, (iii) diṭṭhogha, and (iv) avijjogha.

6. **three forms of existence:** (i) *Kāmabhava*, sensual existence, comprising the eleven realms of sense-desire, a state of existence dominated by pleasures of the senses. This of course implies also corporeal existence; (ii) *Rūpabhava*, the existence with fine materiality, comprising sixteen of the realms of the Brahmas, the upper celestial beings; (iii) *Arūpabhava*, non-corporeal (or formless, non-material) existence, comprising four of the realms of the Upper Brahmās.

Thus spoke the Bhagavā. Delighted, the Venerable Ānanda rejoiced in what the Bhagavā had said.

End of the Āneñjasappāya Sutta, the sixth in this vagga.

7. GAṆAKA MOGGALLĀNA SUTTA

Discourse to Gaṇaka Moggallāna

74. Thus have I heard:

Once the Bhagavā was residing at Pubbārāma, the pinnacled monastery built by Migāramātā (Visākhā) in Sāvatthī. During that time the brahmin Gaṇaka Moggallāna approached the Bhagavā and exchanged greetings with the Bhagavā. After having concluded amiable and courteous greetings, he sat in a suitable place and said thus to the Bhagavā:

"O Gotama, just as successive stages of training, successive stages of performance and successive stages of practice can be seen in the steps (leading) to the top of the staircase of Migāramātā's pinnacled monastery; O Gotama, so also there are successive stages of training, successive stages of performance, and successive stages of practice in the studying of the Vedas by the brahmins; O Gotama, so also there are successive stages of training, successive stages of performance and successive stages of practice in the art of archery; O Gotama, so also there are successive stages of training, successive stages of performance and successive stages of practice in the studying of mathematics for us mathematicians who make our living by it; O Gotama, indeed, when we get a pupil, we initially make him multiply one by one, two by two, three by three, four by four, five by five, six by six, seven by seven, eight by eight, nine by nine and ten by ten. O Gotama, we make him multiply up to a hundred and beyond a hundred. O Gotama, as in these examples, is it possible to prescribe successive stages of training, successive stages of performance and successive stages of practice in this Teaching also?"

75. Brahmin, in this Teaching also, it is possible to prescribe the successive stages of training, successive

stages of performance and successive stages of practice. Brahmin, for example, when a clever horse-trainer gets a thoroughbred horse, he fixes a bridle-bit over its mouth. He then proceeds with what has to be done next. In the same way, Brahmin, when the Tathāgata gets one who ought to be taught, he teaches him initially by saying thus, "Come, bhikkhu. Be endowed with morality, observe restraint according to the Fundamental Principles of Pātimokkha,[1] adhere to right behaviour and lawful resort[2] (in the quest for alms-food), see danger even in the slightest faults; fully observe the precepts (of Discipline).

Brahmin, the bhikkhu is thus endowed with morality, he observes restraint according to the Fundamental Principles of Pātimokkha, he adheres to right behaviour and lawful resort (in the quest for alms-food), he sees danger even in the slightest faults, and he fully observes the precepts (of Discipline). Going one step further, the Tathāgata exhorts the bhikkhu thus, "Come, bhikkhu. Guard the door of the sense-faculties; whenever you see a visible object with the eye, do not take in its characteristics (such as male or female) or its secondary details (such as expression or behaviour). If the faculty of sight is left unguarded, such depraved states of mind as covetousness and dissatisfaction stemming from that would overpower you as you fail to control your senses. So apply yourself to the task of restraint, guard your faculty of sight, gain control over it. Whenever you hear a sound with the ear ...p... Whenever you smell an odour with the nose ...p... Whenever you taste a flavour with the tongue ...p... Whenever you make contact with the body ...p... Whenever you cognize a mind-object with the mind, do not take in its characteristics or its secondary details. If the faculty of mind is left unguarded, such depraved states of mind as covetousness and dissatisfaction stemming from that would overpower you as you fail to

---

1. *Pātimokkha*: a set of fundamental instructions on conduct and attitude to be followed by every bhikkhu.

2. **lawful resort**: *gocara*: The rules of vinaya or discipline prohibit a bhikkhu from standing for alms-food at houses of ill fame or such unsavoury places. Places that are permissible to bhikkhus are called lawful resorts. Going the rounds for alms-food only to resorts permissible to a bhikkhu is the observance of gocara.

control your senses. So apply yourself to the task of restraint, guard your faculty of mind, and gain control over it.

Brahmin, the bhikkhu thus guards the door of sense-faculties. Going one step further, the Tathāgata exhorts the bhikkhu thus, "Come, bhikkhu. Eat in moderation. Take food with proper reflection. Do so not for enjoyment, not for vanity (in strength), not for improvement of the body and not for a better complexion, but only to sustain the physical body, to have just enough nourishment for maintaining life, to appease hunger and to carry out the Noble Practice of Purity. (Reflect thus:) By this alms-food, I shall remove the existing (lit., old) discomfort (of hunger) and shall prevent the arising of new discomfort (from immoderate eating). I shall have just enough nourishment to maintain life and to lead a blameless life in good health'.

Brahmin, the bhikkhu thus knows how to eat in moderation. Going one step further, the Tathāgata exhorts the bhikkhu thus, "Come, bhikkhu. Practise vigilance. By walking and sitting (in meditation) in the day-time cleanse your mind of factors that are obstructions (to spiritual development). By walking and sitting (in meditation) in the first watch of the night cleanse your mind of factors that are obstructions (to spiritual development). In the middle watch of the night, lie down on your right side, in a noble reclining posture, with the left foot placed on and a little beyond the right foot, completely mindful and aware, making a mental note of the time to get up. Get up in the last watch of the night and by walking and sitting (in meditation) cleanse your mind of factors that are obstructions (to spiritual development).

Brahmin, the bhikkhu thus practises vigilance. Going one step further, the Tathāgata exhorts the bhikkhu thus, "Come, bhikkhu. Be endowed with mindfulness and clear comprehension; keep yourself completely aware, in moving forward or back; keep yourself completely aware, in looking forward or sideways; keep yourself completely aware, in bending or stretching your limbs; keep yourself completely aware, in carrying or wearing the great robe (i.e., double-layered robe), alms-bowl and the other two robes; keep yourself completely aware, in eating, drinking, chewing and savouring (food and beverages); keep yourself completely aware, in urinating and defecating; keep yourself completely aware, in walking, standing, sitting, falling asleep, waking, speaking and observing silence.

Brahmin, the bhikkhu is thus endowed with mindfulness and clear comprehension. Going one step further, the Tathāgata exhorts the bhikkhu thus, "Come, bhikkhu. Choose for habitation a lonely spot in the woods, or at the foot of a tree, or on a hillside, or in a gully, or in a mountain cave, or in a cemetery, or in a thicket, or on an open plain, or on a heap of straw.

Brahmin, the bhikkhu thus chooses for habitation a lonely spot in the woods, or at the foot of a tree, or on a hillside, or in a gully, or in a mountain cave, or in a cemetery, or in a thicket, or on an open plain, or on a heap of straw. Returning from the round of alms and having had his meal, he sits down cross-legged and upright and establishes mindfulness in meditation. Then that bhikkhu dissociates himself from coveting the world (of the five aggregates of clinging) and abides with his mind free from covetousness, thereby cleansing himself of covetousness altogether. He dissociates himself from ill will, abides with his mind free from ill will and develops goodwill towards all living beings, thereby cleansing himself of ill will altogether. He dissociates himself from sloth and torpor, abides with his mind free from sloth and torpor, with clear perception, mindfulness and comprehension, thereby cleansing himself of sloth and torpor altogether. He dissociates himself from restlessness and worry and abides with his mind in calmness and develops inner peace, thereby cleansing himself of restlessness and worry altogether. He dissociates himself from doubt, abides with his mind free from doubt, and does not waver (in his faith) in meritorious dhammas, thereby cleansing himself of doubt altogether.

76. Having thus abandoned the five hindrances which are the causes of defilement of the mind and which weaken knowledge, and having detached himself from sensual pleasures and demeritorious factors, that bhikkhu achieves and remains in the first jhāna which has vitakka (initial application of the mind), vicāra (sustained application of the mind) and also has pīti (delightful satisfaction) and sukha (bliss) born of detachment from the hindrances (nīvaraṇas). Having

got rid of vitaka and vicāra, he achieves and remains in the second jhāna with internal serenity ...p... Having detached from pīti as well, he achieves and remains in the third jhāna ...p... By dispelling both pleasure and pain ...p... he achieves and remains in the fourth jhāna.

Brahmin, there are those bhikkhus who are still in training and have not yet attained Arahatship, and who, therefore, are still longing for (attainment of) the incomparable peace of arahatship where there is extinction of (all) bonds[3]. The above is my teaching for those bhikkhus. There are those bhikkhus who are arahats[4], who are rid of āsavas, who have fulfilled magga practice, have completed the task, have laid down the burden (of the five khandhas), have gained arahattaphala, have done away with the fetters binding them to existence, have full knowledge, and have a mind liberated from kilesas. For those bhikkhus these dhammas are conducive to a happy existence in this very life and to the accomplishment of mindfulness and clear comprehension.

When this had been said, the brahmin Gaṇaka Moggallāna asked the Bhagavā thus: "When taught thus by the revered Gotama, when taught thus repeatedly, do all the disciples of the revered Gotama attain Nibbāna, the ultimate goal? Or, are there some bhikkhus who do not so attain?"

"Brahmin, when taught thus by me and when taught thus repeatedly, some of my disciples do attain Nibbāna, the ultimate goal and some do not."

"O Gotama, indeed, Nibbāna exists; the path to Nibbāna exists; and the revered Gotama who exhorts (his disciples to follow the path) exists. Nevertheless, among the disciples of the revered Gotama who are taught thus by the revered Gotama and taught thus repeatedly, some attain Nibbāna, the ultimate goal, and some do not. What is the cause, what is the reason?"

77. "Brahmin, in that case, I will put a question

---

3. **bonds:** *yoga*: the bonds of attachment to (i) sense-pleasures *(kama)*, (ii) existence *(bhava)*, (iii) false views *(diṭṭhi)*, and (iv) ignorance *(avijjā)*.

4. **arahats:** those who are devoid of kilesas.

to you in turn. Answer that question as you like. Brahmin, what do you think of what I am going to say? Are you familiar with the road that leads to Rājagaha?"

"Yes, Sir, I am familiar with the road that leads to Rājagaha."

"Brahmin, what do you think of what I am going to say? Suppose a man wanting to go to Rājagaha were to come to this place. Having approached you, he might ask, 'Sir, I would like to go to Rājagaha. Please show me the road that leads to Rājagaha.' You might say to that man thus, 'Come, O man. This road goes to Rājagaha. Go for awhile by this road. When you have gone for awhile by this road, you will come to see a village by such and such a name. Go a little further by this road. When you have gone a little further by this road, you will come to see a market-town by such and such a name. Go a little further by this road. When you have gone a little further by this road, you will come to see a delightful garden, a delightful thicket, a delightful plain, a delightful lake, all in Rājagaha.' Though directed by you thus, and directed thus repeatedly, that man might take the wrong road and might go in another direction.

"Next, suppose, a second man wanting to go to Rājagaha were to come to this place. Having approached you he might ask, 'Sir, I would like to go to Rājagaha. Please show me the road that leads to Rājagaha.' You might say to that man thus, 'Come, O man. This road goes to Rājagaha. Go for awhile by this road. When you have gone for awhile by this road, you will come to see a village by such and such a name. Go a little further by this road. When you have gone a little further by this road, you will come to see a market-town by such and such a name. Go a little further by this road. When you have gone a little further by this road, you will come to see a delightful garden, a delightful thicket, a delightful plain, a delightful lake, all in Rājagaha.' When directed by you thus, and directed thus repeatedly, he might get to Rājagaha with ease.

"Brahmin, indeed, Rājagaha exists. The road that leads to Rājagaha exists. You who show the man exist. Nevertheless, though directed by you thus, and directed thus repeatedly, one man might take the wrong road and might go in another direction while the other man might reach Rājagaha with ease. What is the cause, what is the reason?" "O Gotama, what can I do in this case? O Gotama, I am one who only shows the way."

Brahmin, in the same way, indeed, Nibbāna exists; the path to Nibbāna exists; I who exhort (my disciples to follow the path to Nibbāna) exist. Nevertheless, among my disciples who are taught thus by me, and taught thus repeatedly, some attain Nibbāna, the ultimate goal and some do not. Brahmin, what can I do in this case? Brahmin, I am the Tathāgata who only shows the way.

78. When this had been said, the brahmin Gaṇaka Moggallāna spoke to the Bhagavā thus, "O Gotama, there are persons who renounce hearth and home for the homeless life of a recluse not from faith, not from conviction, but for livelihood. They are crafty and deceitful, fraudulent, distracted, arrogant, foppish, scurrilous, loose-tongued; they leave the doors of sense-faculties unguarded; they are immoderate in eating, not intently vigilant, indifferent to practice proper to a samaṇa, not keen in observance of the Rules of Discipline, intent on acquiring abundance (of material benefits), lax (in following the Teaching), foremost in regressing (into demeritoriousness), irresponsible in the task of achieving absolute extinction of dukkha (which is Nibbāna), lazy, deficient in energy, unmindful, uncomprehending, unsettled (in mind), straying in mind, unwise and duḷl. The honourable Gotama does not associate with such persons.

"But there are (also) worthy men who renounce their homes for the homeless life of a recluse through faith, who are not crafty, not deceitful, not fraudulent, not distracted, not arrogant, not foppish, not scurrilous, not loose-tongued; they have the doors of sense-faculties guarded, they are moderate in eating, intently vigilant, attentive to practice proper to a samaṇa, keen in observance of the Rules of Discipline, not intent on acquiring abundance (of material benefits), not lax (in following the Teaching), not responsible for any regression (into demeritoriousness), foremost in the task of achieving absolute extinction of dukkha; they are assiduous; their minds are directed to Nibbāna; they are mindful, clear in comprehension, settled (in mind), concentrated (in mind), wise and not dull. The honourable Gotama associates with such persons.

"Just as, O Gotama, of all fragrant roots, black sandalwood is said to be the best; of all fragrant heartwoods, red sandalwood is said to be the best; of all fragrant flowers, jasmin is said to be the best, similarly, the teaching of the revered Gotama is loftier than all other extant teachings.

"O Gotama! Excellent (is the dhamma)! O Gotama! Excellent (is the dhamma)! The Revered Gotama has taught the dhamma in many ways; it is, O Gotama, as if one turns up what lies upside down, as if one uncovers what lies covered, as if one shows the way to another who is lost, as if one holds up a lamp in the darkness for those with eyes to see visible objects. I take refuge in the Revered Gotama; I take refuge in the Dhamma and I take refuge in the Saṁgha. May the revered Gotama take me as a lay disciple who has taken refuge (in the Buddha, the Dhamma and the Saṁgha) from today onwards till the end of life."

End of the Gaṇaka Moggallāna Sutta,
the seventh in this vagga.

8. GOPAKA MOGGALLĀNA SUTTA

Discourse to Gopaka Moggallāna

79. Thus have I heard:

Once, not long after the Buddha's parinibbāna (passing away), the Venerable Ānanda was staying in Rājagaha at the monastery of Bamboo Grove where the black squirrels were fed. At that time King Ajātasattu of Māgadha, son of Queen Vedehī, being apprehensive of (the intention of) King Pajjota[1], had the fortifications of Rājagaha strengthened. It was then that the Venerable Ānanda, having rearranged his robes and taking alms-bowl and great robe, set out early in the morning for Rājagaha on his daily round for alms. It occurred then to the Venerable Ānanda thus, 'It is yet too early to go round for alms-food in Rājagaha. It would be well for me to go to the brahmin Gopaka Moggallāna at his place of work.'

The Venerable Ānanda then went to the brahmin Gopaka Moggallāna at his place of work. Seeing the Venerable Ānanda coming in the distance, the brahmin Gopaka Moggallāna said thus to the Venerable Ānanda: "May the honourable Ānanda be pleased to come. The coming of the honourable Ānanda is good. Honourable Ānanda has taken quite a long time to visit us here. Here is the seat duly prepared. May the honourable Ānanda take the seat." The Venerable Ānanda took the prepared seat while Gopaka Moggallāna, the brahmin,

---

1. **Apprehensive of King Pajjota:** King Pajjota, also known as Canda-pajjota, was a very close friend of King Bimbisāra, father of King Ajātasattu. On hearing that King Bimbisāra was killed by his son, Ajātasattu, King Pajjota declared: "This Ajātasattu has killed my very dear friend to make himself King of Māgadha. I will make him see that here is a very dear friend of King Bimbisāra!" King Ajātasattu took this as a threat to him, and was therefore very apprehensive; but he was not sure of King Pajjota's intention.

took a low seat in a suitable place. The brahmin Gopaka Moggallāna, who was seated in a suitable place, said these words to the Venerable Ānanda: "O Ānanda, the Honourable Gotama, who was worthy of special veneration and was perfectly self-enlightened, was endowed with Sabbaññuta Ñāṇa.[2] Is there a single bhikkhu who also is fully and completely endowed with Sabbaññuta Ñāṇa?"

"Brahmin, the Bhagavā, who was worthy of special veneration and was perfectly self-enlightened, was endowed with Sabbaññuta Ñāṇa. There is not a single bhikkhu who also is fully and completely endowed with Sabbaññuta Ñāṇa. Brahmin, indeed, the Bhagavā caused the Path that had not yet arisen to arise. He caused the Path that had not yet appeared to appear. He proclaimed the Path that had not yet been proclaimed by others. He was one who knew the Path (Maggaññū). He was one who knew the Path clearly (Maggavidū). He was one who was skilled in the Path (Maggakovida). His present day disciples follow the Path and attain the Path (knowledge) afterwards". This was the unfinished conversation of the Venerable Ānanda with the brahmin Gopaka Moggallāna.

At that time the brahmin Vassakāra, Chief Minister of Māgadha, on his regular round of inspection of works in Rājagaha, arrived at the work-place of Gopaka Moggallāna where the Venerable Ānanda was. Approaching the Venerable Ānanda, he exchanged greetings with the Venerable Ānanda; having concluded the amiable and courteous greetings, he sat in a suitable place and said to the Venerable Ānanda thus: "O Ānanda, what were you talking about as you were assembled here? What was the subject of your unfinished conversation before I came?"

"Brahmin, the brahmin Gopaka Moggallāna said to me thus: 'O Ānanda, the honourable Gotama, who was worthy of special veneration and was perfectly self-enlightened, was endowed with Sabbaññuta Ñāṇa. Is there any single bhikkhu who also is fully and completely endowed with Sabbaññuta Ñāṇa?' On this

2. *Sabbaññuta Ñāṇa*: In the text the pāḷi word used is 'dhamma'; according to the Commentary here it means Sabbaññuta Ñāṇa (perfect wisdom).

I said to the brahmin Gopaka Moggallāna thus: 'Brahmin, the Bhagavā, who was worthy of special veneration and was perfectly self-enlightened, was endowed with Sabbaññuta Ñāṇa. There is not a single bhikkhu who also is fully and completely endowed with Sabbaññuta Ñāna. Brahmin, indeed, the Bhagavā caused the Path that had not yet arisen to arise. He caused the Path that had not yet appeared to appear. He proclaimed the Path that had not yet been proclaimed by others. He was one who knew the Path. He was one who knew the Path clearly. He was one who was skilled in the Path. His present day disciples follow the Path and attain the Path (knowledge) afterwards.' Brahmin, this was the unfinished conversation between the brahmin Gopaka Moggallāna and myself before you came in."

80. "O Ānanda, is there a bhikkhu now who would be your refuge and who has been left by the revered Gotama (with these words:) 'This bhikkhu will be your refuge when I have passed away'?" "Brahmin, there is not a single bhikkhu now who would be our refuge and who has been left (with these words:) 'This bhikkhu will be your refuge when I have passed away', by the Bhagavā who knew all, who saw all, who was homage-worthy and who was perfectly self-enlightened."

"O Ānanda, is there a bhikkhu now who would be your refuge and who has been designated by the community of bhikkhus and appointed by several senior bhikkhus as: 'This is the bhikkhu who will be our refuge after the Bhagavā has passed away'?" "Brahmin, there is not a single bhikkhu now who would be our refuge and who has been designated by the community of bhikkhus and appointed by several senior bhikkhus as: 'This is the bhikkhu who will be our refuge after the Bhagavā has passed away'."

"O Ānanda, in the absence of such a refuge, what is the reason for (your) unity?" "Brahmin, it is not that we have no refuge. Brahmin, we do have refuge. The Teaching is our refuge."

"When asked, 'O Ānanda, is there a bhikkhu now who would be your refuge and who has been left by the revered Gotama (with these words): This bhikkhu will be your refuge when I have passed away?' you said, 'Brahmin, there is not a single bhikkhu now who would be our refuge and who has been left (with these words): This bhikkhu will be your refuge when I have passed away, by the Bhagavā, who knew all, who saw all, who was homage-worthy and who was perfectly self-enlightened.'

"When asked, 'O Ānanda, is there a bhikkhu now who would be your refuge, and who is designated by the community of bhikkhus and appointed by several senior bhikkhus as: This is the bhikkhu who will be our refuge after the Bhagavā has passed away?' you said, 'Brahmin, there is not a single bhikkhu now who would be our refuge, and who is designated by the community of bhikkhus and who is appointed by several senior bhikkhus as: This is the bhikkhu who will be our refuge after the Bhagavā has passed away'."

"When asked, 'O Ānanda, in the absence of such a refuge, what is the reason for your unity?' you said, 'Brahmin, it is not that we have no refuge. Brahmin, we do have refuge. The Teaching is our refuge'. O Ānanda, how are we to understand the meaning of these words?"

81. "Brahmin, the Bhagavā who knew all, who saw all, who was homage-worthy and who was perfectly self-enlightened, laid down the rules of discipline for the bhikkhus. He prescribed the Pātimokkha(fundamental precepts for bhikkhus). On sabbath days, those of us who reside within certain limits of a village meet together and a certain bhikkhu who knows the Pātimokkha by heart is requested to recite it. When that bhikkhu recites the Pātimokkha, we ask any bhikkhu who finds himself guilty of an offence by transgression of the rules to act in accordance with the rules (of discipline) and in accordance with the Teaching."

"This is not caused by you honourable ones to be done; this is caused to be done by the rules (of discipline). O Ānanda, is there a particular bhikkhu now whom you respect, esteem, revere and venerate, a bhikkhu whom you depend upon with respect and esteem?" "Brahmin, there is no particular bhikkhu now whom we respect, esteem, revere and venerate, a bhikkhu whom we depend upon with respect and esteem."

"When asked, 'O Ānanda,is there a bhikkhu now who would be your refuge, and who has been left by the Honourable Gotama (with these words): This bhikkhu will be your refuge when I have passed away?' you said, 'Brahmin, there is not a single bhikkhu now who would be our refuge and who has been left (with these words): This bhikkhu will be your refuge when I have passed away, by the Bhagavā, who knew all, who saw all, who was homage-worthy and who was perfectly self-enlightened.'

"When asked, 'O Ānanda, is there a bhikkhu now who would be your refuge and who is designated by the community of bhikkhus and appointed by several senior bhikkhus as: This is the bhikkhu who will be our refuge after the Bhagavā has passed away?' you said: 'Brahmin, there is not a single bhikkhu now who would be our refuge, and who is designated by the community of bhikkhus and who is appointed by several senior bhikkhus as: This is the bhikkhu who will be our refuge after the Bhagavā has passed away.'

"When asked, 'O Ānanda, is there a particular bhikkhu now whom you respect, esteem, revere and venerate, a bhikkhu whom you depend upon with respect and esteem?' you said: 'Brahmin, there is no particular bhikkhu now whom we respect, esteem, revere and venerate, a bhikkhu whom we depend upon with respect and esteem.' O Ānanda, how are we to understand the meaning of these words?"

The Ten Factors (dhammā) Fostering Respect

82. Brahmin, there are ten factors fostering respect expounded by the Bhagavā who knew all, who saw all, who was homage-worthy and who was perfectly self-enlightened. Now we respect, esteem, revere and venerate the one who has these ten factors, and we depend upon him with respect and esteem. Which are the ten factors fostering respect?

In this sāsana, brahmiṇ, the bhikkhu has perfect morality; he observes restraint according to the Fundamental Principles of Pātimokkha; he adheres to right behaviour and lawful resort (in the quest for alms-food); he sees danger even in the slightest faults; and he fully observes the precepts (of Discipline). (1)

He has heard a great deal (of the teaching), retains and accumulates the teachings he has heard; these teachings are excellent in the beginning, excellent in the middle and excellent in the end, complete in meaning and phrasing, setting out the Noble Practice of Purity which is absolutely perfect and absolutely pure. He has heard a great deal of such teachings, commits them to memory, accumulates them by recitation, reflects on them and penetratingly comprehends them through insight. (2)

He is contented with any available robes, alms-food, monastic living place, and medicines and medicinal requisites for curing illness. (3)

He can attain at will, without difficulty and without trouble, the four jhānas which are the results of utmost purity of mind and which bring bliss in this very life. (4)

He enjoys (possession of) various forms of psychic power;[3] from being one, he can become many; from being many he can become one; he can be visible or invisible; he can pass unhindered through walls, enclosures and mountains as though going through space; he can plunge into or out of the earth as though plunging into or out of water; he can walk on water without parting it as though walking on earth; he can travel in space cross-legged just like a winged bird; he can touch and stroke the moon and the sun, so mighty and powerful; and he can gain mastery over his body to reach even up to the world of Brahmās. (5)

He can hear both the sounds of devas and men far or near, with the hearing power which surpasses the hearing-power of men, and which is extremely clear like the divine hearing-power. (6)

He can know discriminatively with his own mind the minds of other beings or individuals; he can know the mind with attachment, rāga,[4] as mind with attach-

3. **psychic power:** *iddhividha*: iddhi means "completion," "accomplishment." It is the power to create marvels.

4. **attachment,** *rāga*: In vipassanā bhāvanā, the bhikkhu is liable to misunderstand attachment. He may think that he is required to be mindful of strong forms of attachment only. He is, in fact, required to be mindful of all forms of attachment – weak, medium, strong. In vipassanā, it is a very important point. Whatever takes place in the six senses, however insignificant, however good or bad it is, he is required to be mindful of it. (attachment = pleasure in or craving for something).

ment; he can know the mind without attachment as mind without attachment; he can know the mind with anger, dosa,[5] as mind with anger; he can know the mind without anger as mind without anger; he can know the mind with bewilderment, moha,[6] as mind with bewilderment; he can know the mind without bewilderment as mind without bewilderment; he can know the indolent mind, saṁkhitta citta,[7] as indolent mind; he can know the distracted mind, vikkhitta citta,[8] as distracted mind; he can know the exalted mind, mahaggata citta,[9] as exalted mind; he can know the unexalted mind, amahaggata citta,[10] as unexalted mind; he

---

5. *dosa:* mental violence, hatred, frustration, desire to ill-treat, desire to destroy, desire to kill, are all covered by this term, dosa.

6. *moha*: (Usually defined as stupidity, dullness of mind, bewilderment, infatuation, delusion.) Moha is a cetasika that makes citta (mind) incapable of choosing between right and wrong, incapable of perceiving the Four Ariya Truths, incapable of practising correctly for the perception of the Four Ariya Truths, incapable of adopting a proper mental attitude. It is called micchāñāṇa, the intellect that is capable of giving only evil counsel in all matters. Moha makes a person blind to the nature and consequences of a demeritorious deed.

7. *saṁkhitta citta*: (lit., shrunken mind); this means indolence, lethargy, slothfulness, lack of interest in anything. (The Commentary)

8. *vikkhitta citta*: A diffused or restless state of mind resulting in lack of concentration. (The Commentary)

9. *mahaggata citta*: The loftiness of mind experienced in rūpa jhāna and arūpa jhāna. (The Commentary).

10. *amahaggata citta*: (kāmāvacara citta): The mind as generally found in the sensuous realms. (The Commentary)

can know the inferior mind, sa-uttara citta,[11] as inferior mind; he can know the superior mind, anuttara citta,[12] as superior mind; he can know the concentrated mind; samāhita citta,[13] as concentrated mind; he can

---

11 & 12. *sa-uttara* and *anuttara* are relative terms, indicating inferior and superior states of mind. A state of mind that has some other state of mind superior to it, and is therefore inferior, is sa-uttara citta; a state of mind that is superior to some other state of mind is anuttara citta. Kāmāvacara citta, the state of mind of the sensuous realms, is inferior to the rūpa and arūpa jhāna states of mind. The rūpa jhāna state of mind is inferior to the arūpa jhāna state of mind, but is superior to the kāmāvacara state of mind. In vipassanā practice, the arūpa jhāna state of mind is superior to both the rūpa jhāna and the kāmāvacara states of mind. Within the stages of the jhānas themselves, each jhāna is relatively inferior or superior, progressing to the nevasaññānāsaññāyatanajhāna which is the highest state of mind.

An ordinary yogī who has no experience of jhāna cannot concentrate on the mahaggata or anuttara states of mind.

As a matter of fact, anuttara is normally an epithet for Lokuttara citta or Magga-phala citta. However, in vipassanā practice, the yogī can concentrate only on the five upādānakkhandhas, the five Aggregates which form the objects of Clinging. He cannot concentrate on Magga-phala citta. Therefore, jhānas are given the epithe. anuttara. (The Commentary)

13. *samāhita citta*: the mind that has samādhi, which is mental concentration on an object. According to the Commentary, samāhita citta has (i) upacāra samādhi, and (ii) appanā samādhi, (i.e., jhāna). Upacāra samādhi is samādhi that precedes, and is close to appanā samādhi, helping the latter to take place. Appanā samādhi fixes the mind on the mental object. The mind with upacāra samādhi generally belongs to the sensuous state of existence. The mind with appanā samādhi belongs to the rūpa (fine material) and arūpa (non-material) jhānas.

know the unconcentrated mind, asamāhita citta,[14] as unconcentrated mind; he can know the liberated mind, vimutta citta,[15] as liberated mind; and he can know the unliberated mind, avimutta citta,[16] as unliberated mind. (7)

He can recollect many and varied existences of the past.[17] And what is that? It is the recollection of one past existence,[18] or two, or three, or four, or five, or ten, or twenty, or thirty, or forty, or fifty, or a hundred, or a thousand, or a hundred thousand existences, or existences in many cycles of dissolution, or in many cycles of development, or in many cycles of the rounds of development and dissolution, in this way: 'In that past existence I was known by such a name; I was born into such a clan; I was of such an appearance; I was thus nourished; I enjoyed pleasure thus; I suffered pain thus; my life-span was such; I died in that existence; then I was born in another existence; in that (new) existence, I was known by such a name; I was born into such a clan; I was of such an appearance; I was thus nourished; I enjoyed pleasure thus; I suffered pain thus; my life-span was such; I died in

---

14. *asamāhita citta*: The mind without the two kinds of samādhi. (The Commentary)

15. *vimutta citta*: Here it means the mind temporarily liberated from defilements (kilesas). (The Commentary)

16. *avimutta citta*: The mind not liberated from defilements. (The Commentary)

17. See Appendix A2 of "Ten Suttas from Dīgha Nikāya".

18. **Existence:** *jāti*: Existence means that sequence of mental and physical phenomena that begins with birth-consciousness and ends with death-consciousness.

that existence; and then I was born in this existence.' He can recollect thus his many and varied past existences, together with their circumstances and related facts. (8)

He can with the psychic power of divine sight, which is extremely clear, surpassing the sight of men, see beings in the process of passing away and arising, inferior or superior beings, beautiful or ugly beings and beings with good or bad destinations; and he can know how beings arise according to their own kamma--actions. (9)

He can, by means of abhiññā,[19] special apperception, personally and in this very life, realize, attain to and remain in the emancipation of mind (cetovimutti)[20] and in the emancipation by insight (paññāvimutti)[21] free of āsavas (defilements that befuddle the mind) through their destruction. (10)

Brahmin, these are the ten factors fostering respect expounded by the Bhagavā who knew all, who saw all, who was homage-worthy and who was perfectly self-enlightened. Now, we respect, esteem, revere and venerate the one who has these ten factors, and we depend upon him with respect and esteem.

83. When this was said, the Chief Minister of Māgadha, brahmin Vassakāra, said to General Upananda thus, "Honourable General, what do you think of this? If the worthy ones respect those who are worthy of respect, esteem those who are worthy of esteem, revere those who are worthy of reverence, and venerate those who are worthy of veneration, they are indeed respecting those who are worthy of respect, esteeming those who are worthy of esteem, revering those who are worthy of reverence, and venerating those who are worthy of veneration. If they do not respect, esteem,

---

19. *abhiññā*: Arahatta Magga ñāṇa: Fourth-Stage Insight into Nibbāna. This is the interpretation of abhiññā in this context.

20. *cetovimutti*: i.e., Arahatta Phala samādhi: Concentration of mind, free of passion or craving, pertaining to Fourth-Stage Fruition.

21. *paññāvimutti*: i.e., Arahatta Phala paññā: Insight-Wisdom pertaining to Fourth-Stage Fruition.

revere and venerate those who have these ten factors fostering respect, what kind of person should they respect, esteem, revere and venerate and depend upon?"

Then the Chief Minister of Māgadha, brahmin Vassakāra, said to the Venerable Ānanda thus, "Where does the honourable Ānanda reside now?" "Brahmin, I reside now in the Veḷuvana monastery". "O Ānanda, is the Veḷuvana Bamboo Grove delightful, quiet, free from noise, free from the coming and going of people, suitable for privacy, suitable for solitary seclusion?" "Brahmin, the Veḷuvana Bamboo Grove is delightful, quiet, free from noise, free from the coming and going of people, suitable for privacy and suitable for solitary seclusion. Why is it so? It is due to people like you who take care and look after (the Veluvana Bamboo Grove)."

"O Ānanda, the Veḷuvana Bamboo Grove is indeed delightful, quiet, free from noise, free from the coming and going of people, suitable for privacy, suitable for solitary seclusion. Why is it so? It is due to your revered selves who are in the habit of abiding in jhāna absorption. Your revered selves have indeed attained jhāna and are in the habit of abiding in jhāna absorption.

"O Ānanda, once the honourable Gotama was residing at the pinnacled monastery in Mahāvana Wood of Vesālī. O Ānanda, at that time I approached the honourable Gotama at that pinnacled monastery in Mahāvana Wood. When thus approached, that honourable Gotama spoke in various ways about jhāna (mental absorption). That honourable Gotama had attained jhāna and was in the habit of abiding in the mental absorption (jhāna). That honourable Gotama praised all forms of jhāna."

84. "Brahmin, in fact the Bhagavā does not praise all forms of jhāna nor does he not praise all forms of jhāna. Brahmin, what form of jhāna is not praised by the Bhagavā? Brahmin, in this world, someone who lives with a mind overwhelmed and oppressed by craving for sensual pleasure does not understand fundamentally and truly the way to escape from craving for sensual pleasure that has arisen in him. In contemplating, that person contemplates, variously contemplates,

repeatedly contemplates with craving for sensual pleasure. He who lives with a mind overwhelmed and oppressed by ill will does not understand fundamentally and truly the way to escape from ill will that has arisen in him. In contemplating, that person contemplates, variously contemplates, repeatedly contemplates with ill will. He who lives with a mind overwhelmed and oppressed by sloth and torpor does not understand fundamentally and truly the way to escape from sloth and torpor that has arisen in him. In contemplating, that person contemplates, variously contemplates, repeatedly contemplates with sloth and torpor. He who lives with a mind overwhelmed and oppressed by distraction and worry does not understand fundamentally and truly the way to escape from distraction and worry that has arisen in him. In contemplating, that person contemplates, variously contemplates, repeatedly contemplates with distraction and worry. He who lives with a mind overwhelmed and oppressed by uncertainty does not understand fundamentally and truly the way to escape from uncertainty that has arisen in him. In contemplating, that person contemplates, variously contemplates, repeatedly contemplates with uncertainty. Brahmin, the Bhagavā does not praise these forms of jhāna (mental absorptions).

"Brahmin, which form of jhāna does the Bhagavā praise? Brahmin, in this Teaching, the bhikkhu, being detached from sensual pleasures and demeritorious factors, achieves and remains in the first jhāna which has vitakka (initial application of the mind), vicāra (sustained application of the mind), and which has pīti (delightful satisfaction) and sukha (bliss) born of detachment from hindrances (nīvaraṇas). Then having got rid of vitakka and vicāra he achieves and remains in the second jhāna with internal tranquillity, with enhancement of one-pointedness of mind, devoid of vitakka and vicāra, but with pīti and sukha born of concentration ..... in the third jhāna ..... in the fourth jhāna. Brahmin, the Bhagavā praises these forms of jhāna."

"O Ānanda, the honourable Gotama disparages the jhānas that should be disparaged, praises the jhānas that should be praised. O Ānanda, let me take leave of you. We have many things to do." "Brahmin, you may go when you wish." Then the Chief Minister of

Māgadha, brahmin Vassakāra, pleased and delighted with what the Venerable Ānanda said, rose from his seat and departed.

Not long after the departure of the Chief Minister of Māgadha, the brahmin Vassakāra, the brahmin Gopaka Moggallāna addressed the Venerable Ānanda as follows: "We have asked the honourable Ānanda a question, which the Venerable Ānanda has not answered yet." "Brahmin, haven't I answered your question thus? 'The Bhagavā, by virtue of his being endowed with Sabbaññuta Ñāṇa, was worthy of special veneration and perfectly self-enlightened. There is not a single bhikkhu who also is fully and completely endowed with Sabbaññuta Ñāṇa. Brahmin, indeed, the Bhagavā caused the Path that had not yet arisen to arise. He caused the Path that had not yet appeared to appear. He proclaimed the Path that had not yet been proclaimed by others. He was one who knew the Path (Maggaññū). He was one who knew the Path clearly (Maggavidū). He was one who was skilled in the Path (Maggakovida). His present day disciples follow the Path and attain the Path (Knowledge) afterwards."

End of the Gopaka Moggallāna Sutta,
the eighth in this vagga.

1. MAHĀPUṆṆAMA SUTTA

The Greater Discourse Given on a Full Moon Night

85. Thus have I heard:

Once the Bhagavā was residing at Pubbārāma, the pinnacled monastery built by Migāramātā (Visākhā), in Sāvatthī. At that time, on the night of the fifteenth day which is a full moon day and an uposatha (sabbath) day,[1] the Bhagavā was seated in the open air, surrounded by a company of bhikkhus. Then, one of the bhikkhus, rising from his seat and arranging his robe so as to cover his left shoulder with it, paid homage to the Bhagavā with joined palms raised (to the forehead) and addressed the Bhagavā as follows:

"Venerable Sir, if you would allow me, I would like to put a question to the Bhagavā." "Bhikkhu, should you desire to ask, remain seated at your place and ask the question you want."

86. Thereupon, the bhikkhu, remaining seated at his place, put the following question to the Bhagavā: "Venerable Sir, are these the five aggregates which are the objects of clinging, namely, the aggregate of corporeality which is the object of clinging, the aggregate of sensation which is the object of clinging, the aggregate of perception which is the object of clinging, the aggregate of volitional activities which is the object of clinging, and the aggregate of consciousness which is the object of clinging?"

---

1. an *uposatha* (sabbath) day:

In the Buddha's Teaching the days on which the eight moral precepts are observed are called uposatha (sabbath) days. The eighth and the fifteenth days of the waxing half of the lunar month as well as the eighth and the fourteenth or the fifteenth days of the waning half of the lunar month are uposatha days.

"Bhikkhus, these are the five aggregates which are the objects of clinging,[2] namely, the aggregate of corporeality which is the object of clinging, the aggregate of sensation which is the object of clinging, the aggregate of perception which is the object of clinging, the aggregate of volitional activities which is the object of clinging and the aggregate of consciousness which is the object of clinging."

"Very well, Venerable Sir", said the bhikkhu, delighted with what the Bhagavā had said, and having expressed his satisfaction asked the Bhagavā a further question. "Venerable Sir, what is the root-cause of these five aggregates which are the objects of clinging?" "Bhikkhu, Craving is the root-cause of these five aggregates which are the objects of clinging." "Venerable Sir, is that clinging[3] itself the five aggregates which are the objects of clinging? Or is clinging apart from the five aggregates which are the objects of clinging?" "Bhikkhu, that clinging is not the same as those five aggregates which are the objects of clinging, nor is it apart from them. Bhikkhu, there is the craving for the five aggregates which are the objects of clinging. This craving for the five aggregates is clinging."

"Venerable Sir, can this craving for the five aggregates which are the objects of clinging be in different forms?" "Bhikkhu, it could be" said the Bhagavā. "Bhikkhu, in this matter, it occurs to some person thus, 'May I have such and such an appearance in the future','May I have such and such sensation in the future', 'May I have such and such perception in the future', 'May I have such and such volitional activities in the future', 'May I have such and such consciousness in future.' Thus, craving for the five aggregates which are the objects of clinging can be in different forms."

"Venerable Sir, for what reason are the aggregates (khandhas) called aggregates?" "Bhikkhu, whatever

---

2. **the five aggregates which are the objects of clinging:** pañcupādānakkhandhā: The five aggregates (khandhā) are the objects of craving and wrong view which have the tendency to cling tenaciously to the object of attention. Hence these aggregates are called the five aggregates which are the objects of clinging.

3. **clinging,** here, is equated with Craving.

corporeality there is, whether past, present or future, whether internal or external, whether gross or delicate, whether inferior or superior, whether far or near, all that corporeality is called the aggregate of corporeality. Whatever sensation there is, whether past, present or future, whether internal or external, whether gross or delicate, whether inferior or superior, whether far or near, all that sensation is called the aggregate of sensation. Whatever perception there is, whether past, present or future, ...p... whether far or near, all that perception is called the aggregate of perception. Whatever volitional activities there are, whether past, present or future, whether internal or external, whether gross or delicate, whether inferior or superior, whether far or near, all those volitional activities are called the aggregate of volitional activities. Whatever consciousness there is, whether past, present or future, whether internal or external, whether gross or delicate, whether inferior or superior, whether far or near all that consciousness is called the aggregate of consciousness. Bhikkhu, for this reason are the aggregates called aggregates."

"Venerable Sir, what is the cause and what is the condition, by which the aggregate of corporeality can be known? What is the cause and what is the condition, by which the aggregate of sensation can be known? What is the cause and what is the condition, by which the aggregate of perception can be known? What is the cause and what is the condition, by which the aggregate of volitional activities can be known? What is the cause and what is the condition, by which the aggregate of consciousness can be known?"

"Bhikkhu, the four great primary elements are the cause and the condition by which the aggregate of corporeality can be known. Contact is the cause and the condition by which the aggregate of sensation can be known. Contact is the cause and the condition by which the aggregate of perception can be known. Contact is the cause and the condition by which the aggregate of volitional activities can be known. Mind-and-matter is the cause and the condition by which the aggregate of consciousness can be known."

87. "Venerable Sir, how does the view of sakkāya (i.e., sakkāya-diṭṭhi) come to be?" "Bhikkhu in this

matter, an ignorant worldling who habitually disregards the ariyas, who is not proficient in the teachings of the ariyas, who is not trained and disciplined in the teachings of the ariyas, who habitually disregards men of virtue, who is not proficient in the teachings of men of virtue, who is not trained and disciplined in the teachings of men of virtue, regards corporeality as atta, Self,[4] or regards (the remaining aggregates forming) the atta as having corporeality,[5] or regards corporeality, (as existing) in atta, or atta (as existing) in corporeality; regards sensation as atta, Self, or regards (the remaining aggregates forming) the atta as having sensation, or regards sensation (as existing) in atta, or atta (as existing) in sensation; regards perception as atta, Self, or regards (the remaining aggregates forming) the atta as having perception, or regards perception (as existing) in atta, or atta (as existing) in perception; regards volitional activities as atta, Self, or regards (the remaining aggregates forming) the atta as having volitional activities, or regards volitional activities (as existing) in atta, or atta (as existing) in volitional activities; regards consciousness as atta, Self, or regards (the remaining aggregates forming) the atta as having consciousness, or regards consciousness (as existing) in atta, or atta (as existing) in consciousness.[6] Thus, bhikkhu, does the view of sakkāya come to be."

4. The view that corporeality and atta are identical, as the flame and the light it sheds are wrongly taken to be identical.

5. The view that only the mental aggregates are atta which has corporeality, as a tree has its shadow.

6. In considering corporeality as (being identical with) atta, only corporeality by itself is taken as atta. In considering atta as possessing corporeality, or as containing corporeality, or as being contained in corporeality, atta is equated only with nāma, the mental component (mind) of mind-and-body. So also when sensation (or perception, or volitional activity, or consciousness) is considered as (being identical with) atta, only the mental component (mind) is taken as atta. But in considering atta as possessing sensation (or perception, or volitional activity, or consciousness), or as containing, or as being contained in any one of these four, both mind and body (i.e., the mental component and corporeality conjointly) are taken as atta. The view that corporeality, or sensation, or perception, or volitional activity, or consciousness, is (identical with) atta, is the annihilation view.

   The view that atta possesses or contains, or is contained in any one of these five khandhas, is the view that the separate and distinct atta is eternal, (known as the eternity view).

"Venerable Sir, how does the view of sakkāya not come to be?" "Bhikkhu, in this matter, a learned man, an ariya disciple, who pays attention to the ariyas, who is proficient in the teachings of the ariyas, who is trained and disciplined in the teachings of the ariyas, who pays attention to men of virtue, who is proficient in the teachings of men of virtue, does not regard corporeality as atta, Self, does not regard the remaining aggregates as atta having corporeality, does not regard corporeality (as existing) in atta, does not regard atta (as existing) in corporeality; does not regard sensation as atta, Self, does not regard the remaining aggregates as atta having sensation, does not regard sensation (as existing) in atta, does not regard atta (as existing) in sensation; does not regard perception as atta, Self, does not regard the remaining aggregates as atta having perception, does not regard perception (as existing) in atta, does not regard atta (as existing) in perception; does not regard volitional activities as atta, Self, does not regard the remaining aggregates as atta having volitional activities, does not regard volitional activities (as existing) in atta, does not regard atta (as existing) in volitional activities; does not regard consciousness as atta, Self, does not regard the remaining aggregates as atta having consciousness, does not regard consciousness (as existing) in atta, does not regard atta (as existing) in consciousness. Thus, bhikkhu, does the view of sakkāya not come to be."

88. "Venerable Sir, what is the enjoyableness of corporeality, what is its fault, what is the freedom from attachment to it? What is the enjoyableness of sensation, what is its fault, what is the freedom from attachment to it? What is the enjoyableness of perception, what is its fault, what is the freedom from attachment to it? What is the enjoyableness of volitional activity, what is its fault, what is the freedom from attachment to it? What is the enjoyableness of consciousness, what is its fault, what is the freedom from attachment to it?" "Bhikkhu, the happiness and satisfaction that arise due to that corporeality are the enjoyableness of corporeality. The impermanency, the suffering and changeableness of corporeality are its faults. The elimination and the abandonment of craving for corporeality are the freedom from attachment to it.

Bhikkhu, the happiness and satisfaction that arise due to that sensation ..... that perception .....those volitional activities ..... . The happiness and satisfaction that arise due to that consciousness are the enjoyableness of consciousness. The impermanency, the suffering and the changeableness of consciousness are its faults. The elimination and the abandonment of craving for consciousness are the freedom from attachment to it."

89. "Venerable Sir, with respect to one's own body as well as to another's which has consciousness, and with respect to all material objects, what must one know and what must one see for the concept 'My Self, mine, and I' not to arise in him?" "Bhikkhu, whatever corporeality there is, whether past, present or future, whether internal or external, whether gross or delicate, whether inferior or superior, whether far or near, one perceives fundamentally and truly with Insight-wisdom, thus, 'This is not mine; this is not 'I'; this is not my Self (atta)'; whatever sensation there is .....; whatever perception there is .....; whatever volitional activities there are .....; whatever consciousness there is, whether past, present or future, whether internal or external, whether gross or delicate, whether inferior or superior, whether far or near, one perceives fundamentally and truly with Insight-wisdom, thus, 'This is not mine; this is not 'I'; this is not my Self'. Bhikkhu, in such a one who knows and sees in that manner with respect to one's own body as well as to another's which has consciousness, and with respect to all material objects, the concept 'my self, mine and I' does not arise."

90. Then, it occurred to a certain bhikkhu thus: 'Oh, it is said that corporeality is not atta, sensation is not atta, perception is not atta, volitional activities are not atta, consciousness is not atta. This being so, which atta is there that can be affected by acts done by what is not atta?'[7] Then the Bhagavā, knowing what had occurred in the bhikkhu's mind, said to the bhikkhus: "Bhikkhus, it is possible that in this matter some empty man (who is devoid of any chance of attaining magga and phala), who is overwhelmed by ignorance,

7. **what is not atta:** *anatta*: The mental and physical aggregates (khandhas) which are devoid of atta.

might think with a mind obsessed by Craving, thus: 'Oh, it is said that corporeality is not atta, sensation is not atta, perception is not atta, volitional activities are not atta, and consciousness is not atta. This being so, which atta is there that can be affected by acts done by what is not atta?' And he might consider that he should go beyond the Buddha's Teaching. Bhikkhus, I have repeatedly taught you (regarding this matter) in various discourses."

"Bhikkhus, what do you think of this? Is corporeality permanent or impermanent?" "Impermanent, Venerable Sir." "That which is impermanent, is it painful or pleasant?" "Painful, Venerable Sir." "Is it proper to consider what is impermanent, painful and subject to change, as: 'This is mine; this is I; this is my Self (atta)?'" "Indeed no, Venerable Sir." "Bhikkhus, what do you think of this? Is sensation ...p... Is Perception ...p... Are volitional activities ...p... Is consciousness permanent or impermanent?" "Impermanent, Venerable Sir." "That which is impermanent, is it painful or pleasant?" "Painful, Venerable Sir." "Is it proper to consider what is impermanent, painful and subject to change, as: 'This is mine; this is I; this is my Self (atta)?'" "Indeed no, Venerable Sir."

Therefore, whatever corporeality there is, whether past, present or future, whether internal or external, whether gross or delicate, whether inferior or superior, and whether far or near, should be perceived, as it really is with Insight-wisdom thus: 'This is not mine; this is not I; this is not my Self (atta).' Whatever sensation ...p.... whatever perception ...p.... whatever volitional activities ...p.... whatever consciousness there is, whether past, present or future, internal or external, gross or delicate, inferior or superior, far or near, should be perceived, as it really is, with Insight-wisdom thus: 'This is not mine; this is not I; this is not my Self (atta)'.

Bhikkhus, on perceiving thus, the well-instructed ariya disciple becomes disgusted with corporeality, with sensation, with perception, with volitional activities, and with consciousness. On being disgusted (thus), he is detached from passion. On being detached from passion, he is liberated. On being liberated, knowledge of liberation arises. He knows, clearly: 'Rebirth is ended; the

Noble Practice of Purity has been accomplished; what is to be done for the attainment of Magga Insight has been done; nothing else remains to be done for such attainment.'

Thus spoke the Bhagavā. Delighted, those bhikkhus rejoiced in what the Bhagavā had said. When this discourse in the form of question and answer has been delivered, the minds of the sixty bhikkhus were freed from Clinging and released from the āsavas.

End of the Mahāpuṇṇama Sutta,
The Ninth in this vagga.

Namo tassa bhagavato arahato sammāsambuddhassa

(ii) ANUPADA VAGGA

2. Chabbisodhana Sutta
5. Bahudhātuka Sutta
7. Mahācattārīsaka Sutta
8. Ānāpānassati Sutta
9. Kāyagatāsati Sutta

2. CHABBISODHANA SUTTA

Discourse on Six Ways of Testing Arahatship

98. Thus have I heard:

Once the Bhagavā was residing at the Jetavana monastery of Anāthapiṇḍika in Sāvatthī. Then the Bhagavā addressed the bhikkhus, saying: "Bhikkhus!" The bhikkhus replied to the Bhagavā: "Venerable Sir!" The Bhagavā spoke thus:

Bhikkhus, in this Teaching a bhikkhu claims the attainment of arahatship, saying, 'Rebirth is ended. The Noble Practice of Purity has been accomplished. What is to be done (for the attainment of Magga Insight) has been done. Nothing else remains to be done (for such attainment). I know this.'

Bhikkhus, the words of that bhikkhu should neither be approved nor rejected. Without approving or rejecting, you should question him thus: 'Friend, the Bhagavā who knows all, who sees all, who is worthy of special veneration and who is perfectly self-enlightened, has taught well these four kinds of statements. Which are the four? They are: to speak of what is seen as seen, what is heard as heard, what is sensed as sensed, and what is cognized as cognized. Friend, these are the four kinds of statements taught well by the Bhagavā who knows all, who sees all, who is worthy of special veneration, and who is perfectly self-enlightened. Regarding these four kinds of statements, by knowing how and by seeing how, is the mind of the venerable one freed from Clinging and released from āsavas?'

Bhikkhus, the bhikkhu who is rid of āsavas, who has fulfilled Magga Practice, who has completed the task, who has laid down the burden (of the five khandhas), who has gained Arahattaphala, who has done away with the fetters binding him to existence, who has full knowledge, and who has a mind liberated from kilesas, would answer in this way: 'Friend, with regard to what I see I do not cling to it, I do not reject it, I am not attached to it, I am not bound to it, I am not fettered to it, I do not associate with it, and I abide with a mind unrestricted by it. Friend, with regard to what I hear ...p... Friend, with regard to what I sense ...p... Friend, with regard to what I cognize I do not cling to it, I do not reject it, I am not attached to it, I am not bound to it, I am not fettered to it, I do not associate with it, and I abide with a mind unrestricted by it. Friend, knowing thus and seeing thus, with regard to these four kinds of statements, my mind is freed from Clinging and is released from āsavas.'

Bhikkhus, you should rejoice at the words of that bhikkhu and express satisfaction by saying, 'Good!' Having rejoiced at his words and having expressed satisfaction by saying 'Good', you should ask him a further question thus:

99. 'Friend, the Bhagavā who knows all, who sees all, who is worthy of special veneration, and who is perfectly self-enlightened, has taught well the five aggregates which are the objects of Clinging. Which are the five? They are: the aggregate of corporeality which is the object of clinging, the aggregate of sensation which is the object of clinging, the aggregate of perception which is the object of clinging, the aggregate of volitional activities which is the object of clinging, and the aggregate of consciousness which is the object of clinging. Friend, these are the five aggregates which are the objects of clinging taught well by the Bhagavā who knows all, who sees all, who is worthy of special veneration and who is perfectly self-enlightened. Regarding these five aggregates which are the objects of clinging, by knowing how, and by seeing how, is the mind of the venerable one freed from Clinging and released from āsavas?'

Bhikkhus, the bhikkhu who is rid of āsavas, who has fulfilled Magga Practice, who has completed the task, who has laid down the burden (of the five khandhas),who has gained Arahattaphala, who has done away with the fetters binding him to existence, who has full knowledge and who has a mind liberated from kilesas, would answer in this way: 'Friend, because of the knowledge that corporeality lacks strength, is subject to dissolution and is devoid of comfort, there is extinction, absence, cessation, renunciation of and release from adherence and clinging to corporeality, which forms the basis of, which is permeated by, and in which lies latent (demeritorious) thought; thus I know that my mind is liberated. Friend, because of the knowledge that sensation ...p... Friend, because of the knowledge that perception ...p... Friend, because of the knowledge that volitional activities ...p... Friend, because of the knowledge that consciousness lacks strength, is subject to dissolution and is devoid of comfort, there is extinction, absence, cessation, renunciation of and release from adherence and clinging to consciousness which forms the basis of, which is permeated by, and in which lies latent (demeritorious) thought; thus I know that my mind is liberated. Friend, knowing thus and seeing thus, with regard to these five aggregates which are the objects of clinging, my mind is freed from Clinging and is released from āsavas.'

Bhikkhus, you should rejoice at the words of that bhikkhu and express satisfaction by saying, 'Good!' Having rejoiced at his words and having expressed satisfaction by saying, 'Good', you should ask him a further question thus:

100. 'Friend, the Bhagavā who knows all, who sees all, who is worthy of special veneration and who is perfectly self-enlightened has taught well the six elements. Which are the six? They are: the element of solidity, the element of fluidity and cohesion, the element of heat, the element of motion, the element of space[1] and the element of consciousness. Friend, these are the six elements taught well by the Bhagavā who knows all, who sees all, who is worthy of special veneration and who is perfectly self-enlightened.

'Regarding these six elements, by knowing how and by seeing how is the mind of the venerable one

1. the element of space *(ākāsa)* is explained as 'that which cannot be subjected to any marking'. One cannot write on or put any mark on space, since space is void and empty. Corporeal or material particles that make up any form have interstices or space between them, though this may not be apparent to the naked eye.

freed from Clinging and released from āsavas?'

Bhikkhus, the bhikkhu who is rid of āsavas, who has fulfilled Magga Practice, who has completed the task, who has laid down the burden (of the five khandhas),who has gained Arahattaphala, who has done away with the fetters binding him to existence, who has full knowledge, and who has a mind liberated from kilesas, would answer in this way: 'Friend, I do not take the element of solidity as Self, atta. Neither do I take factors dependent on the element of solidity as Self, atta. Because of extinction, absence, cessation, renunciation of and release from Clinging, which cause the mind to settle on, adhere to and lie latent in factors dependent on the element of solidity, I know that my mind is liberated. Friend, I do not take the element of fluidity and cohesion ...p... Friend, I do not take the element of heat ...p... Friend, I do not take the element of motion ...p... Friend, I do not take the element of space ...p... Friend, I do not take the the element of consciousness as Self. Neither do I take factors dependent on the element of consciousness as Self. Because of extinction, absence, cessation, renunciation of and release from Clinging which cause the mind to settle on, adhere to and lie latent in factors dependent on the element of consciousness, I know that my mind is liberated. Friend, knowing thus and seeing thus, with regard to these six elements, my mind is freed from Clinging and released from āsavas.'

Bhikkhus, you should rejoice at the words of that bhikkhu and express satisfaction by saying, 'Good!' Having rejoiced at his words and having expressed satisfaction by saying, 'Good', you should ask him a further question thus:

101. 'Friend, the Bhagavā who knows all, who sees all, who is worthy of special veneration and who is perfectly self-enlightened, has taught well the six (pairs of) sense-bases, internal and external. Which are the six? They are: eye and visible object, ear and sound, nose and odour, tongue and taste, body and tangible object, mind and cognizable object. Friend, these are the six (pairs of) sense-bases, internal and external, taught well by the Bhagavā who knows all, who sees all, who is worthy of special veneration, and who is

perfectly self-enlightened. Regarding these six (pairs of) sense-bases, by knowing how and by seeing how, is the mind of the venerable one freed from Clinging and released from āsavas?'

Bhikkhus, the bhikkhu who is rid of āsavas, who has fulfilled Magga Practice, who has completed the task, who has laid down the burden (of the five khandhas), who has gained Arahattaphala, who has done away with the fetters binding him to existence, who has full knowledge, and who has a mind liberated from kilesas, would answer in this way:

'Friend, regarding the eye, the visible object, the eye-consciousness, and the factors that are to be known together with eye-consciousness, there is extinction, absence, cessation, renunciation of and release from the desire, the attachment, the delight, the craving and the adherence and clinging to them, which form the basis of, which are permeated by, and in which lies latent (demeritorious) thought; thus I know that my mind is liberated. Friend, regarding the ear, the sound, the ear-consciousness ...p... Friend, regarding the nose, the odour, the nose-consciousness, ...p... Friend, regarding the tongue, the taste, the tongue--consciousness ...p... Friend, regarding the body, the tangible object, the body-consciousness ...p... Friend, regarding the mind, the cognizable object, the mind--consciousness and the factors that are to be known together with the mind-consciousness, there is extinction, absence, cessation, renunciation of and release from the desire, the attachment, the delight, the craving, and the adherence and clinging to them, which form the basis of, which are permeated by, and in which lies latent (demeritorious) thought; thus I know that my mind is liberated. Friend, knowing thus and seeing thus with regard to these six (pairs of) sense-bases, internal and external, my mind is freed from Clinging and released from āsavas.'

Bhikkhus, you should rejoice at the words of that bhikkhu and express satisfaction by saying, 'Good!' Having rejoiced at his words and having expressed satisfaction by saying, 'Good', you should ask him a further question thus:

102. 'With respect to one's own body as well as another's which has consciousness, and with respect to all material objects, by knowing how and by seeing how, has the venerable one given up the concept, 'my Self, Mine and I'?

Bhikkhus, the bhikkhu who is rid of āsavas, who has fulfilled Magga Practice, who has completed the task, who has laid down the burden (of the five khandhas), who has gained Arahattaphala, who has done away with the fetters binding him to existence, who has full knowledge, and who has a mind liberated from kilesas, would answer in this way: 'Friend, I did not 'know' and I did not 'see' while I was in my former lay life. The Tathāgata or a disciple of the Tathāgata taught me the dhamma. On hearing the dhamma I develop faith in the Tathāgata. When faith is thus developed, I consider thus:

> "Confined is the life of a householder; it is a path laden with dust (of defilement). A samaṇa's life is like an open plain. Difficult it is for a layman to pursue the Noble Practice in all its fullness, in all its purity, like a polished conch. Now, it were better for me to shave off my hair and beard, don the bark-dyed robe, renounce hearth and home, and become a recluse leading the homeless life."

'Afterwards, I gave up my wealth, great or small, leaving my relatives, be they few or be they many, shaved off my hair and beard, donned the bark-dyed robe, renounced hearth and home, and became a recluse leading the homeless life.

'Having entered the Order, I observed the precepts and the rule of life of bhikkhus. I abandoned all thoughts of taking life and abstained from destruction of life, setting aside the stick and sword, ashamed to do evil, I was compassionate and dwelt with solicitude for the welfare of all living beings.

'I abandoned all thoughts of taking what was not given and abstained from taking what was not given. I accepted only what was given, wishing to receive only what I was given. I established myself in purity by abstaining from committing theft.

'I abandoned all thoughts of leading a life of unchastity and practised chastity, remaining virtuous and abstinent from sexual intercourse, the practice of lay people.

'I abandoned all thoughts of telling lies and abstained from telling lies, speaking only the truth, combining truth with truth, remaining steadfast (in truth), trustworthy and not deceiving.

'I abandoned all thoughts of slandering and abstained from slander. Hearing things from these people I did not relate them to those people to sow the seed of discord among them. Hearing things from those people I did not relate them to these people to sow the seed of discord among them. I reconciled those who were at variance. I encouraged those who were in accord. I delighted in unity, loved it and rejoiced in it. I spoke to create harmony.

'I abandoned all thoughts of speaking harshly and abstained from harsh speech. I spoke only blameless words, pleasing to the ear, affectionate, going to the heart, courteous, pleasing to many and heartening to many.

'I abandoned all thoughts of talking frivolously and abstained from frivolous talk. My speech was appropriate to the occasion, being truthful, beneficial, consistent with the Doctrine and the Discipline, memorable, timely and opportune, with reasons, confined within limits and conducive to welfare.

'I abstained from destroying all seeds and vegetation.

'I took only one meal a day, not taking food at night and fasting after mid-day.

'I abstained from dancing, singing, enjoying music and watching (entertainments) that is a stumbling block to the attainment of morality.

'I abstained from wearing flowers, using perfumes and anointing with unguents.

'I abstained from the use of high and luxurious beds and seats.

'I abstained from the acceptance of gold and silver.

'I abstained from the acceptance of uncooked cereals.

'I abstained from the acceptance of uncooked meat.

'I abstained from the acceptance of women and maidens.

'I abstained from the acceptance of male and female slaves.

'I abstained from the acceptance of goats and sheep.

'I abstained from the acceptance of chickens and pigs.

'I abstained from the acceptance of elephants, cattle, horses and mares.

'I abstained from the acceptance of cultivated or uncultivated land.

'I abstained from acting as messenger or courier.

'I abstained from buying and selling.

'I abstained from using false weights and measures and counterfeits.

'I abstained from such dishonest practices as bribery, cheating and fraud.

'I abstained from maiming, murdering, holding persons in captivity, committing highway robbery, plundering villages and engaging in dacoity.

'I remained contented with robes just sufficient to protect my body and with food just sufficient to sustain me. Wherever I went, I carried with me only my requisites. Just as a winged bird, wherever it flies, flies only with its burden of wings, so too I was contented with my robes that protect my body and with the food that sustained me; wherever I went I properly carried with me only my requisites. Thus fully equipped with this group of noble morality, I enjoyed blameless happiness within myself.'

103. 'Whenever I saw a visible object with the eye, I did not take in its characteristics (such as male

or female), nor its secondary details (such as expression or behaviour). If the faculty of sight was left unguarded, such depraved states of mind as covetousness and dissatisfaction stemming from that would overpower me as I failed to control my senses. So I applied myself to the task of restraining my faculty of sight, kept watch on it, and gained control over it.

'Whenever I heard a sound with the ear ...p...

'Whenever I smelled an odour with the nose ...p...

'Whenever I tasted a flavour with the tongue ...p...

'Whenever I made contact with the body ...p...

'Whenever I cognized a mind-object with the mind, I did not take in its characteristics (such as pleasing or unpleasing), nor its secondary details. If the faculty of mind was left unguarded, such depraved states of mind as covetousness and dissatisfaction stemming from that would overpower me as I failed to control my senses. So I applied myself to the task of restraining my faculty of mind, kept watch on it, and gained control over it.

'And I, endowed with this noble control of the sense faculties, enjoyed within myself happiness unalloyed (with defilements of the mind).

'I kept myself completely aware, in moving forward or back, kept myself completely aware, in looking forward or sideways; kept myself completely aware, in bending or stretching my limbs; kept myself completely aware, in carrying or wearing the great robe (i.e., double-layered robe), alms-bowl and the other two robes; kept myself completely aware, in eating, drinking, chewing and savouring (food and beverages); kept myself completely aware, in urinating and defecating; kept myself completely aware, in walking, standing, sitting, falling asleep, waking, speaking and observing silence.

'Then I, endowed with this noble group of moral precepts, this noble contentedness, this noble self--control, and this noble mindfulness and clear comprehension, chose for habitation a lonely spot in the woods or at the foot of a tree or on a hillside, or in a gully, or in a mountain cave, or in a cemetery, or in a thicket, or on an open plain, or on a heap of straw.

'Returning from the round of alms and having had my meal, I sat down cross-legged and upright and established mindfulness in meditation. Then I dissociated myself from coveting the world (i.e., of the five aggregates which are the objects of Clinging) and abided with my mind free from covetousness, thereby cleansing myself of covetousness altogether. I dissociated myself from ill will, abided with my mind free from ill will and developed goodwill towards all living beings, thereby cleansing myself of ill will altogether. I dissociated myself from sloth and torpor, abided with my mind free from sloth and torpor with clear perception, mindfulness and comprehension, thereby cleansing myself of sloth and torpor altogether. I dissociated myself from restlessness and worry and abided with my mind in calmness and developed inner peace, thereby cleansing myself of restlessness and worry altogether. I dissociated myself from doubt, abided with my mind free from doubt, and did not waver (in my faith) in meritorious dhammas, thereby cleansing myself of doubt altogether.'

104. 'Having got rid of these five nīvaraṇas, hindrances, that cause defilement of the mind and the weakening of wisdom, and having become detached from sensual pleasures and demeritorious factors, I entered upon and abided in the first jhāna which has vitakka (initial application of mind) and vicāra (sustained application of mind) and which has pīti (delightful satisfaction) and sukha (bliss) born of detachment from the nīvaraṇas, hindrances.

'Having got rid of vitakka and vicāra, I entered upon and abided in the second jhāna, with internal tranquillity, with enhancement of one-pointedness of mind, devoid of vitakka and vicāra, but with pīti and sukha born of concentration ...p... abided in the third jhāna ...p... abided in the fourth jhāna.

'When the settled mind has thus become perfectly pure, cleansed, unsullied, uncontaminated, malleable, ready for application, firm and imperturbable, I directed it towards (attainment of) Āsavakkhaya ñāṇa, the Insight which uproots the āsavas.

'I knew fundamentally and truly: "This is dukkha"; I knew fundamentally and truly: "This is the cause of dukkha"; I knew fundamentally and truly: "This is the extinction of dukkha"; I knew fundamentally and truly: "This is the practice leading to the extinction of dukkha"; I knew fundamentally and truly: "These are the āsavas"; I knew fundamentally and truly: "This is the cause of the āsavas"; I knew fundamentally and truly: "This is the extinction of the āsavas"; I knew fundamentally and truly: "This is the practice leading to the extinction of the āsavas". Knowing thus and seeing thus, my mind became liberated from kāmāsava, the defilement of sense-desire, bhavāsava, the defilement of hankering after (better) existence, and avijjāsava, the defilement of ignorance of the Four Ariya Truths. When (the mind was thus) liberated there occurred the knowledge "it is liberated." I knew "Rebirth is ended; the Noble Practice of Purity has been accomplished; what is to be done (for the attainment of Magga Insight) has been done; nothing else remains to be done (for such attainment)".

'With respect to one's own body as well as another's which has consciousness, and with respect to all material objects, by knowing thus and by seeing thus I have given up the concept," my Self, Mine and I".'

Bhikkhus, you should rejoice at the words of that bhikkhu and express satisfaction by saying, 'Good!' Having rejoiced at his words and having expressed satisfaction by saying 'Good', you should acclaim thus: 'Friends! It is of benefit, a great benefit to us in having the chance to see such a personage as the venerable one among the companions in the practice of the dhamma'.

Thus spoke the Bhagavā. Delighted, the bhikkhus rejoiced in what the Bhagavā had said.

End of the Chabbisodhana Sutta,
the second in this vagga.

5. BAHUDHĀTUKA SUTTA

Discourse on Various Elements

124. Thus have I heard:

Once the Bhagavā was residing at the Jetavana monastery of Anāthapiṇḍika in Sāvatthī. On that occasion the Bhagavā addressed the bhikkhus, saying: "Bhikkhus!" The bhikkhus replied to the Bhagavā: "Venerable Sir!" The Bhagavā spoke thus:

Bhikkhus, all fears arise on account of the foolish, not on account of the wise. All dangers arise on account of the foolish, not on account of the wise. All troubles arise on account of the foolish, not on account of the wise. Just as a fire spreads from a thatch-roofed or grass-roofed house to gabled houses that are plastered both within and without, that are not exposed to the wind, that have secure doors, and closed windows, and burns them down, similarly, all fears arise on account of the foolish, not on account of the wise; all dangers arise on account of the foolish, not on account of the wise; all troubles arise on account of the foolish, not on account of the wise. Bhikkhus, in this way, fear is caused by the foolish, not by the wise; danger is caused by the foolish, not by the wise; trouble is caused by the foolish, not by the wise. Bhikkhus, there is no fear on account of the wise; there is no danger on account of the wise; there is no trouble on account of the wise. Bhikkhus, let us therefore be wise ones who are given to reflection. Bhikkhus, you should conduct yourselves accordingly.

When this was said, the Venerable Ānanda asked the Bhagavā thus: "Venerable Sir, for what reason may one be called 'a wise and reflective bhikkhu'?" "Ānanda, a bhikkhu is skilled in understanding the Elements, is skilled in understanding the sense-bases, is skilled in understanding the Theory of Cause and Effect, is skilled in understanding the possibility and impossibility of things. Ānanda, for this reason, that bhikkhu may be called 'a wise and reflective bhikkhu'."

125. "Venerable Sir, for what reason may one be called 'a bhikkhu skilled in understanding the Elements'?" "Ānanda, the Elements are these eighteen: the element of eye, the element of visible object and the element of eye-consciousness; the element of ear, the element of sound and the element of ear-consciousness; the element of nose, the element of odour and the element of nose--consciousness; the element of tongue, the element of taste and the element of tongue-consciousness; the element of body, the element of tangible object and the element of body-consciousness; the element of mind, the element of cognizable object and the element of mind--consciousness. Ānanda, a bhikkhu knows and sees with Insight these eighteen elements. Ānanda, for this reason, that bhikkhu may be called 'a bhikkhu skilled in understanding the Elements'." (1)

"Venerable Sir, is there any other reason by which one may be called 'a bhikkhu skilled in understanding the Elements'?" "Yes, Ānanda. There are these six elements: the element of solidity, the element of fluidity and cohesion, the element of heat,[1] the element of motion, the element of space, the element of consciousness. Ānanda, a bhikkhu knows and sees with Insight these six elements. Ānanda, for this reason, that bhikkhu may be called 'a bhikkhu skilled in understanding the Elements'." (2)

"Venerable Sir, is there any other reason by which one may be called 'a bhikkhu skilled in understanding the Elements'?" "Yes, Ānanda. There are these six elements: the element of pleasure, the element of pain, the element of gladness, the element of sadness, the element of equanimity and the element of ignorance. Ānanda, a bhikkhu knows and sees with Insight these six elements. Ānanda, for this reason, that bhikkhu may be called 'a bhikkhu skilled in understanding the Elements'." (3)

---

1. the element of heat *(tejo dhātu)*, sometimes rendered 'thermal element', has the dual aspect of heat and cold, just as the word 'temperature' has.

"Venerable Sir, is there any other reason by which one may be called 'a bhikkhu skilled in understanding the Elements'?" "Yes, Ānanda. There are these six elements: the element of sense-pleasure, the element of liberation (from sense-pleasures), the element of ill will, the element of goodwill, the element of harmfulness, and the element of compassion. Ānanda, a bhikkhu knows and sees with Insight these six elements. Ānanda, for this reason, that bhikkhu may be called 'a bhikkhu skilled in understanding the Elements'." (4)

"Venerable Sir, is there any other reason by which one may be called 'a bhikkhu skilled in understanding the Elements'?" "Yes, Ānanda. There are these three elements: The element of sense-pleasure, the element of fine-materiality, the element of non-materiality.[2] Ānanda, a bhikkhu knows and sees with Insight these three elements. Ānanda, for this reason, that bhikkhu may be called 'a bhikkhu skilled in understanding the Elements.'" (5)

"Venerable Sir, is there any other reason by which one may be called 'a bhikkhu skilled in understanding the Elements'?" "Yes, Ānanda. There are these two elements: the element of the conditioned (i.e. produced by a cause or a combination of causes) and the element of the unconditioned (i.e. not produced by any cause). Ānanda, a bhikkhu knows and sees with Insight these two elements. Ānanda, for this reason, that bhikkhu may be called 'a bhikkhu skilled in understanding the Elements'. (6)

126. "Venerable Sir, for what reason may one be called 'a bhikkhu skilled in understanding the Sense-bases'?" "Ānanda, there are these six (pairs of) Sense-bases, internal and external. They are: eye and visible object; ear and sound; nose and odour; tongue and taste; body and tangible object; mind and cognizable object. Ānanda, a bhikkhu knows and sees with Insight these six (pairs of) Sense-bases, internal and external. Ānanda, for this reason, that bhikkhu may be called 'a bhikkhu skilled in understanding the Sense-bases'."

---

2. Five khandhas in the sensuous sphere, five khandhas in the fifteen fine-material spheres and the four mental khandhas in the non-material sphere , respectively.

"Venerable Sir, for what reason may one be called 'a bhikkhu skilled in understanding the Theory of Cause and Effect'?" In this matter, a bhikkhu knows thus: 'when this (cause) exists, that (effect) comes to be. Because of the occurrence of this (cause), that (effect) appears. When this (cause) does not exist, that (effect) does not come to be. When this (cause) ceases, that (effect) does not arise. So it is that dependent on ignorance, volitional activities arise; dependent on volitional activities, consciousness arises; dependent on consciousness, mind-and-body (nāmarūpa) arises; dependent on nāmarūpa, the six sense-bases arise; dependent on the six sense-bases, Contact arises; dependent on Contact, Sensation arises; dependent on Sensation, Craving arises; dependent on Craving, Clinging arises; dependent on Clinging, bhava (kamma-actions causing further existence) arises; dependent on bhava, rebirth arises; dependent on rebirth, there arise ageing, death, grief, lamentation, pain, distress and despair. In this way occurs the arising of this entire mass of pure dukkha.

'Only with the total cessation of ignorance through arahatta magga, volitional activities cease; with the cessation of volitional activities, consciousness ceases; with the cessation of consciousness, mind-and-body (nāmarūpa) ceases; with the cessation of nāmarūpa, the six sense-bases cease; with the cessation of the six sense-bases, Contact ceases; with the cessation of Contact, Sensation ceases; with cessation of Sensation, Craving ceases; with the cessation of Craving, Clinging ceases; with the cessation of Clinging, bhava (kamma--actions causing further existence) ceases; with the cessation of bhava, rebirth ceases; with the cessation of rebirth, ageing, death, grief, lamentation, pain, distress and despair cease. In this way occurs the cessation of this entire mass of pure dukkha'. Ānanda, for this reason, that bhikkhu may be called 'a bhikkhu skilled in understanding the Theory of Cause and Effect.'"

127. "Venerable Sir, for what reason may one be called 'a bhikkhu skilled in understanding the possibility and impossibility of things'?" "Ānanda, in this matter, for a person who has attained sotāpatti magga[3] there is

3. a person who has attained sotāpatti magga: in the Pāli text, *diṭṭhi sampanno puggalo*, lit., a person who is endowed with right view. This is interpreted as a person who has entered the Stream, i.e., one who has attained sotāpatti magga.

no reason or possibility that he would take any conditioned phenomenon as being permanent; the bhikkhu knows that there is no such possibility. But, for a common worldling, there is the possibility that he might take a conditioned phenomenon as being permanent; that bhikkhu also knows that there is such a possibility. For a person who has attained sotāpatti magga, there is no reason or possibility that he would take any conditioned phenomenon as being pleasant; that bhikkhu knows that there is no such possibility. But, for a common worldling, there is the possibility that he might take a conditioned phenomenon as being pleasant; that bhikkhu also knows that there is such a possibility. For a person who has attained sotāpatti magga, there is no reason or possibility that he would take any conditioned phenomenon as Self, atta; that bhikkhu knows that there is no such possibility. But, for a common worldling, there is the possibility that he might take a conditioned phenomenon as Self, atta; that bhikkhu also knows that there is such a possibility.

128. For a person who has attained sotāpatti magga, there is no reason or possibility that he would kill his mother; that bhikkhu knows that there is no such possibility. But, for a common worldling, there is the possibility that he might kill his mother; that bhikkhu also knows that there is such a possibility. For a person who has attained sotāpatti magga, there is no reason or possibility that he would kill his father; that bhikkhu knows that there is no such possibility. But, for a common worldling, there is the possibility that he might kill his father; that bhikkhu also knows that there is such a possibility. For a person who has attained sotāpatti magga, there is no reason or possibility that he would kill an arahat; that bhikkhu knows that there is no such possibility. But, for a common worldling, there is the possibility that he might kill an arahat; that bhikkhu also knows that there is such a possibility. For a person who has attained sotāpatti magga, there is no reason or possibility that he would, with intent to kill, wound[4] the

4. Wound: *lohita uppāda*; lit., causing the blood to appear. Nobody's effort could rupture the skin of the Buddha and cause blood to flow. Only a bruise could result. When Devadatta tried to kill the Buddha by letting a rock fall from a cliff, there resulted only a bruise on the Buddha's toe. Nevertheless Devadatta was guilty of the lohituppādaka kamma, action causing the blood to appear, i.e., shedding the blood of the Buddha.

Tathāgata; that bhikkhu knows that there is no such possibility. But, for a common worldling, there is the possibility that he might, with intent to kill, wound the Tathāgata; that bhikkhu also knows that there is such a possibility. For a person who has attained sotāpatti magga, there is no reason or possibility that he would cause a schism amongst the Order; that bhikkhu knows that there is no such possibility. But, for a common worldling, there is the possibility that he might cause a schism amongst the Order; that bhikkhu also knows that there is such a possibility. For a person who has attained sotāpatti magga, there is no reason or possibility that he would indicate anyone else (but the Buddha) as the Teacher; that bhikkhu knows that there is no such possibility. But, for a common worldling, there is the possibility that he might indicate someone else (other than the Buddha) as the Teacher; that bhikkhu also knows that there is such a possibility.

129. There is no reason or possibility that two Buddhas, worthy of special veneration and perfectly self-enlightened, would appear contemporaneously in a single world-system; that bhikkhu knows that there is no such possibility. But, there is the possibility that a single Buddha, worthy of special veneration and perfectly self--enlightened, might appear in a single world-system; that bhikkhu also knows that there is such a possibility. There is no reason or possibility that two universal monarchs would appear comtemporaneously in a single world-system; that bhikkhu knows that there is no such possibility. But, there is the possibility that a single universal monarch might appear in a single world-system; that bhikkhu also knows that there is such a possibility.

130. There is no reason or possibility that a woman would become a Buddha, worthy of special veneration and perfectly self-enlightened; that bhikkhu knows that there is no such possibility. But, there is the possibility that a man might become a Buddha, worthy of special veneration and perfectly self-enlightened; that bhikkhu also knows that there is such a possibility. There is no reason or possibility that a woman would become a universal monarch; that bhikkhu knows that there is no such possibility. But, there is the possibility that a man might become a universal monarch; that bhikkhu also knows that there is such a possibility. There is no reason

or possibility that a woman would become a Sakka (king of devas), would become a Māra (the Evil One), or would become a Mahābrahmā (Great Brahmā); that bhikkhu knows that there is no such possibility. But, there is the possibility that a man might become a Sakka (king of devas), or might become a Māra (the Evil one), or might become a Mahābrahmā (Great Brahmā); that bhikkhu also knows that there is such a possibility.

131. There is no reason or possibility that an evil bodily act would give rise to a result that is desirable, delightful, pleasing; that bhikkhu knows that there is no such possibility. But, there is the possibility that an evil bodily act might give rise to a result that is undesirable, undelightful, unpleasing; that bhikkhu also knows that there is such a possibility. There is no reason or possibility that an evil verbal act ...p... There is no reason or possibility that an evil mental act would give rise to a result that is desirable, delightful, pleasing; that bhikkhu knows that there is no such possibility. But, there is the possibility that an evil mental act might give rise to a result that is undersirable, undelightful, unpleasing; that bhikkhu also knows that there is such a possibility. There is no reason or possibility that a good bodily act would give rise to a result that is undesirable, undelightful, unpleasing; that bhikkhu knows that there is no such possibility. But, there is the possibility that a good bodily act might give rise to a result that is desirable, delightful, pleasing; that bhikkhu also knows that there is such a possibility. There is no reason or possibility that a good verbal act ...p... There is no reason or possibility that a good mental act would give rise to a result that is undesirable, undelightful, unpleasing; that bhikkhu knows that there is no such possibility. But, there is the possibility that a good mental act might give rise to a result that is desirable, delightful, pleasing; that bhikkhu also knows that there is such a possibility.

There is no reason or possibility that a person who has committed an evil bodily act would, as a result or consequence of that act, be reborn in a good destination, a fortunate celestial (deva) realm after the death and dissolution of the body; that bhikkhu knows that there is no such possibility. But, there is the possibility that a person who has committed an evil bodily act might, as a result or consequence of that act, be reborn in miserable existences (apāya), wretched destinations (duggatiṁ), states of ruin (vinipāta), realms of continuous suffering (niraya) after the death and dissolution of the body; that bhikkhu also knows that there is such a possibility. There is no reason or possibility that a person who has committed an evil verbal act ...p... There is no reason or possibility that a person who has committed an evil mental act would, as a result or consequence of that act, be reborn in a good destination, a fortunate celestial (deva) realm after the death and dissolution of the body; that bhikkhu knows that there is no such possibility. But, there is the possibility that a person who has committed an evil mental act might, as a result or consequence of that act, be reborn in miserable existences, wretched destinations, states of ruin, realms of continuous suffering after the death and dissolution of the body; that bhikkhu also knows that there is such a possibility. There is no reason or possibility that a person who has done a good bodily act would, as a result or consequence of that act, be reborn in miserable existences, wretched destinations, states of ruin, realms of continuous suffering after the death and dissolution of the body; that bhikkhu knows that there is no such possibility. But, there is the possibility that a person who has done a good bodily act might, as a result or consequence of that act, be reborn in a good destination, a fortunate celestial (deva) realm after the death and dissolution of the body; that bhikkhu also knows that there is such a possibility. There is no reason or possibility that a person who has done a good verbal act ...p... There is no reason or possibility that a person who has done a good mental act would, as a result or consequence of that act, be reborn in miserable existences, wretched destinations, states of ruin, realms of continuous suffering after the death and dissolution of the body; that bhikkhu knows that there is no such possibility. But, there is the possibility that a person who has done a good mental act might, as a result or consequence of that act, be reborn in a good destination, a fortunate celestial (deva) realm after the death and dissolution of the body; that bhikkhu also knows that there is such a possibility. Ānanda, for this reason, that bhikkhu may be called 'a bhikkhu skilled in understanding the possibility and impossibility of things'.

132. When this had been said, the Venerable Ānanda addressed the Bhagavā thus: "Marvellous indeed, Venerable Sir! Extraordinary indeed, Venerable Sir! What,

Venerable Sir, is the name of this exposition of the dhamma?" "Ānanda!" said the Bhagavā, "Bear in mind that this exposition of the dhamma is called, for these reasons,[5] Bahudhātuka (Various Elements), as well as Catuparivatta (Four Aspects), as well as Dhammadāsa (Mirror of Wisdom), as well as Amatadundubhi (A Big Drum Proclaiming the Dhamma on the Deathless), as well as Anuttarasaṅgāmavijaya (Incomparable Victory in Battle).

Thus spoke the Bhagavā. Delighted, the Venerable Ānanda rejoiced in what the Bhagavā had said.

End of the Bahudhātuka Sutta, the fifth in this vagga.

---

5. for these reasons: Because this discourse deals with various elements, it is called Bahudhātuka; because this discourse deals with Elements, Sense-bases, Cause and Effect, and possibility and impossibility of things, it is called Catuparivatta.

7. MAHĀ CATTĀRĪSAKA SUTTA

Discourse on the Forty Factors

136. Thus have I heard:

Once the Bhagavā was staying at the Jetavana monastery of Anāthapiṇḍika in Sāvatthī. On that occasion the Bhagavā addressed the bhikkhus saying: "Bhikkhus!" The bhikkhus replied to the Bhagavā: "Venerable Sir!" The Bhagavā spoke thus:

"Bhikkhus, I shall expound to you on the faultless Right Concentration[1] with its cause and its accompaniments. Listen and pay good attention. I shall speak." "Very well, Venerable Sir," replied the bhikkhus to the Bhagavā who then delivered this discourse.

Bhikkhus, what is the faultless Right Concentration with its cause and its accompaniments? What are its cause and its accompaniments? They are: Right View, Right Thought, Right Speech, Right Action, Right Livelihood, Right Effort and Right Mindfulness. Bhikkhus, this state of one-pointedness of mind accompanied by these seven factors is called the faultless Right concentration with its cause and its accompaniments. Bhikkhus, among these factors, Right View leads the way. Bhikkhus, how does Right View lead the way? One knows the Wrong View as Wrong View; one knows the Right View as Right View. Knowing thus is the Right View of that person.

Bhikkhus, what is Wrong View? 'There is no (consequence to) alms-giving, sacrificial offerings or pious donation. A good or bad action produces no direct or indirect results. This world does not exist, nor do

1. faultless Right Concentration: *ariya samādhi*: *Ariya* is explained by the Commentary as *niddosa*, faultless, *lokuttara*, transcendental. Here Right Concentration means *magga samādhi* or concentration pertaining to the Path.

other worlds. There is no mother, no father (that is, all good or evil done to them produce no result). There is no rebirth of beings after death. In the world, there are no samanas or brāhmanas, established in the Ariya Path and accomplished in good practice, who, through Magga Insight (abhiññā) realized by themselves, can expound on this world and other worlds.' Bhikkhus, this is Wrong View.

Bhikkhus, what is Right View? Bhikkhus, I teach that there are two kinds of Right View. Bhikkhus, there is the Right View which is associated with āsavas (defilements that befuddle the mind), is connected with meritorious factors and which results in the coming into (repeated) existence of the aggregates, khandhā. Bhikkhus, there is the (other) Right View which is faultless, which is free of āsavas, and which, transcending the mundane, is part of the Ariya Path. Bhikkhus, what is the Right View which is associated with āsavas, is connected with meritorious factors and which results in the coming into (repeated) existence of the aggregates? 'There is (consequence to) alms-giving, sacrificial offering and pious donation. A good or bad action produces direct or indirect results. This world exists and so also do other worlds. There is mother and father (that is, all good or evil done to them produce results). There is rebirth of beings after death. In the world, there are samanas or brāhmanas, established in the Ariya Path and accomplished in good practice, who, through Magga Insight (abhiññā) realized by themselves, can expound on this world or other worlds.' Bhikkhus, this is the Right View which is associated with āsavas, is connected with meritorious factors and which results in the coming into (repeated) existence of the aggregates.

Bhikkhus, what is the (other) Right View which is faultless, which is free of āsavas, and which, transcending the mundane, is part of the Ariya Path? Bhikkhus, there is the insight which is the faculty of wisdom, which is the power of wisdom, which is the enlightenment-factor of investigative knowledge, which is the Right View and which is a constituent of the Ariya Path, possessed by one whose mind is faultless, is free of āsavas, who has attained the Ariya Path and who cultivates Magga Insight. Bhikkhus, this is called the Right View which is faultless, which is free of āsavas, and which, transcending the mundane, is part of the

Ariya Path. That bhikkhu strives to get rid of Wrong View and strives for Right View to arise. Such striving is the Right Effort of that bhikkhu. That bhikkhu, established in mindfulness, avoids Wrong View. Established in mindfulness, he abides endowed with Right View. Such mindfulness is the Right Mindfulness of that bhikkhu. Right View,[2] Right Effort and Right Mindfulness, these three factors always lead to and accompany Right View.

137. Bhikkhus, among the factors (of the Ariya Path), Right View leads the way. Bhikkhus, how does Right View lead the way? One knows Wrong Thinking as Wrong Thinking and Right Thinking as Right Thinking. Knowing thus is the Right View of that person. Bhikkhus, what is Wrong Thinking? Bhikkhus, thinking associated with sense-pleasures, with ill will and with harmfulness is Wrong Thinking.

Bhikkhus, what is Right Thinking? Bhikkhus, I teach that there are two kinds of Right Thinking. Bhikkhus, there is the Right Thinking which is associated with āsavas, is connected with meritorious factors, and which results in the coming into (repeated) existence of the aggregates. Bhikkhus, there is the (other) Right Thinking which is faultless, which is free of āsavas, and which, transcending the mundane, is part of the Ariya Path. Bhikkhus, what is the Right Thinking which is associated with āsavas, is connected with meritorious factors, and which results in the coming into (repeated) existence of the aggregates? Bhikkhus, thinking associated with liberation (from sense-pleasures), with non--destructiveness and with compassion is Right Thinking which is associated with āsavas, is connected with meritorious factors, and which results in the coming into (repeated) existence of the aggregates.

Bhikkhus, what is the (other) Right Thinking which is faultless, which is free of āsavas, and which, transcending the mundane, is part of the Ariya Path?

---

2. Right View: The Right View mentioned here is the right view gained through vipassanā Insight, i.e., the first kind of Right View expounded by the Buddha in this Sutta. This vipassanā Right View inevitably leads to and is a forerunner of the Right View gained through Magga Insight which is the second kind of Right View. Right Effort and Right Mindfulness simultaneously accompany Magga Right View.

Bhikkhus, there is thinking which is initial application of the mind, which is effective thinking, which is application of the mind to the object of thinking, which is effectively applying the mind to the object of thinking, which is focussing the mind on the object of thinking and which initiates the act of speech, by one whose mind is faultless, is free of āsavas, who has attained the Ariya Path and who cultivates Magga Insight. Bhikkhus, this is Right Thinking which is faultless, which is free of āsavas, and which, transcending the mundane, is part of the Ariya Path. That bhikkhu strives to get rid of Wrong Thinking and strives for Right Thinking to arise. Such striving is the Right Effort of that bhikkhu. That bhikkhu, established in mindfulness, avoids Wrong Thinking. Established in mindfulness, he abides endowed with Right Thinking. Such mindfulness is the Right Mindfulness of that bhikkhu. Right View, Right Effort and Right Mindfulness, these three factors always lead to and accompany Right Thinking.

138. Bhikkhus, among the factors (of the Ariya Path), Right View leads the way. Bhikkhus, how does Right View lead the way? One knows Wrong Speech as Wrong Speech and Right Speech as Right Speech. Knowing thus is the Right View of that person. Bhikkhus, what is Wrong Speech? Bhikkhus, false speech, malicious speech, harsh speech, or frivolous speech is Wrong Speech. Bhikkhus, what is Right Speech? Bhikkhus, I teach that there are two kinds of Right Speech. There is the Right Speech which is associated with āsavas, is connected with meritorious factors, and which results in the coming into (respeated) existence of the aggregates. Bhikkhus, there is the (other) Right Speech which is faultless, which is free of āsavas, and which, transcending the mundane, is part of the Ariya Path. Bhikkhus, what is the Right Speech which is associated with āsavas, is connected with meritorious factors, and which results in the coming into (repeated) existence of the aggregates? Bhikkhus, abstaining from false speech, malicious speech, harsh speech, or frivolous speech is the Right Speech which is associated with āsavas, is connected with meritorious factors, and which results in the coming into (repeated) existence of the aggregates.

Bhikkhus, what is the (other) Right Speech which is faultless, which is free of āsavas, and which, transcending the mundane, is part of the Ariya Path?

Bhikkhus, there is the total and absolute abstention from the four kinds of Wrong Speech and eradication of the same by one whose mind is faultless, is free of āsavas, who has attained the Ariya Path, and who cultivates Magga Insight. Bhikkhus, such abstention is the Right Speech which is faultless, which is free of āsavas, and which, transcending the mundane, is part of the Ariya Path. That bhikkhu strives to get rid of Wrong Speech and strives for Right Speech to arise. Such striving is the Right Effort of that bhikkhu. That bhikkhu, established in mindfulness, avoids Wrong Speech. Established in mindfulness, he abides endowed with Right Speech. Such mindfulness is the Right Mindfulness of that bhikkhu. Right View, Right Effort and Right Mindfulness, these three factors always lead to and accompany Right Speech.

139. Bhikkhus, among the factors (of the Ariya Path), Right View leads the way. Bhikkhus, how does Right View lead the way? One knows Wrong Action as Wrong Action and Right Action as Right Action. Knowing thus is the Right View of that person. Bhikkhus, what is Wrong Action? Bhikkhus, destroying life, taking what is not given, or indulging in wrong sensual pleasures is Wrong Action. Bhikkhus, what is Right Action? Bhikkhus, I teach that there are two kinds of Right Action. There is the Right Action which is associated with āsavas, is connected with meritorious factors, and which results in the coming into (repeated) existence of the aggregates. Bhikkhus, there is the (other) Right Action which is faultless, which is free of āsavas, and which, transcending the mundane, is part of the Ariya Path. Bhikkhus, what is the Right Action which is associated with āsavas, is connected with meritorious factors and which results in the coming into (repeated) existence of the aggregates? Bhikkhus, abstaining from destroying life, from taking what is not given, or from indulging in wrong sensual pleasures is the Right Action which is associated with āsavas, is connected with meritorious factors, and which results in the coming into (repeated) existence of the aggregates.

Bhikkhus, what is the (other) Right Action which is faultless, which is free of āsavas and which, transcending the mundane, is part of the Ariya Path? Bhikkhus, there is the total and absolute abstention from the three kinds of bodily misdeeds and eradication of the same by one whose mind is faultless, is free of āsavas, who has attained the Ariya Path and who cultivates Magga Insight. Bhikkhus, such abstention is the Right Action which is faultless, which is free of āsavas, and which, transcending the mundane, is part of the Ariya Path. That bhikkhu strives to get rid of Wrong Action and strives for Right Action to arise. Such striving is the Right Effort of that bhikkhu. That bhikkhu, established in mindfulness, avoids Wrong Action. Established in mindfulness, he abides endowed with Right Action. Such mindfulness is the Right Mindfulness of that bhikkhu. Right View, Right Effort and Right Mindfulness, these three factors always lead to and accompany Right Action.

140. Bhikkhus, among the factors (of the Ariya Path), Right View leads the way. Bhikkhus, how does Right View lead the way? One knows Wrong Livelihood as Wrong Livelihood and Right Livelihood as Right Livelihood. Knowing thus is the Right View of that person.

Bhikkhus, what is Wrong Livelihood? Bhikkhus, deceitful pretension (to attainments), flattery (for gain), subtle insinuation by signs and indications (for gain), using pressure (to get offerings), or the seeking of more gain by cunning offer of gifts is Wrong Livelihood.

Bhikkhus, what is Right Livelihood? Bhikkhus, I teach that there are two kinds of Right Livelihood. There is the Right Livelihood which is associated with āsavas, is connected with meritorious factors, and which results in the coming into (repeated) existence of the aggregates. Bhikkhus, there is the (other) Right Livelihood which is faultless, which is free of āsavas, and which, transcending the mundane, is part of the Ariya Path.

Bhikkhus, what is the Right Livelihood which is associated with āsavas, is connected with meritorious factors, and which results in the coming into (repeated) existence of the aggregates? Bhikkhus, in this matter, the ariya disciple avoids Wrong Livelihood and adopts Right Livelihood. Bhikkhus, this is the Right Livelihood which is associated with āsavas, is connected with meritorious factors, and which results in the coming into (repeated) existence of the aggregates.

Bhikkhus, what is the (other) Right Livelihood which is faultless, which is free of āsavas and which, transcending the mundane, is part of the Ariya Path.

Bhikkhus, there is the total and absolute abstention from Wrong Livelihood and eradication of the same by one whose mind is faultless, is free of āsavas, who has attained the Ariya Path, and who cultivates Magga Insight. Bhikkhus, such abstention is the Right Livelihood which is faultless, free of āsavas and which, transcending the mundane, is part of the Ariya Path. That bhikkhu strives to get rid of Wrong Livelihood and strives for Right Livelihood to arise. Such striving is the Right Effort of that bhikkhu. That bhikkhu, established in mindfulness, avoids Wrong Livelihood. Established in mindfulness, he abides endowed with Right Livelihood. Such mindfulness is the Right Mindfulness of that bhikkhu. Right View, Right Effort and Right Mindfulness, these three factors always lead to and accompany Right Livelihood.

141. Bhikkhus, among the factors (of the Ariya Path), Right View leads the way. Bhikkhus, how does Right View lead the way? Bhikkhus, in one who has Right View, there can arise Right Thinking. In one who has Right Thinking, there can arise Right Speech. In one who has Right Speech, there can arise Right Action. In one who has Right Action, there can arise Right Livelihood. In one who has Right Livelihood, there can arise Right Effort. In one who has Right Effort, there can arise Right Mindfulness. In one who has Right Mindfulness, there can arise Right Concentration. In one who has Right Concentration, there can arise Right Knowledge. In one who has Right Knowledge, there can arise Right Liberation (which means attainment of Arahattaphala). Bhikkhus, thus one who is still in training (sekkha) for perfection is endowed with eight factors; and the Arahat is endowed with ten factors.[3] (Among these factors it is Right Knowledge which brings about the freedom from various evil and demeritorious factors and the attainment of perfect mental development.)*

---

3. The person still in training *(sekkha)* who is established in the eight constituents of the Path, by attaining the two additional factors of *sammā-ñāṇa (paccavekkhaṇa-ñāṇa)* and the fruition that liberates one from defilements *(sammā-vimutti)*, becomes an arahat who is endowed with the ten factors.

* Parenthesis as indicated in Pāli Text.

142. Bhikkhus, among the factors (of the Ariya Path) Right View leads the way. Bhikkhus, how does Right View lead the way? Bhikkhus, in one who has Right View, Wrong View is destroyed. In such a person, various evil and demeritorious factors arising from Wrong View are also destroyed. Owing to Right View, various meritorious factors come to perfection in mental development (through meditation). Bhikkhus, in one who has Right Thinking, Wrong Thinking is destroyed ...p... Bhikkhus, in one who has Right Speech, Wrong Speech is destroyed .... Bhikkhus, in one who has Right Action, Wrong Action is destroyed ...... Bhikkhus, in one who has Right Livelihood, Wrong Livelihood is destroyed .... Bhikkhus, in one who has Right Effort, Wrong Effort is destroyed .... Bhikkhus, in one who has Right Mindfulness, Wrong Mindfulness is destroyed. .... Bhikkhus, in one who has Right Concentration, Wrong Concentration is destroyed .... Bhikkhus, in one who has Right Knowledge, Wrong Knowledge is destroyed .... Bhikkhus, in one who has attained Right Liberation (which means attainment of Arahattaphala), Wrong (concept of) Liberation is destroyed. In such a person, various evil and demeritorious factors arising from Wrong (concept of) Liberation are destroyed too. Also, owing to Right Liberation, various meritorious factors come to perfection in mental development (through meditation).

Bhikkhus, I have discoursed on the forty factors[4] comprising twenty meritorious and twenty demeritorious factors. Neither samaṇa nor brāhmaṇa nor deva nor māra nor Brahmā nor any one else in the world can take exception to this.

143. Bhikkhus, if any samaṇa or brāhmaṇa were to think it fit to criticize and disavow this discourse called Mahācattārīsaka, he would, in this very life, be subject to censure or justified condemnation on ten grounds. If the revered one were to disparage Right View, it would be tantamount to venerating and praising those samaṇas and brāhmaṇas who believe in Wrong View. If the revered one were to disparage Right Thinking, it would be tantamount to venerating and praising those

---

4. the forty factors: In the Pāli text, *Mahācattārīsaka*. The forty factors are the expansion of the eight factors of the Path. Therefore the epithet *mahā* is used, meaning here 'many' or 'various.'

samaṇas and brāhmaṇas who believe in Wrong Thinking. If the revered one were to disparage Right Speech ...p... If the revered one were to disparage Right Action .... If the revered one were to disparage Right Effort .... If the revered one were to disparage Right Mindfulness .... If the revered one were to disparage Right Concentration .... If the revered one were to disparage Right Knowledge .... If the revered one were to disparage Right Liberation (which means attainment of Arahattaphala), it would be tantamount to venerating and praising those samaṇas and brāhmaṇas who believe in the Wrong (concept of) Liberation.

Bhikkhus, if any samaṇa or brāhmaṇa were to think it fit to criticize and disavow this discourse called Mahācattārīsaka, he would, in this very life, be subject to censure or justified condemnation on ten grounus. Bhikkhus, even Vassa and Bhañña, the two residents of Ukkala village who believe in the Doctrine of Ahetuka (no past cause), the Doctrine of Akiriya (mere action without any effect), and the Doctrine of Natthika (no resultant in future existence) think that the discourse called Mahācattārīsaka should not be criticized and disavowed. Why is it so? Because they are afraid of being blamed, of being assailed and of being reproved by others.

Thus spoke the Bhagavā. Delighted, those bhikkhus rejoiced in what the Bhagavā had said.

End of the Mahācattārīsaka Sutta,
the seventh in this vagga.

8. ĀNĀPĀNASSATI SUTTA

Discourse on Mindfulness of In-coming and Out-going Breath

144. Thus have I heard:

Once the Bhagavā was residing with many of the most eminent senior disciples at Pubbārāma, the pinnacled monastery built by Migāramātā (Visākhā) in Sāvatthī. In residence with him were the Venerable Sāriputta, the Venerable Mahā Moggallāna, the Venerable Mahā Kassapa, the Venerable Mahā Kaccāyana, the Venerable Mahā Koṭṭhika, the Venerable Mahā Kappina, the Venerable Mahā Cunda, the Venerable Anuruddha, the Venerable Revata, the Venerable Ānanda and many other most eminent senior disciples.

On that occasion, the senior bhikkhus were giving advice and instruction to the junior bhikkhus. Some senior bhikkhus gave advice and instruction to ten bhikkhus; some senior bhikkhus gave advice and instruction to twenty bhikkhus; some senior bhikkhus gave advice and instruction to thirty bhikkhus; some senior bhikkhus gave advice and instruction to forty bhikkhus. On being thus advised and instructed by the senior bhikkhus, the junior bhikkhus came to acquire further knowledge which was superior to what they had learnt before.[1]

145. At that time, on the night of the fifteenth day of the month, the full moon day, an uposatha day which (also) happened to be the Pavāraṇā Day,[2] the

1. This means that the junior bhikkhus came to acquire further knowledge such as that of the preparation for meditation, the knowledge which is superior to the observance of moral discipline, etc., already known to them.

2. Pavāraṇā Day: A ceremony at the end of the rains retreat period *(vassa)* at which the bhikkhus in a certain community gather together and invite each other to give admonition for any transgression of the rules of discipline which, one sees or hears or has reason to believe, has been committed.

Bhagavā was sitting in the open air surrounded by a company of bhikkhus. Then, glancing round at the silent and quiet gathering of bhikkhus, the Bhagavā addressed them, saying: "Bhikkhus, I approve of this practice (of yours). And, bhikkhus, there is approval in my mind for this practice (of yours). Therefore, bhikkhus, strive your utmost to attain that which has not yet been attained, to obtain that which has not yet been obtained, and to realize that which has not yet been realized.[3] I shall tarry here in this city of Sāvatthī (postponing the Pavāraṇā ceremony) to the next full moon day at the end of the four-month rainy season when the white lotus blooms."

The bhikkhus living in the countryside heard: 'The Bhagavā would be tarrying in Sāvatthī till the end of the four-month rainy season when the white lotus blooms.' And the bhikkhus living in the countryside went to Sāvatthī to pay homage to the Bhagavā. The senior bhikkhus strove their utmost to give advice and instruction to the junior bhikkhus. Some senior bhikkhus gave advice and instruction to ten bhikkhus; some senior bhikkhus gave advice and instruction to twenty bhikkhus; some senior bhikkhus gave advice and instruction to thirty bhikkhus; and some senior bhikkhus gave advice and instruction to forty bhikkhus. On being thus advised and instructed by the senior bhikkhus, the junior bhikkhus came to acquire further knowledge which was superior to what they had learnt before.

146. At that time, on the night of the fifteenth day of the month, an uposatha day and the full moon day at the end of the four-month rainy season when the white lotus blooms, the Bhagavā was sitting in the open air surrounded by a company of bhikkhus. Then, glancing round at the silent and quiet company of bhikkhus, the Bhagavā addressed them, saying: "Bhikkhus, there is no worthlessness or inferiority in this gathering; bhikkhus, this gathering is pure and is full of essence.

"Bhikkhus, a gathering of such nature is worthy of offerings brought even from afar, is worthy of offerings specially set aside for guests, is worthy of

---

3. By what has not yet been attained, obtained and realized: is meant Arahattaphala.

offerings donated for well-being in the future existences; it is worthy of receiving obeisance; it is the incomparable fertile field for all to sow the seeds of merit. Bhikkhus, this company of bhikkhus is of such a character.

"Bhikkhus, a small amount of offering given to a gathering of such nature brings much merit; a large amount of offering brings much more merit. Bhikkhus, this company of bhikkhus is of such a character.

"Bhikkhus, it is a rare opportunity for people to see a gathering of such nature. Bhikkhus, this company of bhikkhus is of such a character.

"Bhikkhus, to pay homage to a gathering of such nature, it is worthwhile travelling for many yojanas[4] carrying provisions. Bhikkhus, this company of bhikkhus is of such a character."

147. Bhikkhus, in this company of bhikkhus, there are bhikkhus who are devoid of kilesas (defilements), who are rid of āsavas (defilements that befuddle the mind), who have fulfilled magga practice, have completed their task, have laid down the burden (of the five khandhas), have achieved the benefit (of Arahattaphala), have done away with the fetters binding them to existence, have full knowledge, and have a mind liberated from kilesas. Bhikkhus, in this company of bhikkhus, there are such bhikkhus.

Bhikkhus, in this company of bhikkhus, there are bhikkhus who, through the total destruction of the five fetters[5] that lead to (rebirth in) the lower planes (of sensual existence), will have a spontaneous rebirth (in the abode of brahmās) and, not being liable to return from that realm, will realize parinibbāna there. Bhikkhus, in this company of bhikkhus, there are such bhikkhus.

---

4. yojana: A unit of distance variously estimated as a distance between seven miles and twelve miles.

5. the five fetters: (i) *Sakkāyadiṭṭhi*, the view of individuality which wrongly takes any or all of the five aggregates of mind and matter as atta (Self), jīva (Soul), and satta (being). (ii) *Vicikicchā*, doubts in the Buddha, the Dhamma and the Saṁgha. (iii) *Sīlabbataparāmasa*, belief in efficacy of practices and paths other than the Ariya Path of Eight Constituents. (iv) *Kāmarāga*, craving for kāmabhava, sensual existence. (v) *Byāpāda*, ill will.

Bhikkhus, in this company of bhikkhus, there are bhikkhus who are Once-Returners (sakadāgāmīs), who, through the total destruction of the three fetters[6] and through lessening of attachment, anger and bewilderment, will return only once to this world and make an end of the cycle of dukkha. Bhikkhus, in this company of bhikkhus, there are such bhikkhus.

Bhikkhus, in this company of bhikkhus, there are bhikkhus who are Stream-Winners (sotāpannas) who, through the total destruction of three fetters, are not liable to fall into realms of misery and suffering, are definitely assured of a good destination and of attaining the three higher levels of Insight (magga). Bhikkhus, in this company of bhikkhus, there are such bhikkhus.

Bhikkhus, in this company of bhikkhus, there are bhikkhus who abide in the cultivation of the Four Methods of Steadfast Mindfulness (Satipaṭṭhāna). Bhikkhus, in this company of bhikkhus, there are such bhikkhus.

Bhikkhus, in this company of bhikkhus, there are bhikkhus who abide in the cultivation of the Four Supreme Efforts (Sammappadhāna) ...p... the Four Bases of Psychic Potency (Iddhipāda) ...p... the Five Faculties (Indriya) ...p... the Five Powers (Bala) ...p... the Seven Factors of Enlightenment (Bojjhaṅga) ...p... who abide in the cultivation of the Ariya Path of Eight Constituents (Aṭṭhaṅgika Magga). Bhikkhus, in this company of bhikkhus, there are such bhikkhus.

Bhikkhus, in this company of bhikkhus, there are bhikkhus who abide in the cultivation of goodwill (mettā), who abide in the cultivation of compassion (karuṇā), who abide in the cultivation of sympathetic joy (muditā), who abide in the cultivation of equanimity (upekkhā), who abide in the cultivation of meditation on foulness (asubha), who abide in the cultivation of meditation on the concept of impermanence. Bhikkhus, in this company of bhikkhus, there are such bhikkhus.

Bhikkhus, in this company of bhikkhus, there are bhikkhus who abide in the cultivation of mindfulness of in-coming breath and out-going breath. Bhikkhus, if one

---

6. the three fetters: the first three fetters mentioned in footnote No. 5.

cultivates and repeatedly practises mindfulness of the in-coming breath and out-going breath, it would prove immensely fruitful and highly beneficial. Bhikkhus, by cultivating and repeatedly practising mindfulness of the in-coming breath and out-going breath, the practice of the Four Methods of Steadfast Mindfulness is accomplished. By cultivating and repeatedly practising the Four Methods of Steadfast Mindfulness, the Seven Factors of Enlightenment are fulfilled. By cultivating and repeatedly practising the Seven Factors of Enlightenment, Emancipation by arahatta magga and arahatta phala is attained.

148. Bhikkhus, how should mindfulness of the in-coming breath and out-going breath be cultivated and how should it be repeatedly practised to be immensely fruitful and highly beneficial? In this Teaching, bhikkhus, the bhikkhu goes to the forest, or to the foot of a tree, or to a secluded place, sits cross-legged, keeps his body erect and establishes mindfulness, orientating it (towards the object of concentration). Then that bhikkhu breathes in with entire mindfulness, and breathes out with entire mindfulness. When he makes a long inhalation, he knows: "I make a long inhalation." When he makes a long exhalation, he knows: "I make a long exhalation." When he makes a short inhalation, he knows: "I make a short inhalation." When he makes a short exhalation, he knows: "I make a short exhalation." He trains himself to be clearly conscious of the whole stretch of the in-coming breath (at its beginning, at its middle and at its end). He trains himself to be clearly conscious of the whole stretch of the out--going breath (at its beginning, at its middle and at its end). He trains himself to calm down the strong inhalation as he breathes in. He trains himself to calm down the strong exhalation as he breathes out.

He trains himself to be clearly conscious of pīti (joyful satisfaction) as he inhales. He trains himself to be clearly conscious of pīti (joyful satisfaction) as he exhales. He trains himself to be clearly conscious of sukha (bliss) as he inhales. He trains himself to be clearly conscious of sukha (bliss) as he exhales. He trains himself to be clearly conscious of volitional activities (of sensation and perception) as he inhales. He trains himself to be clearly conscious of volitional activities as he exhales. He trains himself to calm down volitional activities as he inhales. He trains himself to calm down volitional activities as he exhales.

He trains himself to be clearly conscious of the mind as he inhales. He trains himself to be clearly conscious of the mind as he exhales. He trains himself to inhale with gladdened mind. He trains himself to exhale with gladdened mind.

He trains himself to inhale with settled mind.[7] He trains himself to exhale with settled mind. He trains himself to inhale with mind liberated (from defilements). He trains himself to exhale with mind liberated (from defilements).

He trains himself to inhale with repeated contemplation of impermanence. He trains himself to exhale with repeated contemplation of impermanence. He trains himself to inhale with repeated contemplation of destruction of attachment. He trains himself to exhale with repeated contemplation of destruction of attachment.[8] He trains himself to inhale with repeated contemplation of cessation (of conditioned and compounded factors). He trains himself to exhale with repeated contemplation of cessation (of conditioned and compounded factors). He trains himself to inhale with repeated contemplation of the discarding of defilements. He trains himself to exhale with repeated contemplation of the discarding of defilements.

Bhikkhus! Mindfulness of inhalation and exhalation, when thus cultivated and thus repeatedly practised, is immensely fruitful and highly beneficial.

149. Bhikkhus, in what manner is the Practice of the Four Methods of Steadfast Mindfulness accomplished by cultivating and repeatedly practising mindfulness of the in-coming breath and out-going breath? Bhikkhus, when the bhikkhu makes a long inhalation, he knows: "I make a long inhalation." When he makes a long exhalation, he knows: "I make a long exhalation." When

---

7. settled mind: *samādaha citta,* equivalent to *samāhita citta,* mind settled on an object of concentration.

8. Attachment *(rāga)* is almost synonymous with craving (*taṇhā*). Destruction of attachment (rāga) and cessation of conditioned and compounded factors are of the same nature and imply the realization of Nibbāna. Discarding of defilements also implies realization of magga and Nibbāna.

he makes a short inhalation, he knows: "I make a short inhalation." When he makes a short exhalation, he knows: "I make a short exhalation."

He trains himself to be clearly conscious of the whole stretch of the in-coming breath (at its beginning, at its middle and at its end). He trains himself to be clearly conscious of the whole stretch of the out-going breath (at its beginning, at its middle and at its end). He trains himself to calm down the strong inhalation as he breathes in. He trains himself to calm down the strong exhalation as he breathes out.

At that time, bhikkhus, that bhikkhu keeps his mind steadfastly on the body (kāya), with diligence, comprehension and mindfulness, (and perceives its impermanent, insecure, soulless and unpleasant nature), thus keeping away covetousness and distress pertaining to the five khandha aggregates which are the objects of Clinging.[9] Bhikkhus, I teach the in-coming breath and the out-going breath as being one of the kāyas.[10] For that reason, bhikkhus, the bhikkhu keeps his mind steadfastly on the body (kāya), with diligence, comprehension and mindfulness (and perceives its impermanent, insecure, soulless and unpleasant nature), thus keeping away covetousness and distress pertaining to the five khandha aggregates which are the objects of Clinging.(1)

Bhikkhus, the bhikkhu trains himself to be clearly conscious of pīti (joyful satisfaction) as he inhales. He trains himself to be clearly conscious of pīti (joyful satisfaction) as he exhales. He trains himself to be clearly conscious of sukha (bliss) as he inhales. He trains himself to be. clearly conscious of sukha (bliss) as he exhales. He trains himself to be clearly conscious of volitional activities (of sensation and perception) as he inhales. He trains himself to be clearly conscious of volitional activities as he exhales.

---

9. the five khandha ..... of Clinging: In the Pāḷi text *loka;* interpreted by the Commentary in the Mahāsatipaṭṭhāna Sutta as rendered here.

10. *Kāya* in the sense of material body can be reduced to the four great primary elements, literally translated as 'earth, water, fire and air', --- *'pathavī, āpo, tejo* and *vāyo'*. By identifying kāya with those four elements, kāya is classified into four kinds.

The in-coming breath and out-going breath come under vāyo kāya.

He trains himself to calm down volitional activities as he inhales. He trains himself to calm down volitional activities as he exhales.

At that time, bhikkhus, that bhikkhu keeps his mind steadfastly on sensation (vedanā), with diligence, comprehension and mindfulness, (and perceives its impermanent, insecure, soulless and unpleasant nature), thus keeping away covetousness and distress pertaining to the five khandha aggregates which are the objects of Clinging. Bhikkhus, I teach proper reflection on the in-coming breath and the out-going breath as being one of the Sensations (vedanā).[11] For that reason, bhikkhus, the bhikkhu keeps his mind steadfastly on Sensation (vedanā), with diligence, comprehension and mindfulness (and perceives its impermanent, insecure, soulless and unpleasant nature), thus keeping away covetousness and distress pertaining to the five khandha aggregates which are the objects of Clinging. (2)

Bhikkhus, the bhikkhu trains himself to be clearly conscious of the mind as he inhales. He trains himself to be clearly conscious of the mind as he exhales. He trains himself to inhale with gladdened mind. He trains himself to exhale with gladdened mind. He trains himself to inhale with settled mind. He trains himself to exhale with settled mind. He trains himself to inhale with mind liberated (from defilements). He trains himself to exhale with mind liberated (from defilements).

At that time, bhikkhus, that bhikkhu concentrates steadfastly on the mind (citta), with diligence, comprehension and mindfulness, (and perceives its impermanent, insecure, soulless and unpleasant nature), thus keeping away covetousness and distress pertaining to the five khandha aggregates which are the objects of Clinging. Bhikkhus, I do not teach mindfulness of the in-coming breath and out-going breath to one who is given to forgetfulness and is lacking in clear comprehension. For that reason, bhikkhus, that bhikkhu concentrates steadfastly on the mind (citta) with diligence, comprehension and mindfulness, (and perceives

11. one of the sensations (vedanās): Sensation is classified into three, namely, pleasant sensation (sukha vedanā), unpleasant sensation (dukkha vedanā) and neither pleasant nor unpleasant sensation (upekkhā vedanā). Here pleasant sensation is meant.

its impermanent, insecure, soulless and unpleasant nature), thus keeping away covetousness and distress pertaining to the five khandha aggregates which are the objects of Clinging. (3)

Bhikkhus, the bhikkhu trains himself to inhale with repeated contemplation of impermanence. He trains himself to exhale with repeated contemplation of impermanence. He trains himself to inhale with repeated contemplation of destruction of attachment. He trains himself to exhale with repeated contemplation of destruction of attachment. He trains himself to inhale with repeated contemplation of cessation (of conditioned and compounded factors). He trains himself to exhale with repeated contemplation of cessation (of conditioned and compounded factors). He trains himself to inhale with repeated contemplation of the discarding of defilements. He trains himself to exhale with repeated contemplation of the discarding of defilements.

At that time, bhikkhus, that bhikkhu keeps his mind steadfastly on the dhammā,[12] with diligence, comprehension and mindfulness, (and perceives their impermanent, insecure, soulless and unpleasant nature), thus keeping away covetousness and distress pertaining to the five khandha aggregates which are the objects of Clinging. That bhikkhu abandons covetousness and distress; and seeing that abandonment with insight, there is complete equanimity in him. For that reason, bhikkhus, the bhikkhu keeps his mind steadfastly on the dhammā, with diligence, comprehension and mindfulness (and perceives their impermanent, insecure, soulless and unpleasant nature), thus keeping away covetousness and distress pertaining to the five khandha aggregates which are the objects of Clinging. (4)

Bhikkhus, by thus cultivating and by thus repeatedly practising mindfulness of the in-coming breath and out-going breath, the practice of the Four Methods of Steadfast Mindfulness is accomplished.

150. Bhikkhus, in what manner are the Seven Factors of Enlightenment fulfilled by cultivating and repeatedly practising the Four Methods of Steadfast

12. keeps his mind ..... on the dhammā: Being completely aware of the absence in him of covetousness and distress, i.e., sense-desire and ill-will which are two of the five hindrances (nīvaraṇas).

Mindfulness? Bhikkhus, the bhikkhu keeps his mind steadfastly on the body (kāya), with diligence, comprehension and mindfulness (and perceives its impermanent, insecure, soulless and unpleasant nature), thus keeping away covetousness and distress pertaining to the five khandha aggregates which are the objects of Clinging. At that time, the mindfulness of that bhikkhu is established without remission. Bhikkhus, when the mindfulness of that bhikkhu is established without remission, the enlightenment-factor of mindfulness of that bhikkhu is developed; the bhikkhu repeatedly cultivates the enlightenment-factor of mindfulness; and cultivation of the enlightenment-factor of mindfulness of that bhikkhu is completed. (1)

That bhikkhu, who is thus established in mindfulness, reflects on, examines and investigates that dhamma (i.e., the phenomenon of inhaling and exhaling) with vipassanā insight. Bhikkhus, when the bhikkhu, who is thus established in mindfulness, reflects on, examines and investigates that dhamma with vipassanā insight, the enlightenment-factor of investigative knowledge of phenomena of that bhikkhu is developed; the bhikkhu repeatedly cultivates the enlightenment-factor of investigative knowledge of phenomena; and the cultivation of the enlightenment-factor of investigative knowledge of phenomena of that bhikkhu is completed. (2)

In that bhikkhu, who has thus reflected on, examined and investigated that dhamma with vipassanā insight, unrelenting effort is developed. Bhikkhus, when the unrelenting effort of the bhikkhu, who has thus reflected on, examined and investigated that dhamma with vipassanā insight, is developed, the enlightenment-factor of effort of that bhikkhu is developed; the bhikkhu repeatedly cultivates the enlightenment-factor of effort; and the cultivation of the enlightenment-factor of effort of that bhikkhu is completed. (3)

To the bhikkhu who is endowed with unrelenting effort there arises pīti (joyful satisfaction) that is free from defilements. Bhikkhus, when pīti that is free from defilements arises in that bhikkhu who is endowed with unrelenting effort, the enlightenment-factor of delightful satisfaction of that bhikkhu is developed; the bhikkhu repeatedly cultivates the enlightenment-factor of delightful satisfaction; and the cultivation of the enlightenment-factor of delightful satisfaction of that bhikkhu is completed. (4)

The bhikkhu who has a mind filled with pīti (delightful satisfaction) is calm in body* and mind. Bhikkhus, when the bhikkhu who has a mind filled with pīti is calm in body and mind, the enlightenment-factor of serenity of that bhikkhu is developed; the bhikkhu repeatedly cultivates the enlightenment-factor of serenity; and the cultivation of the enlightenment-factor of serenity of that bhikkhu is completed. (5)

The mind of the bhikkhu, who is calm in body and is happy, is established in concentration. Bhikkhus, when the mind of that bhikkhu, who is calm in body and is happy, is established in concentration, the enlightenment-factor of concentration of that bhikkhu is developed; the bhikkhu repeatedly cultivates the enlightenment-factor of concentration; and the cultivation of the enlightenment-factor of concentration of that bhikkhu is completed. (6)

The bhikkhu views with perfect equanimity the mind thus established in concentration. Bhikkhus, when that bhikkhu views with perfect equanimity the mind thus established in concentration, the enlightenment-factor of equanimity of that bhikkhu is developed; the bhikkhu repeatedly cultivates the enlightenment-factor of equanimity; and the cultivation of the enlightenment-factor of equanimity of that bhikkhu is completed. (7)

151. Bhikkhus, the bhikkhu keeps his mind steadfastly on Sensation ...p... Bhikkhus, the bhikkhu concentrates steadfastly on the mind ...p... Bhikkhus, the bhikkhu keeps his mind steadfastly on the dhammā, with diligence, comprehension and mindfulness, (and perceives their impermanent, insecure, soulless and unpleasant nature), thus keeping away covetousness and distress pertaining to the five khandha aggregates which are the objects of Clinging. At that time, the mindfulness of that bhikkhu is established without remission. Bhikkhus, when the mindfulness of the bhikkhu is established without remission the enlightenment-factor of mindfulness of that bhikkhu is developed; the bhikkhu repeatedly cultivates the enlightenment-factor of mindfulness; and the cultivation of the enlightenment-factor of mindfulness of that bhikkhu is completed. (1)

---

* Body: By this is meant here the body of mental concomitants, specifically, sensation, perception and volitional activities. The same applies to 'body' in the next paragraph.

That bhikkhu, who is thus established in mindfulness, reflects on, examines and investigates that dhamma (i.e., the phenomenon of inhaling and exhaling) with vipassanā insight. Bhikkhus, when the bhikkhu, who is thus established in mindfulness, reflects on, examines and investigates that dhamma with vipassanā insight, the enlightenment-factor of the investigative knowledge of phenomena of that bhikkhu is developed; the bhikkhu repeatedly cultivates the enlightenment-factor of investigative knowledge of phenomena; and the cultivation of the enlightenment factor of investigative knowledge of phenomena of that bhikkhu is completed. (2)

In that bhikkhu, who has thus reflected on, examined and investigated that dhamma with vipassanā insight, unrelenting effort is developed. Bhikkhus, when the unrelenting effort of the bhikkhu, who has thus reflected on, examined and investigated that dhamma with vipassanā insight, is developed, the enlightenment-factor of effort of that bhikkhu is developed; the bhikkhu repeatedly cultivates the enlightenment-factor of effort; and the cultivation of the enlightenment factor of effort of that bhikkhu is completed. (3)

To the bhikkhu who is endowed with unrelenting effort there arises pīti (joyful satisfaction) that is free from defilements. Bhikkhus, when pīti that is free from defilements arises in that bhikkhu who is endowed with unrelenting effort, the enlightenment-factor of delightful satisfaction of that bhikkhu is developed; the bhikkhu repeatedly cultivates the enlightenment-factor of delightful satisfaction; and the cultivation of the enlightenment-factor of delightful satisfaction of that bhikkhu is completed. (4)

The bhikkhu who has a mind filled with delightful satisfaction is calm in body and mind. Bhikkhus, when the bhikkhu, who has a mind filled with delightful satisfaction, is calm in body and mind, the enlightenment-factor of serenity of that bhikkhu is developed; the bhikkhu repeatedly cultivates the enlightenment-factor of serenity; and the cultivation of the enlightenment--factor of serenity of that bhikkhu is completed. (5)

The mind of the bhikkhu, who is calm in body and is happy, is established in concentration. Bhikkhus, when the mind of that bhikkhu, who is calm in body and is happy, is established in concentration, the enlightenment-factor of concentration of that bhikkhu is developed; the bhikkhu repeatedly cultivates the enlightenment-factor of concentration; and the cultivation of the enlightenment-factor of concentration of that bhikkhu is completed. (6)

That bhikkhu views with perfect equanimity the mind thus established in concentration. Bhikkhus, when that bhikkhu views with perfect equanimity the mind thus established in concentration, the enlightenment--factor of equanimity of that bhikkhu is developed; the bhikkhu repeatedly cultivates the enlightenment-factor of equanimity; and the cultivation of the enlightenment--factor of equanimity of that bhikkhu is completed. Bhikkhus, by thus cultivating and by thus repeatedly practising meditation on the Four Methods of Steadfast Mindfulness, the Seven Factors of Enlightenment are fulfilled. (7)

152. Bhikkhus, in what manner is the Emancipation through insight-wisdom attained by cultivating and by repeatedly practising the Seven Factors of Enlightenment? Bhikkhus, in this Teaching, the bhikkhu cultivates the enlightenment-factor of mindfulness that is directed to detachment (viveka) from defilements, freedom from attachment (virāga), cessation (nirodha) of defilements, and that promotes and develops the uprooting of defilements and speedy attainment of Nibbāna (vossagga). He cultivates the enlightenment-factor of investigative knowledge of phenomena ...p... He cultivates the enlightenment-factor of effort ...p... He cultivates the enlightenment-factor of delightful satisfaction ...p... He cultivates the enlightenment-factor of serenity ...p... He cultivates the enlightenment-factor of concentration ...p... He cultivates the enlightenment-factor of equanimity that is directed to detachment from defilements, freedom from attachment, cessation of defilements, and that promotes and develops the uprooting of defilements and speedy attainment of Nibbāna. Bhikkhus, the Emancipation through Insight-wisdom is attained by thus cultivating and by thus repeatedly practising the Seven Factors of Enlightenment.

Thus spoke the Bhagavā. Delighted with what the Bhagavā had said, the bhikkhus received it with gladness.

End of the Ānāpānassati Sutta,
the eighth in this vagga.

9. KĀYAGATĀSATI SUTTA

Discourse on Mindfulness of the Body

153. Thus have I heard:

Once the Bhagavā was staying at the Jetavana monastery of Anāthapindika in Sāvatthī. On that occasion, the following unfinished conversation arose among many bhikkhus who had had their alms-food, had left the place (of the meal) and gathered in the assembly-hall: 'Friends! How wonderful! And, indeed, how marvellous, friends, that what has never happened before has now happened! The Bhagavā who knows all and sees all, who is worthy of special veneration and who is perfectly self-enlightened, has taught that mindfulness of the body, if cultivated and if repeatedly practised, is immensely fruitful and highly beneficial. Then in the evening before the conversation of those bhikkhus had finished, the Bhagavā rose from his solitary retreat, approached the assembly-hall and took the seat prepared for him. After taking the seat, the Bhagavā asked the bhikkhus:

"Bhikkhus, what were you talking about as you are assembled here? What was the subject of your unfinished conversation before I came?" "Venerable Sir, the conversation which we were having in this assembly--hall where we have gathered after having had our alms-food and left the place (of the meal) is this: 'Friends! How wonderful! And, indeed, how marvellous, friends, that what has never happened before has now happened! The Bhagavā who knows all and sees all, and who is worthy of special veneration and who is perfectly self-enlightened, has taught that mindfulness of the body, if cultivated and if repeatedly practised, is immensely fruitful and highly beneficial.' Venerable Sir, this was the unfinished conversation before the Bhagavā came in."

154. Bhikkhus, how should mindfulness of the body be cultivated and how should it be repeatedly practised to be immensely fruitful and highly beneficial? In this Teaching, bhikkhus, the bhikkhu goes to the forest or to the foot of a tree or to a secluded place, sits cross-legged, keeps his body erect and establishes mindfulness, orientating it (towards the object of concentration). Then, that bhikkhu breathes in with entire mindfulness, and breathes out with entire mindfulness. When he makes a long inhalation, he knows: "I make a long inhalation." When he makes a long exhalation, he knows: "I make a long exhalation." When he makes a short inhalation, he knows: "I make a short inhalation." When he makes a short exhalation, he knows: "I make a short exhalation." He trains himself to be clearly conscious of the whole stretch of the in-coming breath (at its beginning, at its middle and at its end). He trains himself to be clearly conscious of the whole stretch of the out-going breath (at its beginning, at its middle and at its end). He trains himself to calm down the strong inhalation as he breathes in. He trains himself to calm down the strong exhalation as he breathes out. While the bhikkhu is thus abiding in mindfulness and diligence, directing his mind (to Nibbāna), thoughts based on and directed to sensual pleasures disappear. Because of the disappearance of such thoughts, his mind is well established on and is well absorbed only in the object of meditation, is fixed one-pointedly and is set up well only on it. Bhikkhus, thus does the bhikkhu cultivate mindfulness of the body. (1)

And again, bhikkhus, the bhikkhu, when walking, is conscious of walking; or when standing, he is conscious of standing; or when sitting, he is conscious of sitting; or when lying down, he is conscious of lying down; or in whatever movement or posture his body is, he is conscious of it. While the bhikkhu is thus abiding in mindfulness and diligence, directing his mind (to Nibbāna), thoughts based on and directed to sensual pleasures disappear. Because of the disappearance of such thoughts, his mind is well established on and is well absorbed only in the object of meditation, is fixed one-pointedly and is set up well only on it. Bhikkhus, thus does the bhikkhu cultivate mindfulness of the body. (2)

And again, bhikkhus, the bhikkhu in moving forward and in moving back, does so with clear comprehension; in looking straight ahead and sideways, he does so with clear comprehension; in bending and in stretching his limbs, he does so with clear comprehension; in carrying or wearing the great robe, alms-bowl and the other two robes, he does so with clear comprehension; in eating, drinking, chewing and savouring, he does so with clear comprehension; in defecating and urinating, he does so with clear comprehension; in walking, standing, sitting, falling asleep, waking, speaking or in keeping silent, he does so with clear comprehension. While the bhikkhu is thus abiding in mindfulness and diligence, directing his mind (to Nibbāna), thoughts based on and directed to sensual pleasures disappear. Because of the disappearance of such thoughts, his mind is well established on and is well absorbed only in the object of meditation, is fixed one-pointedly and is set up well only on it. Bhikkhus, thus does the bhikkhu cultivate mindfulness of the body. (3)

And again, bhikkhus, the bhikkhu examines and reflects closely upon this very body, from the soles of the feet up and from the tips of the hair down, enclosed by the skin and full of manifold impurities, (thinking thus:) "There are in this body: hair of the head, hairs of the body, nails, teeth, skin, flesh, sinews, bones, marrow, kidneys, heart, liver, membranes (including the pleura, diaphragm and other forms of membranes in the body), spleen, lungs, large intestine, small intestine, contents of the stomach,faeces, (brain),[1] bile, phlegm, pus, blood, sweat, solid fat, tears, liquid fat, saliva, nasal mucus, synovic fluid (i.e., lubricating oil of the joints) and urine."

Just as if, bhikkhus, there were a bag with an opening at each end, full of various kinds of grain such as hill-paddy, paddy, green gram, cow-pea, sesame and husked rice; and as if a man with normal vision, having opened it, should examine and reflect (on the contents) thus: "This is hill-paddy, this is paddy, this is green gram, this is cow-pea, this is sesame, this is husked rice," even so, bhikkhus, the bhikkhu examines and

---

1. "the brain" is not included in the Pāḷi Text of this sutta, but is included in the Paṭisambhidā Magga.

reflects on this very body, from the soles of the feet up and from the tips of the hair down, enclosed by the skin and full of manifold impurities, (thinking thus:) "There are in this body: hair of the head, hairs of the body, nails, teeth, skin, flesh, sinews, bones, marrow, kidneys, heart, liver, membranes (including the pleura, diaphragm and other forms of membranes in the body), spleen, lungs, large intestine, small intestine, contents of the stomach, faeces, (brain), bile, phlegm, pus, blood, sweat, solid fat, tears, liquid fat, saliva, nasal mucus, synovic fluid (i.e., lubricating oil of the joints) and urine." While the bhikkhu is thus abiding in mindfulness and diligence, directing his mind (to Nibbāna), thoughts based on and directed to sensual pleasures disappear. Because of the disappearance of such thoughts, his mind is well established on and is well absorbed only in the object of meditation, is fixed one-pointedly and is set up well only on it. Bhikkhus, thus does the bhikkhu cultivate mindfulness of the body. (4)

And again, bhikkhus, the bhikkhu examines and reflects on this very body, in whatever position it remains or is placed, as composed of the primary elements:[2] "There are in this body (only) the earth element, the water element, the fire element, and the air element."

Just as if, bhikkhus, a skilful butcher or a butcher's apprentice, having slaughtered a cow and cut it up into portions, should be sitting at the junction of

2. the primary elements: *dhātu*, element, is a force of Nature which behaves in accordance with the laws of Nature. The four primary elements, literally translated above for the sake of brevity as 'earth, water, fire, and air', are:

(1) *Pathavī-dhātu*: a force of Nature that has the attribute of causing hardness. (It is sometimes translated as the element of solidity or of extension);

(2) *Āpo-dhātu* : a force of Nature that has the attributes of causing cohesion and of causing fluidity. (It is sometimes translated as the element of cohesion);

(3) *Tejo-dhātu* : a force of Nature that has the attributes of causing heat or cold, i.e., thermal energy. (It is sometimes translated as the element of heat);

(4) *Vāyo-dhātu* : a force of Nature that has the attribute of causing motion or impetus. (It is sometimes translated as the element of motion).

four main roads, (so that only pieces of meat are seen and not the cow as such), even so, the bhikkhu examines and reflects on this very body in whatever position it remains or is placed, as composed of the primary elements: "There are in this body (only) the earth element, the water element, the fire element, and the air element." While the bhikkhu is thus abiding in mindfulness and diligence, directing his mind (to Nibbāna), thoughts based on and directed to sensual pleasures disappear. Because of the disappearance of such thoughts, his mind is well established on and is well absorbed only in the object of meditation, is fixed one-pointedly and is set up well only on it. Bhikkhus, thus does the bhikkhu cultivate mindfulness of the body. (5)

And again, bhikkhus, as if the bhikkhu is seeing a body, one day dead, or two days dead, or three days dead, swollen, turning black and blue, and festering, abandoned in the charnel-ground, he applies (this perception) to his own body thus: "Indeed, this body of mine, too, is of the same nature; it will become like that; it cannot escape such a fate." While the bhikkhu is thus abiding in mindfulness and diligence, directing his mind (to Nibbāna), thoughts based on and directed to sensual pleasures disappear. Because of the disappearance of such thoughts, his mind is well established on and is well absorbed only in the object of meditation, is fixed one-pointedly and is set up well only on it. Bhikkhus, thus does the bhikkhu cultivate mindfulness of the body. (6)

And again, bhikkhus, as if the bhikkhu is seeing a body abandoned in the charnel-ground, being devoured by crows, being devoured by hawks, being devoured by vultures, being devoured by herons, being devoured by dogs, being devoured by tigers, being devoured by leopards, being devoured by jackals, or being devoured by various kinds of worms, he applies (this perception) to his own body thus: "Indeed, this body of mine, too, is of the same nature; it will become like that; it cannot escape such a fate." While the bhikkhu is thus abiding in mindfulness ...p... Bhikkhus, thus does the bhikkhu cultivate mindfulness of the body. (7)

And again, bhikkhus, as if the bhikkhu is seeing a body abandoned in the charnel-ground – (reduced to) a skeleton held together by the tendons, with some flesh and blood still adhering to it ...., (reduced to) a skeleton held together by the tendons, blood-besmeared, fleshless ..., (reduced to) a skeleton still held together by the tendons, without flesh and blood .... (reduced to) loose bones scattered in all directions, – at one place bones of a hand, at another place bones of a foot, at another place ankle-bones, at another place shin-bones, at another place thigh-bones, at another place hip-bones, at another place rib-bones, at another place spinal-bones, at another place shoulder-bones, at another place neck-bones, at another place jawbone, at another place the teeth, at another place the skull, he applies (this perception) to his own body thus: "Indeed, this body of mine, too, is of the same nature; it will become like that; it cannot escape such a fate." While the bhikkhu is thus abiding in mindfulness ...p... Bhikkhus, thus does the bhikkhu cultivate mindfulness of the body. (8-11)

And again, bhikkhus, as if the bhikkhu is seeing a body abandoned in the charnel-ground –

(reduced to) bleached bones of conch-like colour .....,

(reduced to) bones more than a year old, lying in a heap .....,

(reduced to) rotted bones crumbling to dust, he applies (this perception) to his own body thus: "Indeed, this body of mine, too, is of the same nature; it will become like that; it cannot escape such a fate." While the bhikkhu is thus abiding in mindfulness ...p... Bhikkhus, thus does the bhikkhu cultivate mindfulness of the body (12-14).

155. And again, bhikkhus, the bhikkhu being detached from sensual pleasures and demeritorious factors, achieves and remains in the first jhāna ...p..* He soaks, drenches, permeates, and suffuses his body with pīti (delightful satisfaction) and sukha (bliss), born of detachment from the hindrances. There is no place in his body not suffused with pīti and sukha, born of detachment from the hindrances.

Bhikkhus, take the example of a skilful bath--attendant or his assistant, who strews bath-powder in

* Repeat as in paras 51 and 84 of Mūlapaṇṇāsa, on the jhānas.

a brass dish, sprinkles and sprinkles water on it and makes it into a mass. That mass of bath-powder is permeated, is soaked and is suffused inside and out with viscous water; there is no oozing of water.

Bhikkhus, in the same way, the bhikkhu soaks, drenches, permeates and suffuses his body with pīti and sukha, born of detachment from the hindrances. There is no place in his body not suffused with pīti and sukha, born of detachment from the hindrances. While the bhikkhu is thus abiding in mindfulness ...p... Bhikkhus, thus does the bhikkhu cultivate mindfulness of the body. (15)

And again, bhikkhus, the bhikkhu, having got rid of vitakka (initial application of the mind) and vicāra (sustained application of the mind), achieves and remains in the second jhāna ...p... He soaks, drenches, permeates and suffuses his body with pīti and sukha, born of concentration. There is no place in his body not suffused with pīti and sukha, born of concentration.

Bhikkhus, take the example of a deep lake with water welling up from a spring below. There is no inlet from either east or west or north or south. It does not rain heavily or regularly there. And yet cool water which wells up from that spring soaks, drenches, permeates and suffuses the lake and there is no place in that lake not suffused with it. Bhikkhus, in the same way, that bhikkhu soaks, drenches, permeates and suffuses his body with pīti and sukha, born of concentration. There is no place in his body not suffused with them. While the bhikkhu is thus abiding in mindfulness ...p... Bhikkhus, thus does the bhikkhu cultivate mindfulness of the body. (16)

And again, bhikkhus, having been detached from pīti, that bhikkhu dwells in equanimity with mindfulness and clear comprehension and experiences sukha in mind and body. He achieves and remains in the third jhāna, that which causes a person who attains it to be praised by the Ariyas as one who has equanimity and mindfulness, one who abides in sukha. He soaks, drenches, permeates and suffuses his body with sukha detached from pīti. There is no place in his body not suffused with sukha detached from pīti.

Bhikkhus, take the example of uppala, paduma and puṇḍarika lotus in a pond where they grow in the water and thrive in it. Even when they are submerged, they thrive under water, soaked, drenched, permeated and suffused from root to apex with cool water. There is no spot in the whole plant of an uppala, paduma or puṇḍarika lotuses not suffused with it. Bhikkhus, in the same way, the bhikkhu soaks, drenches, permeates and suffuses his body with sukha detached from pīti; and there is no place in his body which is not suffused with sukha detached from pīti. While the bhikkhu is thus abiding in mindfulness ...p... Bhikkhus, thus does the bhikkhu cultivate mindfulness of the body. (17)

And again, bhikkhus, by dispelling both pleasure and pain, (and by the previous disappearance of gladness and sadness) * that bhikkhu achieves and remains in the fourth jhāna, (without pleasure and pain, a state of equanimity and absolute purity of mindfulness).* That bhikkhu dwells suffusing his body with a mind which is pure and stainless. There is no place in his body which is not suffused with it. Bhikkhus, take the example of a man sitting wrapped up head to foot in a white cloth leaving no place on his whole body uncovered by it.[3] Bhikkhus, in the same way that bhikkhu dwells suffusing his body with a mind which is pure and stainless. There is no place in his body which is not suffused with it. While the bhikkhu was thus abiding in mindfulness and diligence, directing his mind (to Nibbāna), thoughts based on and directed to sensual pleasures disappear. Because of the disappearance of such thoughts, his mind is well established on and is well absorbed only in the object of meditation, is fixed one-pointedly and is set up well only on it. Bhikkhus, thus does the bhikkhu cultivate mindfulness of the body. (18)

156. Bhikkhus, when a certain person cultivates and repeatedly practises mindfulness of the body, all meritorious factors that are conducive to true knowledge (vijjā) are included in the meditation practice of that person. For example, bhikkhus, when a certain person thinks of the great ocean, all small rivers flowing into

---

* In the Pāḷi text, the words within the two brackets are indicated only by one *peyyāla*.

3. In this comparison, body warmth, generated by the body which is covered from head to foot, is meant. (The Commentary of Sīlakkhandha Vagga Pāḷi).

the ocean are included in his thought. Similarly, bhikkhus, when a certain person cultivates and repeatedly practises mindfulness of the body, all meritorious factors that are conducive to true knowledge are included in the meditation practice of that person.

Bhikkhus, if a certain person does not cultivate and does not repeatedly practise mindfulness of the body, defilements[4] get a chance and an opportunity to arise in him. Suppose, bhikkhus, a man were to drop a heavy stone on a moist heap of earth. Bhikkhus, what do you think of this? Would that heavy stone get a chance to enter into the moist heap of earth? "Yes, Venerable Sir." Similarly, bhikkhus, if a certain person does not cultivate and does not repeatedly practise mindfulness of the body, defilements get a chance and an opportunity to arise in him.

Suppose, bhikkhus, there were a dry, sapless piece of firewood. Then, there might come a man bringing a fire-making stick, thinking: 'I will make a fire. I will produce heat.' Bhikkhus, what do you think of this? Could that man make a fire and produce heat by rubbing the fire-making stick against this dry sapless piece of firewood? "Yes, Venerable Sir." Bhikkhus Similarly, if a certain person does not cultivate and does not repeatedly practise mindfulness of the body, defilements get a chance and an opportunity to arise in him.

Suppose, bhikkhus, there were an empty water-pot placed on a circular rest. Then, there might come a man carrying water. Bhikkhus, what do you think of this? Would that man find a place to pour the water into? "Yes, Venerable Sir." Similarly, bhikkhus, if a certain person does not cultivate and does not repeatedly practise mindfulness of the body, defilements get a chance and an opportunity to arise in him.

157. Bhikkhus, when a certain person cultivates and repeatedly practises mindfulness of the body, defilements will get no chance or opportunity to arise in him.

---

4. defilements: In the Pāḷi text, māra. Here it means *kilesa māra*, simply rendered defilements.

Suppose, bhikkhus, a man were to throw a light ball of thread at a door-panel all of heartwood. Bhikkhus, what do you think of this? Would that man make the light ball of thread find an entry into that door-panel all of heartwood? "No, Venerable Sir." Similarly, bhikkhus, when a certain person cultivates and repeatedly practises mindfulness of the body, defilements will get no chance or opportunity to arise in him.

Suppose, bhikkhus, there were a wet, sappy piece of firewood. Then, there might come a man bringing a fire-making stick, thinking: 'I will make a fire. I will produce heat'. Bhikkhus, what do you think of this? Would that man make fire and produce heat by rubbing the fire-making stick against the wet and sappy piece of firewood? "No, Venerable Sir." Similarly, bhikkhus, when a certain person cultivates and repeatedly practises mindfulness of the body, defilements will get no chance or opportunity to arise in him.

Suppose, bhikkhus, there were a waterpot, filled with water full to the brim so that a crow can drink out of it, placed on a circular rest. Then, there might come a man carrying water. Bhikkhus, what do you think of this? Would that man find a place to pour the water into? "No, Venerable Sir." Similarly, bhikkhus, when a certain person cultivates and repeatedly practises mindfulness of the body, defilements will get no chance or opportunity to arise in him.

158. Bhikkhus, when a certain person cultivates and repeatedly practises mindfulness of the body, should that person wish to realize by means of abhiññā (Magga Insight) such dhammas that are to be realized by means of abhiññā, he will personally experience the fulfilment of the wish whenever there is the (proper) basis (for its fulfilment).

Suppose, bhikkhus, there were a waterpot, filled with water full to the brim so that a crow can drink out of it, placed on a circular rest. Then, a strong man might move that waterpot to anywhere he desires. Will the water be carried along (with the waterpot)? "Yes, Venerable Sir." Similarly, bhikkhus, when a certain person cultivates and repeatedly practises mindfulness of the body, should that person wish to realize by means of abhiññā (Magga Insight) such dhammas that are to be realized by means of abhiññā, he will personally experience the fulfilment of the wish whenever there is the (proper) basis (for its fulfilment).

Suppose, bhikkhus, there were a pond with a bund on a level piece of ground, filled with water full to the brim so that a crow can drink out of it. Then, a strong man might break the bund of that pond from any side as he desires. Would the water from the pond flow out? "Yes, Venerable Sir." Similarly, bhikkhus, when a certain person cultivates and repeatedly practises mindfulness of the body, should that person wish to realize by means of abhiññā such dhammas that are to be realized by means of abhiññā, he will personally experience the fulfilment of the wish whenever there is the (proper) basis (for its fulfilment).

Suppose, bhikkhus, there were a chariot on even ground at the crossing of four roads, harnessed with thoroughbred steeds, with the whip lying ready. A skilled charioteer might get on to the chariot, holding the reins with the left hand and the whip with the right, and might drive it as he wishes, forwards and backwards, by any road he likes.

Similarly, bhikkhus, when a certain person cultivates and repeatedly practises mindfulness of the body, should that person wish to realize by means of abhiññā such dhammas that are to be realized by means of abhiññā, he will personally experience the fulfilment of the wish whenever there is the (proper) basis (for its fulfilment).

159. Bhikkhus, if mindfulness of the body is frequently undertaken, cultivated and repeatedly practised, mastered, made the basis, made a habit, practised for a long time and well undertaken ten advantages would certainly accrue.

A person (practising thus) can withstand displeasure (in meritoriousness) or pleasure (in enjoyment of sense-objects), and he cannot be overcome by displeasure, having conquered any displeasure that arises. (1)

He can withstand fear and dismay, and he cannot be overcome by fear and dismay, having conquered fear and dismay. (2)

He can endure cold, heat, hunger, thirst, gadflies, mosquitoes, wind, heat of the sun, snakes, scorpions and lice. He can endure ill-spoken and unwholesome words. He has the nature of being able to endure severe, cruel, excruciatingly sharp, disagreeable, unpleasant, deadly and painful sensations which arise in the body. (3)

He can attain at will, without difficulty and without trouble, the four jhānas (of rūpāvacara, appertaining to rūpa or Corporeal Sphere), which are the products of the purest mind, and by which one lives blissfully in this very life. (4)

He enjoys possession of the various forms of psychic power[5]; having been one, he can become many; from being many he can become one; he can be visible ...p...* He can gain mastery over his body to reach even up to the world of the brahmās. (5)

He can hear both the sounds of devas and men, far or near, with the hearing-power which surpasses the hearing-power of men, and which is extremely clear like the divine hearing-power. (6)

He knows discriminatively with his own mind the minds of other beings or individuals; he knows the mind with attachment, rāga, as mind with attachment ...p...; mind without attachment ......; the mind with anger ......; the mind without anger ......; the mind with bewilderment ......; the mind without bewilderment .....; the lethargic mind ......; the distracted mind ......; the exalted mind ......; the unexalted mind ......; the inferior mind ......; the superior mind ......; the concentrated mind ......; the unconcentrated mind ......; the liberated mind ......; and he knows the unliberated mind as unliberated mind. (7)

He can recollect many and varied existences of the past. And what is that? It is the recollection of one past existence, or two past existences ...p... He can recollect his many and varied past existences, together with their circumstances and related facts. (8)

5. psychic power: *iddhividha: iddhi* means 'completion', 'accomplishment.' It is the power to create marvels.

* See para 82 of Gopaka Moggallāna Sutta, also for the following sub-paragraphs.

He can, with the psychic power of divine sight, which is extremely clear, surpassing the sight of men, see beings in the process of passing away and arising, inferior or superior beings, beautiful or ugly beings, and beings with good or bad destinations and he knows how beings arise according to their own kamma-actions.(9)

He can, by means of abhiññā, special apperception, personally and in this very life, realize, attain to and remain in the emancipation of mind (cetovimutti) and in the emancipation by insight (paññāvimutti), free of āsavas (defilements that befuddle the mind) through their destruction. (10)

Bhikkhus, if mindfulness of the body is frequently undertaken, cultivated and repeatedly practised, mastered, made the basis, made a habit, practised for a long time and well undertaken, these ten advantages would certainly accrue.

Thus the Bhagavā said. Delighted, the bhikkhus rejoiced at the words of the Bhagavā.

End of the Kāyagatāsati Sutta,
the ninth in this vagga.

Namo tassa bhagavato arahato sammāsambuddhassa

(iii) SUÑÑATAVAGGA

3. Acchariya-abbhuta Sutta
4. Bākula Sutta
10. Devadūta Sutta

3. ACCHARIYA-ABBHUTA SUTTA

Discourse on the Marvellous and the Extraordinary

197. Thus have I heard:

Once the Bhagavā was staying at the Jetavana monastery of Anāthapiṇḍika in Sāvatthī. On that occasion, the following conversation arose among many bhikkhus who had had their alms-food, had left the place (of the meal) and gathered in the assembly-hall: "Friends! How marvellous! And, indeed, how extraordinary, friends, is the power and greatness of the Tathāgata! Regarding even the Buddhas of the past who had realized Nibbāna, who had cut off the factors that prolong saṁsāra,[1] who had cut off the round of existences, who had put an end to the round of existences, who had overcome all dukkha, the Tathāgata could reflect and know thus: 'Those Bhagavās belonged to such and such castes; those Bhagavās were known by such and such names; those Bhagavās were born into such and such clans; those Bhagavās were endowed with such and such morality; those Bhagavās were endowed with such and such concentration;[2] those Bhagavās were endowed with such and such wisdom (paññā); those Bhagavās used to dwell in such a way (remaining in the sustained attainment of cessation of consciousness); those Bhagavās were endowed with such and such kinds

1. factors that prolong saṁsāra: *papañca:* According to the Commentary, they are tanhā (craving), māna (conceit) and diṭṭhi (wrong view).

2. concentration: In the Text the word used is dhammā. But the Commentary explains it as both mundane and supramundane concentration.

of emancipation (vimutti)'.[3]" When this was said, the Venerable Ānanda said to those bhikkhus thus: "Friends, the Tathāgatas are marvellous and they are endowed with marvellous phenomena. Friends, the Tathāgatas are extraordinary and they are endowed with extraordinary phenomena." This was the unfinished conversation of those bhikkhus.

198. Then, in the evening the Bhagavā rose from his solitary retreat, approached the assembly-hall and took the seat prepared for him. After taking the seat, the Bhagavā asked the bhikkhus: "Bhikkhus, what are you talking about now as you are assembled here? What is the subject of your unfinished conversation?" "Venerable Sir, the conversation which we were having in the assembly-hall where we have gathered after having had our alms-food and left the place (of the meal) is this: 'Friends! How marvellous! And, indeed, how extraordinary, friends, is the power and greatness of the Tathāgata! Regarding even the Buddhas of the past who had realized Nibbāna, who had cut off the factors that prolong saṁsāra, who had cut off the round of existences, who had put an end to the round of existences, who had overcome all dukkha, the Tathāgata could reflect and know thus: 'Those Bhagavās belonged to such and such castes; were known by such and such names; were born into such and such clans; were endowed with such and such morality; were endowed with such and such concentration; were endowed with

3. There are five kinds of vimutti (emancipation):

(i) *Vikkhambhana vimutti*: freedom from the defilements for a long time due to the attainment of jhāna samāpatti (sustained mental absorption);

(ii) *Tadaṅga vimutti*: momentary freedom from the view and belief that conditioned phenomena are permanent, pleasant, etc., this freedom is achieved while contemplating their inpermanent, insecure and soulless nature;

(iii) *Samuccheda vimutti*: freedom brought about by the uprooting of defilements on attainment of the four maggas.

(iv) *Paṭipassaddhi vimutti*: freedom from defilements brought about by the four Fruitions following the attainment of maggas.

(v) *Nissaraṇa vimutti*: freedom from defilements brought about by the realization of Nibbāna.

such and such wisdom; used to dwell in such a way (remaining in the sustained attainment of cessation of consciousness); were endowed with such and such kinds of emancipation.' Venerable Sir, when this was said, the Venerable Ānanda said to us thus: 'Friends, the Tathāgatas are marvellous and they are endowed with marvellous phenomena. Friends, the Tathāgatas are extraordinary and they are endowed with extraordinary phenomena.' This, Venerable Sir, was our unfinished conversation before the Bhagavā came in."

199. Thereupon, the Bhagavā said to the Venerable Ānanda: "If that be so, Ānanda, let the marvellous and extraordinary phenomena of the Tathāgata be made evident to the fullest extent."

"Venerable Sir, I have heard and received this from the Bhagavā himself: 'Ānanda, the Bodhisatta was born in the Tusita deva realm, mindful and fully aware.' In fact, Venerable Sir, the Bodhisatta was born in the Tusita deva realm, mindful and fully aware. Venerable Sir, I bear this in mind as a marvellous and extraordinary phenomenon concerning the Bhagavā. (1)

"Venerable Sir, I have heard and received this from the Bhagavā himself: 'Ānanda, the Bodhisatta lived in the Tusita deva realm, mindful and fully aware.' In fact, Venerable Sir, the Bodhisatta lived in the Tusita deva realm, mindful and fully aware. Venerable Sir, I bear this in mind as a marvellous and extraordinary phenomenon concerning the Bhagavā."(2)

200. "Venerable Sir, I have heard and received this from the Bhagavā himself: 'Ānanda, the Bodhisatta lived his full life-span in the Tusita deva realm. In fact, Venerable Sir, the Bodhisatta lived his full life-span in the Tusita deva realm. Venerable Sir, I bear this in mind as a marvellous and extraordinary phenomenon concerning the Bhagavā. (3)

"Venerable Sir, I have heard and received this from the Bhagavā himself: 'Ānanda, the Bodhisatta passed away in the Tusita deva realm and was conceived in his mother's womb, mindful and fully aware.' In fact, Venerable Sir, the Bodhisatta passed away in the Tusita deva realm and was conceived in his mother's womb, mindful and fully aware. Venerable Sir, I bear this in mind as a marvellous and extraordinary phenomenon concerning the Bhagavā." (4)

201. "Venerable Sir, I have heard and received this from the Bhagavā himself: 'When the Bodhisatta was conceived in his mother's womb after passing away in the Tusita deva realm, there appeared an illimitable radiant light surpassing the radiance of the devas, in this world of devas, māras and brahmās, and in the human world comprising samaṇas, brāhmaṇas, rulers and men. This illimitable radiant light, which appeared in the world, and which surpassed the radiance of the devas also appeared in the lokantara nether regions which are great voids between worlds, abysses of space, pitch dark and totally lacking in visibility where even the powerful and majestic sun and moon cannot spread their light. And the beings in those lokantara nether regions saw one another by this light and came to know (thus): "O Friends! There are also other beings existing here!" Also the ten thousand universes trembled, quaked and shook violently as this illimitable radiant light, surpassing the radiance of the devas, appeared in the world.' In fact, Venerable Sir, ...p... Venerable Sir, I bear this in mind as a marvellous and extraordinary phenomenon concerning the Bhagavā." (5)

202. "Venerable Sir, I have heard and received this from the Bhagavā himself: 'Ānanda, when the Bodhisatta was conceived in his mother's womb, four devas[4] came to guard the four quarters, in order that no one, whether human or non-human, shall harm the Bodhisatta or his mother.' In fact, Venerable Sir, ...p... Venerable Sir, I bear this in mind as a marvellous and extraordinary phenomenon concerning the Bhagavā." (6)

203. "Venerable Sir, I have heard and received this from the Bhagavā himself: 'Ānanda, when the Bodhisatta was conceived in his mother's womb, the Bodhisatta's mother observed moral precepts on her own. She abstained from taking of life, abstained from taking what was not given, abstained from sexual misconduct, abstained from false speech, and abstained from taking

---

4. four devas: The four chief devas of the lowest of the six deva realms (Catumahārājika devas). (The Commentary)

intoxicants.' In fact, Venerable Sir, ...p... Venerable Sir, I bear this in mind as a marvellous and extraordinary phenomenon concerning the Bhagavā. (7)

"Venerable Sir, I have heard and received this from the Bhagavā himself: 'Ānanda, when the Bodhisatta was conceived in his mother's womb there did not arise in the Bodhisatta's mother any thought associated with sensual desire for any man. Also, no man could approach the Bodhisatta's mother with sensual desire.' In fact, Venerable Sir, ...p... Venerable Sir, I bear this in mind as a marvellous and extraordinary phenomenon concerning the Bhagavā. (8)

"Venerable Sir, I have heard and received this from the Bhagavā himself: 'Ānanda, when the Bodhisatta was conceived in his mother's womb, the Bodhisatta's mother received the five kinds of sense-pleasure[5] in abundance. Fully endowed with these five kinds of sense-pleasure, she lived in pleasant satisfaction.' In fact, Venerable Sir, ...p... Venerable Sir, I bear this in mind as a marvellous and extraordinary phenomenon concerning the Bhagavā."(9)

204. "Venerable Sir, I have heard and received this from the Bhagavā himself: 'Ānanda, when the Bodhisatta was conceived in his mother's womb, no ailment arose in the Bodhisatta's mother. The Bodhisatta's mother was not subject to bodily fatigue and she was at ease. The Bodhisatta's mother could see the Bodhisatta in her womb, complete with all the limbs, great and small, and perfect in all the sense--organs. Ānanda, take the example of a Veḷuriya gem, briliant, genuine, eight-faceted, well-cut, which is threaded with a dark-blue, or yellow, or red, or white, or light-yellow string. A man with normal vision placing it on his palm, might reflect thus: "This gem is briliant, genuine, eight-faceted and well-cut. It is threaded with a dark-blue, or yellow, or red, or white, or light-yellow string." Ānanda, in the same way, when the Bodhisatta was conceived in his mother's womb, no ailment arose in the Bodhisatta's mother. The

5. the five kinds of sense-pleasure: This refers to the pleasure derived from the many valuable presents and gifts received from neighbouring rulers while Queen Māyā was pregnant with the Bodhisatta.

Bodhisatta's mother was not subject to bodily fatigue and she was at ease. The Bodhisatta's mother could see the Bodhisatta in her womb, complete with all the limbs, great and small, and perfect in all the sense--organs.' In fact, Venerable Sir, ...p... Venerable Sir, I bear this in mind as a marvellous and extraordinary phenomenon concerning the Bhagavā." (10)

205. "Venerable Sir, I have heard and received this from the Bhagavā himself: 'Ānanda, seven days after the Bodhisatta was born, the Bodhisatta's mother died and was reborn in the Tusita deva realm.' In fact, Venerable Sir, ...p... Venerable Sir, I bear this in mind as a marvellous and extraordinary phenomenon concerning the Bhagavā. (11)

"Venerable Sir, I have heard and received this from the Bhagavā himself: 'Ānanda, other women might give birth after carrying the foetus for nine or ten months. The Bodhisatta's mother did not give birth to the Bodhisatta in this way. She gave birth to the Bodhisatta only after carrying a full ten months.' In fact, Venerable Sir, ...p... Venerable Sir, I bear this in mind as a marvellous and extraordinary phenomenon concerning the Bhagavā. (12)

"Venerable Sir, I have heard and received this from the Bhagavā himself: 'Ānanda, the Bodhisatta's mother did not give birth to the Bodhisatta while sitting or lying as in the case of other women. She gave birth to the Bodhisatta while standing.' In fact, Venerable Sir, ...p... Venerable Sir, I bear this in mind as a marvellous and extraordinary phenomenon concerning the Bhagavā. (13)

"Venerable Sir, I have heard and received this from the Bhagavā himself: 'When the Bodhisatta was delivered from his mother's womb, the devas[6] received him first. Human beings received him later.' In fact, Venerable Sir, ...p... Venerable Sir, I bear this in mind as a marvellous and extraordinary phenomenon concerning the Bhagavā." (14)

---

6. According to the Commentary, the devas here are those brahmās of the Suddhāvāsa Brahmā realm who are arahats (*khīṇāsavā suddhāvāsa brahmās*).

206. "Venerable Sir, I have heard and received this from the Bhagavā himself: 'Ānanda, when the Bodhisatta was delivered from his mother's womb, he did not touch the ground. Four devas[7] received him and put him before the mother, saying: O Queen, rejoice! A mighty and majestic son has been born to you!' In fact, Venerable Sir, ...p... Venerable Sir, I bear this in mind as a marvellous and extraordinary phenomenon concerning the Bhagavā. (15)

"Venerable Sir, I have heard and received this from the Bhagavā himself: 'Ānanda, when the Bodhisatta was delivered from his mother's womb, he came forth perfectly clean. He was delivered without being smeared with any watery matter, nor with mucus, nor with blood, nor with any impurities. He was perfectly clean. Ānanda, take the example of a precious gem placed on cloth made in Kāsi. The gem is not soiled by the Kāsi cloth, nor is the Kāsi cloth soiled by the gem. Why is it so? It is because both are clean. Ānanda, in the same way, when the Bodhisatta was delivered from his mother's womb, he came forth perfectly clean. He was delivered without being smeared with any watery matter, nor with mucus, nor with blood, nor with any impurities. He was perfectly clean.' In fact, Venerable Sir, ...p... Venerable Sir, I bear this in mind as a marvellous and extraordinary phenomenon concerning the Bhagavā. (16)

"Venerable Sir, I have heard and received this from the Bhagavā himself: 'Ānanda, when the Bodhisatta was delivered from the mother's womb, two streams of water appeared in the sky. One was cold and the other was warm. Both the Bodhisatta and his mother were washed with these streams of water.' In fact, Venerable Sir, ...p... Venerable Sir, I bear this in mind as a marvellous and extraordinay phenomenon concerning the Bhagavā." (17)

207. "Venerable Sir, I have heard and received this from the Bhagavā himself: 'Ānanda, soon after his birth, the Bodhisatta stood with even feet on the ground, faced northwards and walked seven steps. With a white umbrella over him, he looked in all directions

---

7. four devas: The four Catumahārājika devas. (The Commentary)

and boldly proclaimed thus: "I am the loftiest in the world! I am the greatest in the world! I am the noblest in the world! This is the last existence for me! There is no more rebirth for me." In fact, Venerable Sir, ...p... Venerable Sir, I bear this in mind as a marvellous and extraordinay phenomenon concerning the Bhagavā. (18)

"Venerable Sir, I have heard and received this from the Bhagavā himself: 'Ānanda, when the Bodhisatta was delivered from the mother's womb, there appeared an illimitable radiant light surpassing the radiance of the devas, in this world of devas, māras and brahmās and in the human world comprising samaṇas, brāhmanas, rulers and men. This illimitable radiant light, which appeared in the world and which surpassed the radiance of the devas, also appeared in the lokantara nether regions which are great voids between worlds, abysses of space, pitch dark and totally lacking in visibility, where even the powerful and majestic sun and moon cannot spread their light. And the beings in those lokantara nether regions saw one another by this light and came to know (thus): "O Friends! There are also other beings existing here!" Also the ten thousand universes trembled, quaked and shook violently as this illimitable radiant light, surpassing the radiance of the devas, appeared in the world.' In fact, Venerable Sir, ...p... Venerable Sir, I bear this in mind as a marvellous and extraordinay phenomenon concerning the Bhagavā." (19)

208. Ānanda, that being so, also bear in mind what I am going to say as a marvellous and extraordinary phenomenon concerning the Tathāgata. In this Teaching, Ānanda, the Tathāgata clearly knows the arising, the (momentary) manifestation, and the cessation of sensations. The Tathāgata clearly knows the arising ...p... of perceptions. The Tathāgata clearly knows the arising, the (momentary) manifestation, and the cessation of initial thoughts (vitakkas).[8] Ānanda,

---

8. What is meant here is that the Buddha is always mindful of the arising, the momentary manifestation and the cessation of all conditioned phenomena together with their characteristics, namely, impermanence (anicca), unsatisfactoriness (dukkha) and soullessness (anatta).

also bear this in mind as a marvellous and extraordinary phenomenon concerning Tathāgata.

"In fact, Venerable Sir, the Bhagavā clearly knows the arising, the (momentary) manifestation, and the cessation of sensations. The Bhagavā clearly knows the arising ..... of perceptions. The Bhagavā clearly knows the arising, the (momentary) mainfestation, and the cessation of initial thoughts. Venerable Sir, I bear this in mind as a marvellous and extraordinary phenomenon concerning the Bhagavā." (20)

The Venerable Ānanda spoke these words. The Teacher was pleased. Delighted, those bhikkhus also rejoiced in what the Venerable Ānanda had said.

End the Acchariya - abbhuta Sutta,
the third in this vagga.

4. BĀKULA SUTTA

Discourse Concerning Bākula

209. Thus have I heard:

Once the Venerable Bākula was staying in Rājagaha at the monastery of the Bamboo Grove where black squirrels were fed. On that occasion, the naked ascetic Kassapa who had been a friend of the Venerable Bākula in the latter's lay life came to the Venerable Bākula and exchanged greetings with him. After bringing to an end the courteous and amiable greetings, he sat in a suitable place and said to the Venerable Bākula thus:

"Friend Bākula, for how long have you been a bhikkhu?"

Friend, I have been a bhikkhu for eighty years.

"Friend Bākula, during these eighty years, how many times have you indulged in sexual union?".

Friend Kassapa, you should not have put the question to me thus: 'Friend Bākula, during these eighty years, how many times have you indulged in sexual union?' Friend Kassapa, you should have put the question to me only in this way, 'Friend Bākula, during these eighty years, how many times has consciousness concerning sense-pleasures arisen in you?'

210. Friend, throughout the eighty years of bhikkhuhood, I was not aware that any consciousness concerning sense-pleasures (kāma saññā) has arisen in me. "The fact that the Venerable Bākula was not aware of the arising of any consciousness concerning sense-pleasures throughout the eighty years of bhikkhuhood is noted by us as a marvellous and extraordinary

phenomenon relating to the Venerable Bākula[1]." (1)

Friend, throughout the eighty years of bhikkhuhood, I was not aware that any consciousness concerning ill will (byāpāda saññā) ...p... any consciousness concerning cruelty (vihiṁsā saññā) has arisen in me. "The fact that the Venerable Bākula was not aware of the arising of any perception of cruelty throughout the eighty years of bhikkhuhood is noted by us as a marvellous and extraordinary phenomenon relating to the Venerable Bākula." (2-3)

Friend, throughout the eighty years of bhikkhuhood, I was not aware that any sensual thought (kāmavitakka) has arisen in me. "The fact that the Venerable Bākula was not aware of the arising of any sensual thought throughout the eighty years of bhikkhuhood is noted by us as a marvellous and extraordinary phenomenon relating to the Venerable Bākula." (4)

Friend, throughout the eighty years of bhikkhuhood, I was not aware that any destructive thought (byāpāda vitakka) ...p... any harmful thought (vihiṁsā vitakka) has arisen in me. "The fact that the Venerable Bākula was not aware of the arising of any harmful thought throughout the eighty years of bhikkhuhood is noted by us as a marvellous and extraordinary phenomenon relating to the Venerable Bākula." (5-6)

211. Friend, throughout the eighty years of bhikkhuhood, I was not aware of having attachment to any robe offered by a householder. "The fact that the Venerable Bākula was not aware of having attachment to any robe offered by a householder, throughout the eighty years of bhikkhuhood is noted by us as a marvellous and extraordinary phenomenon relating to the Venerable Bākula." (7)

Friend, throughout the eighty years of bhikkhuhood, I was not aware of having cut robe-material with a knife.[2] "The fact that the Venerable Bākula was not

1. "The fact that ..... relating to the Venerable Bākula": This remark concerning the marvellous and extraordinary phenomenon of the Venerable Bākula and the similar ones appearing in the following paragraphs were made by the bhikkhus participating in the synod.

2. The Venerable Bākula having a large following was well provided with ready-made robes. He did not have to personally cut or sew or dye robe-material as other bhikkhus had to in those days.

aware of having cut robe-material with a knife throughout the eighty years of bhikkhuhood is noted by us as a marvellous and extraordinary phenomenon relating to the Venerable Bākula." (8)

Friend, throughout the eighty years of bhikkhuhood, I was not aware of having sewn a robe with a needle ...p... I was not aware of having dyed a robe ...p... I was not aware of having sewn a kathina-robe ...p... I was not aware of having involved in the making of robes of companion-bhikkhus ...p... I was not aware of having taken delight in an invitation ...p... I was not aware that the thought 'It would be well if someone were to invite me' ever arose in me ...p... I was not aware of having sat in a house ...p... I was not aware of having partaken alms-food in a house ...p... I was not aware of having looked at a woman noticing her characteristics and behaviour ...p... I was not aware of having delivered a discourse to a woman, even a stanza of four lines ...p... I was not aware of having gone near a bhikkhunīs' retreat ...p... I was not aware of having delivered a discourse to a bhikkhunī ...p... I was not aware of having delivered a discourse to a probationer-bhikkhunī ...p... I was not aware of having delivered a discourse to a female novice ...p... I was not aware of having initiated anyone into the Order as a novice ...p... I was not aware of having undertaken the full admission of anyone into the Order as a bhikkhu ...p... I was not aware of having given any instruction (to any member of the Order) ...p... I was not aware of having made a novice serve me ...p... I was not aware of having bathed in a bath-house ...p... I was not aware of having bathed with bath-powder ...p... I was not aware of having made companion-bhikkhus massage my body ...p... I was not aware of having been ill even for the duration taken to draw a drop of milk ...p... I was not aware of having had to take even a bit of herbal medicine ...p... I was not aware of having leaned on a support ...p... I was not aware of having made a bed. "The fact that the Venerable Bākula was not aware of having made a bed throughout the eighty years of bhikkhuhood is noted by us as a marvellous and extraordinary phenomenon relating to the Venerable Bākula." (9-33)

Friend, throughout the eighty years of bhikkhuhood, I was not aware of having taken up residence for rains-retreat near a village "The fact that the Venerable Bākula was not aware of having taken up residence for rains-retreat near a village is noted by us as a marvellous and extraordinary phenomenon relating to the Venerable Bākula." (34)

Friend, after partaking of alms-food from the people only for seven days as a person not yet free from defilements, knowledge of Arahatta Fruition arose in me on the eighth day. "The fact that after partaking of alms-food from the people only for seven days as a person not yet free from defilements, knowledge of Arahatta Fruition arose in the Venerable Bākula on the eighth day is noted by us as a marvellous and extraordinary phenomenon relating to the Venerable Bākula." (35)

212. "Friend Bākula, may I receive initiation and admission into the Order as a bhikkhu under this Teaching." The naked ascetic Kassapa was initiated into the Order and subsequently admitted fully as a bhikkhu under this Teaching. Not long after he had become a bhikkhu, the Venerable Kassapa, remaining alone and secluded, vigilant and zealous, inclining his mind (to Nibbāna), realized by himself through abhiññā, special apperception, here and now, the fruits of the noblest and the most supreme Arahattaphala, the goal of the Practice of Purity, for the sake of which men of good family rightly go forth from household life into homelessness. He knew: 'Rebirth is no more; the Noble Practice has been accomplished; what is to be done (for Magga-Insight) has been done; there is nothing more to do (to attain magga).' And the Venerable Kassapa became one among the arahats.

Thereafter, on a certain occasion, the Venerable Bākula holding his key went from one monastery to another and announced thus: "Revered Ones, come forth! Revered Ones, come forth! Today, I shall realize parinibbāna!" "The fact that the Venerable Bākula holding his key went from one monastery to another and announced thus: 'Revered ones, come forth! Revered ones, come forth! Today, I shall realize parinibbāna!' is noted by us as a marvellous and extraordinary phenomenon relating to the Venerable Bākula." (36)

The Venerable Bākula realized parinibbāna sitting in the midst of the gathering of bhikkhus.[3] "The fact that the Venerable Bākula realized parinibbāna sitting in the midst of the gathering of bhikkhus is noted by us as a marvellous and extraordinary phenomenon relating to the Venerable Bākula." (37)

End of the Bākula Sutta,
the fourth in this Vagga.

---

3. The Venerable Bākula realized parinibbāna by meditating on the element of heat (tejodhātu) causing flames to arise from his body. The flames consumed his body leaving only the relics (dhātus).

10. DEVADŪTA SUTTA

Discourse on the Messengers of Death

261. Thus have I heard:

Once the Bhagavā was residing at the Jetavana monastery of Anāthapiṇḍika in Sāvatthī. Then the Bhagavā addressed the bhikkhus, saying "Bhikkhus!" The bhikkhus answered the Bhagavā, "Venerable Sir! " The Bhagavā spoke thus:

Bhikkhus, suppose there were two houses with doors facing each other. A man with normal vision standing between the two houses could see people entering and leaving those houses, people walking up and down and people going about from one house to the other. Bhikkhus, in the same way, with the power of divine sight, which is extremely clear, surpassing the sight of men, I see beings in the process of passing away and arising, inferior and superior beings, beautiful and ugly beings and beings with good or bad destinations. I know how beings arise according to their own kamma-actions, (thus): "Friends, there were beings who were endowed with goodness done bodily, verbally and mentally. They did not malign the ariyas. They held right views and performed actions according to right views. After death and dissolution of their bodies, they appeared in good destinations, the happy world of the devas.

"Friends, there were also other beings who were endowed with goodness done bodily, verbally and mentally. They did not malign the ariyas. They held right views and performed actions according to right views. After death and dissolution of their bodies, they were reborn in the world of human beings.

"But, friends, there were also beings who were full of evil committed bodily, verbally and mentally. They maligned the ariyas. They held wrong views and performed actions according to wrong views. After death and dissolution of their bodies, they appeared in the realm of ever hungry beings (petas).

"Friends, there were also other beings who were full of evil committed bodily, verbally and mentally. They maligned the ariyas. They held wrong views and performed actions according to wrong views. After death and dissolution of their bodies, they were reborn in the realm of animals.

"Friends, there were also other beings who were full of evil committed bodily, verbally and mentally. They maligned the ariyas. They held wrong views and performed actions according to wrong views. After death and dissolution of their bodies, they appeared in wretched destinations (duggati), in miserable existences (apāya), states of ruin (vinipāta), and realms of continuous suffering (niraya)."

262. Bhikkhus, the guards of niraya held each arm of that person (who had passed into niraya) and showed him to Yama*, a king of niraya (saying:) "O king, this man has not served his mother well, has not served his father well, has not behaved well to the samanas, has not behaved well to the brāhmaṇas and has not been respectful to the elders of his clan. May the king give him punishment." Bhikkhus, with reference to the first messenger of Death (devadūta), King Yama closely questioned, cross-questioned and repeatedly questioned the man thus: "O man, did you not see among men the appearance of the first messenger of Death?" That man replied thus: "Sir, I did not."

Bhikkhus, King Yama then questioned that man thus: "Did you not see among men a young tender infant still on its back lying in its own faeces and urine?" That man replied thus: "Sir, I did."

Bhikkhus, King Yama then questioned that man thus: "O man, as an adult endowed with intelligence, did it not occur to you thus: I also am subject to rebirth and cannot overcome rebirth. I should do good

* Yama, the ruler of niraya, is a vemānika peta with a mansion of his own who alternately enjoys the delights of the deva world and experiences the sufferings of a peta.

actions, physical, verbal and mental'?" That man replied thus: "Sir, it did not. Sir, I had been unmindful."

Bhikkhus, King Yama then said to that man thus: "O man, through unmindfulness, you failed to do good actions, physical, verbal and mental. O man, indeed, you have done (bad deeds) according to your unmindfulness. Indeed, those wrong deeds were not done by your mother, nor by your father, nor by your brother, nor by your sister, nor by your companions, nor by your relatives, nor by samanas and brāhmanas, nor by the devas. You yourself have done those wrong deeds and you yourself shall have to bear the consequence of that." (1)

263. Bhikkhus, having closely questioned, cross--questioned, and repeatedly questioned that man with reference to the first messenger of Death, King Yama closely questioned, cross-questioned, and repeatedly questioned him with reference to the second messenger of Death (thus;) "O man, did you not see among men the appearance of the second messenger of Death?" That man replied thus: "Sir, I did not."

Bhikkhus, King Yama then questioned that man thus: "O man, did you not see among men an old woman or an old man with back bent and crooked as a rafter, staggering with only a staff to rely on, in pain and senile, toothless, with hair grey and thin, bald--headed, wrinkle-skinned and spotted with moles?" That man replied thus: "Sir, I did."

Bhikkhus, King Yama then questioned that man thus: "O man, as an adult endowed with intelligence, did it not occur to you thus: 'I also am subject to old age and cannot overcome old age. I should do good actions, physical, verbal and mental'?" That man replied thus: "Sir, it did not. Sir, I had been unmindful."

Bhikkhus, King Yama then said to that man thus: "O man, through unmindfulness you failed to do good actions, physical, verbal and mental. O man, indeed, you have done (bad deeds) according to your unmindfulness. Indeed, those wrong deeds were not done by your mother, nor by your father, nor by your brother, nor by your sister, nor by your companions, nor by your relatives, nor by samaṇas and brāhmanas, nor by the devas. You yourself have done those wrong deeds and you yourself shall have to bear the consequence of that." (2)

264. Bhikkhus, having closely questioned, cross--questioned, and repeatedly questioned that man with reference to the second messenger of Death, King Yama closely questioned, cross-questioned and repeatedly questioned him with reference to the third messenger of Death (thus:) "O man, did you not see among men the appearance of the third messenger of Death?" That man replied thus: "Sir, I did not,".

Bhikkhus, King Yama then questioned that man thus: "O man, did you not see among men a woman or a man who is afflicted with disease, suffering and seriously ill, lying in his or her own faeces and urine, who has to be raised up and has to be put to bed by others?" That man replied thus: "Sir, I did."

Bhikkhus, King Yama then questioned that man thus: "O man, as an adult endowed with intelligence, did it not occur to you thus: 'I also am subject to illness and cannot overcome illness. I should do good actions, physical, verbal and mental'?" That man replied thus: "Sir, it did not. Sir, I had been unmindful."

Bhikkhus, King Yama then said to that man thus: "O man, through unmindfulness, you failed to do good actions, physical, verbal and mental. O man, indeed, you have done (bad deeds) according to your unmindfulness. Indeed those wrong deeds were not done by your mother, nor by your father, nor by your brother, nor by your sister, nor by your companions, nor by your relatives, nor by samaṇas and brāhmaṇas, nor by the devas. You yourself have done those wrong deeds and you yourself shall have to bear the consequence of that." (3)

265. Bhikkhus, having closely questioned, cross--questioned and repeatedly questioned that man with reference to the third messenger of Death, King Yama closely questioned, cross-questioned, and repeatedly questioned him with reference the fourth messenger of Death (thus:) "O man, did you not see among men the appearance of the fourth messenger of Death?" That man replied thus: "Sir, I did not."

Bhikkhus, King Yama then questioned that man thus: "O man, did you not see among men a thief being seized by the king who meted out various punishments to him — whipping, caning, beating with sticks, cutting off the hands, cutting off the legs, cutting off both hands and legs, cutting off the ears, cutting off the nose, cutting off the ears and the nose, opening the skull, pouring in molten iron into the brain like pouring boiling sour-gruel, scalping the head to look like a conch-shell, filling blood into the mouth which is agape like Rahu's that swallows the sun, making fire-works by wrapping the body in oilcloth and setting it afire, making a flaming torch by wrapping the hands in oilcloth and setting them afire, flaying him so that the skin of the whole body falls down to the ankle looking like a mass of leaves at the base of an arum plant, flaying him upwards from ankle to neck making the skin look like a robe made of bark, making him look like a crawling antelope out of him by impaling him with sticks (in all the four limbs), pulling down the skin, flesh and sinews with iron spikes as sharp as fish-hooks, chopping up the flesh of the body piece by piece, each weighing one tical, beating with iron spikes and sprinkling (the wounds) with salt, impaling him on an iron stake and revolving him around it as if turning a door-bolt in its door-post, reducing his bones into pulp which is formed into the shape of a straw-ring that serves as a stand for the rice-pot, pouring boiling oil over him, causing him to be devoured by dogs, impaling him alive on an iron stake, cutting off the head with the sword?" That man replied thus: "Sir, I did."

Bhikkhus, King Yama then questioned that man thus: "O man, as an adult endowed with intelligence, did it not occur to you thus: 'Friends, those who commit evil deeds are subject to these various forms of punishment in this very life. How much more so it would be in the next existence. I should do good actions, physical, verbal and mental'?" That man replied thus: "Sir, it did not. Sir, I had been unmindful."

Bhikkhus, King Yama then said to that man thus: "O man, through unmindfulness you failed to do good actions, physical, verbal and mental. O man, indeed, you have done (bad deeds) according to your unmindfulness. Indeed, those wrong deeds were not done by your mother, nor by your father, nor by your brother, nor by your sister, nor by your companions, nor by your relatives, nor by samaṇas and brāhmaṇas, nor by the devas. You yourself have done those wrong deeds and you yourself shall have to bear the consequence of that." (4)

266. Bhikkhus, having closely questioned, cross--questioned and repeatedly questioned that man with reference to the fourth messenger of Death; King Yama closely questioned, cross-questioned, and repeatedly questioned him with reference to the fifth messenger of Death (thus:) "O man, did you not see among men the appearance of the fifth messenger of Death?" That man replied thus: "Sir, I did not."

Bhikkhus, King Yama then questioned that man thus: "Did you not see among men (the body of) a woman or a man, one day dead, or two days dead, or three days dead, swollen, turning black and blue and festering?" That man replied thus: "Sir, I did."

Bhikkhus, King Yama then questioned that man thus: "O man, as an adult endowed with intelligence, did it not occur to you thus: 'I also am subject to death and cannot overcome death. I should do good actions, physical, verbal and mental'?" That man replied thus: "Sir, it did not. Sir, I had been unmindful."

Bhikkhus, King Yama then said to that man thus: "O man, through unmindfulness, you failed to do good actions, physical, verbal and mental. O man, indeed, you have done (bad deeds) according to your unmindfulness. Indeed, those wrong deeds were not done by your mother, nor by your father, nor by your brother, nor by your sister, nor by your companions, nor by your relatives, nor by samaṇas and brāhmaṇas, nor by the devas. You yourself have done those wrong deeds and you yourself shall have to bear the consequence of that." (5)

267. Bhikkhus, after closely questioning, cross--questioning and repeatedly questioning that man with reference to the fifth messenger of Death, King Yama remained silent. Bhikkhus, the guards of niraya then meted out to the man the punishment known as the five ways of pinioning. They drove a hot iron spike into one hand and another hot iron spike into the other

hand. They drove a hot iron spike into one leg and another hot iron spike into the other leg. They drove a hot iron spike into the middle of the breast. In that niraya, that man had to undergo severe, excruciatingly sharp, frightening and painful sensations. There was no death for him before the exhaustion of his evil kamma.

Bhikkhus, the guards of niraya made that man lie down and chopped him with machetes ...p...

Bhikkhus, the guards of niraya held that man upside down and chopped him with hatchets ...p...

Bhikkhus, the guards of niraya harnessed that man to a carriage and made him run back and forth on ground blazing red with flames ...p...

Bhikkhus, the guards of niraya made that man go up and come down a big mountain of live coals blazing red with flames ...p...

Bhikkhus, the guards of niraya held that man upside down and dropped him into a hot iron cauldron blazing red with flames. In that niraya, that man was boiled, with foam rising up to the top. In that niraya, while being boiled, with foam rising up to the top, that man appeared at the surface once, sank once and floated sideways once. In that niraya, that man had to undergo severe, excruciatingly sharp, frightening and painful sensations. There was no death for him before the exhaustion of his evil kamma. Bhikkhus, the guards of niraya cast that man into a greater niraya. Bhikkhus, indeed, that great niraya is four-cornered and has four gates, and is divided into equal sections. It is bounded by iron walls and roofed with iron plates. The flooring of that niraya is made of iron, blazing with flames. That niraya extends a hundred yojanas in all directions and exists all the time.

268. Bhikkhus, the flames rising from the eastern wall of that great niraya strike against the western wall. The flames rising from the western wall strike against the eastern wall. The flames rising from the northern wall strike against the southern wall. The flames rising from the southern wall strike against the northern wall. The flames rising from the bottom strike against the top. The flames rising from the top strike against the bottom. In that niraya, that man had to

undergo severe, excruciatingly sharp, frightening and painful sensations. There was no death for him before the exhaustion of his evil kamma.

Bhikkhus, once in a long while, the eastern gate of that great niraya opens. When that gate opened that man ran with great speed to that gate, and had his outer skin burnt, had his inner skin burnt, had his flesh burnt, had his sinews burnt, had his bones smoking. When he lifted his feet, he got burnt in the same way (as when he put them down). Bhikkhus, after a long lapse of time that gate closes. In that niraya, that man had to undergo severe, excruciatingly sharp, frightening and painful sensations. There was no death for him before the exhaustion of his evil kamma.

Bhikkhus, once in a long while, the western gate of that great niraya opens ...p... the northern gate opens ...p... the southern gate opens. When that gate opened, that man ran with great speed to that gate, and had his outer skin burnt, had his inner skin burnt, had his flesh burnt, had his sinews burnt, had his bones smoking. When he lifted his feet, he got burnt in the same way (as when he put them down). Bhikkhus, after a long lapse of time, that gate closes. In that niraya, that man had to undergo severe, excruciatingly sharp, frightening and painful sensations. There was no death for him before the exhaustion of his evil kama.

Bhikkhus, once in a long while, the eastern gate of that great niraya opens. When that gate opened, that man ran with great speed to that gate, and had his outer skin burnt, had his inner skin burnt, had his flesh burnt, had his sinews burnt, had his bones smoking. When he lifted his feet, he got burnt in the same way (as when he put them down). That man then got out through that gate.

269. Bhikkhus, there is the Gūtha niraya (filled with excrement) adjacent to and connected with that great niraya. That man fell into that niraya. Bhikkhus, in that Gūtha niraya, creatures with beaks like needles cut into his outer skin, then cut into his inner skin, then cut into his flesh, then cut into his sinews, then cut into his bones and ate up the marrow. In that niraya, that man had to undergo severe, excruciatingly sharp, frightening and painful sensations. There was no

death for him before the exhaustion of his evil kamma. (1)

Bhikkhus, there is the Kukkula niraya (filled with hot ashes) adjacent to and connected with that Gūtha niraya. That man fell into that niraya. In that niraya, that man had to undergo severe, excruciatingly sharp, frightening and painful sensations. There was no death for him before the exhaustion of his evil kamma. (2)

Bhikkhus, adjacent to and connected with that Kukkula niraya is the niraya of extensive 'forest of silk-cotton trees', rising to a height of one yojana, blazing red with flames and having thorns that are sixteen digit long. That man was made to climb those trees and descend from those trees. In that niraya, that man had to undergo severe, excruciatingly sharp, frightening and painful sensations. There was no death for him before the exhaustion of his evil kamma. (3)

Bhikkhus, adjacent to and connected with that 'forest of silk-cotton trees' is the niraya of the great 'forest of sword-leafed trees'. That man got into that forest. When blown by the wind, the leaves fell and cut the hands of that man, cut off his legs, cut off both his hands and legs, cut off his ears, cut off his nose, cut off both his ears and nose. In that niraya, that man had to undergo severe, excruciatingly sharp, frightening and painful sensations. There was no death for him before the exhaustion of his evil kamma. (4)

Bhikkhus, adjacent to and connected with that 'forest of sword-leafed trees' is the niraya of the great 'river of salt water'. That man fell into that river. He was carried downstream or upstream and both downstream and upstream in that river. In that niraya, that man had to undergo severe, excruciatingly sharp, frightening and painful sensations. There was no death for him before the exhaustion of his evil kamma. (5)

270. Bhikkhus, the guards of niraya pulled up that man with iron hooks, laid him on the bank and asked thus: "O man, what do you want?" That man replied thus: "Sirs, I am hungry". Bhikkhus, the guards of niraya opened his mouth with a hot iron spike, blazing red with flames, and put into his mouth a hot iron-ball, blazing red with flames. The iron-ball burnt his lips,

burnt his mouth, burnt his throat, burnt his chest, and passed out from the bottom carrying with it his large and small intestines. In that niraya, that man had to undergo severe, excruciatingly sharp, frightening and painful sensations. There was no death for him before the exhaustion of his evil kamma.

Bhikkhus, the guards of niraya asked that man thus: "O man, what do you want?" That man replied thus: "Sirs, I am thirsty". Bhikkhus, the guards of niraya opened his mouth with a hot iron spike, blazing red with flames, and poured into his mouth hot molten iron, blazing red with flames. The molten iron burnt his lips, burnt his mouth, burnt his throat, burnt his chest, and passed out from the bottom carrying with it his large and small intestines. In that niraya, that man had to undergo severe, excruciatingly sharp, frightening and painful sensations. There was no death for him before the exhaustion of his evil kamma. Bhikkhus, the guards of niraya cast that man back again into the great Niraya.

Bhikkhus, what happened in the past was that it occurred to King Yama thus: "Friends, those who in this world do evil and demeritorious deeds are subject to such punishments. It would be good if I were to be reborn as a human being, if also there were to appear in the world a Tathāgata who is Homage-Worthy and Perfectly Self-Enlightened, if also I were to pay homage to that Bhagavā, if also the Bhagavā were to expound the dhamma to me, if also I could understand the dhamma of the Bhagavā."

Bhikkhus, I do not expound this after hearing it from other samaṇas or brāhmaṇas. Indeed, only after I have known, seen and found out this matter by myself, do I expound it.

271. Thus said the Bhagavā. After having said this, the Sugata, the Teacher, further uttered these verses:

Though warned by the Messengers of Death,
unmindful some men remain;

Born in bad destinations, for a long time they
grieve in sorrow and pain.

Yet in this world, warned by the Messengers of Death, the Virtuous ones who are serene,

Are never unmindful of the ariyas' teachings.

Seeing danger in Clinging, as the cause of birth and death;

Freed from Clinging, they arrive at the end of birth and death;

Those ariyas who ~~realize~~ Nibbāna, happiness and peace in this very life they have won;

And passing beyond all danger, all dukkha they have overcome.

End of the Devadūta Sutta,
the tenth in this vagga.

Namo tassa bhagavato arahato sammāsambuddhassa

(iv) VIBHAṄGA VAGGA

1. Bhaddekaratta Sutta
5. Cūḷakammavibhaṅga Sutta
7. Saḷāyatanavibhaṅga Sutta
9. Araṇavibhaṅga Sutta
10. Dhātuvibhaṅga Sutta
12. Dakkhiṇāvibhaṅga Sutta

1. BHADDEKARATTA SUTTA

Discourse on One who has an Excellent Night

272. Thus have I heard:

Once the Bhagavā was staying at the Jetavana monastery of Anāthapiṇḍika in Sāvatthī. On that occasion the Bhagavā addressed the bhikkhus, saying: "Bhikkhus!" And they answered him: "Venerable Sir!" The Bhagavā said thus: "Bhikkhus, I shall expound to you both in brief and in detail, a discourse on a *bhaddekaratta*,[1] one who has an excellent night. Listen and bear it well in mind. I shall speak." "Very well, Venerable Sir," replied the bhikkhus to the Bhagavā. Then the Bhagavā spoke these words:

Neither the past (khandhas) should be harked back to, nor the future (khandhas) be hankered after. The past is no more and the future is not yet.[2]

The wise person contemplates the presently arising physical and mental phenomena as and when they arise. He would repeatedly cultivate the development of Insight Knowledge which is immovable and unshakable.

The effort should be made today. One may die tomorrow, who knows? We have no covenant with the King of Death and his many warriors.[3]

---

1. *Bhaddekaratta*: bhaddekaratta: According to the Commentary, bhaddekaratta means 'One who has an excellent night on account of vipassanā practice.'

2. As the five physical and mental aggregates of the past are no more, they should not be harked back to with Craving and wrong view. As the five physical and mental aggregates of the future are not yet, they should not be hankered after with Craving and wrong view.

3. Warriors of the King of Death: they are the causes of death such as fire, poison, weapons, disease, etc.

The tranquil Muni[4] has defined the person who lives thus, diligently meditating day and night as a *bhaddekaratta*.

273. Bhikkhus, how does one hark back to the past? One takes delight in a past appearance, thinking, 'I had such and such an appearance in the past.' One takes delight in a past sensation, thinking, 'I had such and such a sensation in the past.' One takes delight in a past perception, thinking, 'I had such and such a perception in the past.' One takes delight in a past volitional activity, thinking, 'I had such and such a volitional activity in the past.' One takes delight in a past consciousness, thinking, 'I had such and such a consciousness in the past.' Bhikkhus, this is how the past is harked back to.

Bhikkhus, how does one not hark back to the past? One does not take delight in a past appearance, thinking, 'I had such and such an appearance in the past.' One does not take delight in a past sensation, thinking, 'I had such and such a sensation in the past.' One does not take delight in a past perception, thinking, 'I had such and such a perception in the past.' One does not take delight in a past volitional activity, thinking, 'I had such and such a volitional activity in the past.' One does not take delight in a past consciousness, thinking, 'I had such and such a consciousness in the past.' Bhikkhus, this is how the past is not harked back to.

274. Bhikkhus, how does one hanker after the future? One takes delight in a future appearance, thinking, 'May I have such and such an appearance in the future.' One takes delight in a future sensation, thinking, 'May I have such and such a sensation in the future.' One takes delight in a future perception, thinking, 'May I have such and such a perception in the future. One takes delight in a future volitional activity, thinking 'May I have such and such a volitional activity in the future.' One takes delight in a future conscious-

4. Muni: It is one of the epithets of the Buddha. All defilements have become extinct in a Muni, making for tranquillity.

ness, thinking, 'May I have such and such a consciousness in the future.' Bhikkhus, this is how the future is hankered after.

Bhikkhus, how does one not hanker after the future? One does not take delight in a future appearance, thinking, 'May I have such and such an appearance in the future.' One does not take delight in a future sensation, thinking, 'May I have such and such a sensation in the future.' One does not take delight in a future perception, thinking, 'May I have such and such a perception in the future.' One does not take delight in a future volitional activity, thinking, 'May I have such and such a volitional activity in the future.' One does not take delight in a future consciousness, thinking, 'May I have such and such a consciousness in the future.' Bhikkhus, this is how the future is not hankered after.

275. How is one carried away (by Craving and wrong view) in respect of presently arising physical and mental phenomena? Bhikkhus, in this world, an ignorant worldling, who habitually disregards the ariyas, who is not proficient in the teachings of the ariyas, who is not trained and disciplined in the teachings of the ariyas, who habitually disregards men of virtue, who is not proficient in the teachings of men of virtue, who is not trained and disciplined in the teachings of men of virtue, regards corporeality as atta, Self, or regards the remaining aggregates as atta having corporeality,[5] or regards corporeality (as existing) in atta, or atta (as existing) in corporeality; regards sensation ...p...; regards perception ...p...; regards volitional activities ...p...; and regards consciousness as atta, Self, or regards the remaining aggregates as atta having consciousness, or regards consciousness (as existing) in atta, or atta (as existing) in consciousness.[6] Bhikkhus, this is how one is carried away (by Craving and wrong view) in respect of presently arising physical and mental phenomena.

---

5. the view that only the mental aggregates are atta which has corporeality.

6. See f.n.6 to Mahāpuṇṇama Sutta.

Bhikkhus, how is one not carried away (by Craving and wrong view) in respect of presently arising physical and mental phenomena? Bhikkhus, in this world, a learned ariya disciple, who pays attention to the ariyas, who is proficient in the teachings of the ariyas, who is trained and disciplined in the teachings of the ariyas, who pays attention to men of virtue, who is proficient in the teachings of men of virtue, who is trained and disciplined in the teachings of men of virtue, does not regard corporeality as atta, Self, does not regard the remaining aggregates as atta having corporeality, does not regard corporeality (as existing) in atta, does not regard atta (as existing) in corporeality; does not regard sensation ...p...; does not regard perception ...p...; does not regard volitional activities ...p...; does not regard consciousness as atta, Self, does not regard the remaining aggregates as atta having consciousness, does not regard consciousness (as existing) in atta, does not regard atta (as existing) in consciousness. Bhikkhus, this is how one is not carried away (by Craving and wrong view) in respect of presently arising physical and mental phenomena.

Neither the past should be harked back to, nor the future be hankered after. The past is no more and the future is not yet.

The wise person contemplates the presently arising physical and mental phenomena as and when they arise. He would repeatedly cultivate the development of Insight Knowledge which is immovable and unshakable.

The effort should be made today. One may die tomorrow, who knows? We have no covenant with the King of Death and his many warriors.

The tranquil Muni has defined the person who lives thus, diligently meditating day and night, as a *bhaddekaratta*.

Bhikkhus, this is what I meant when I said that I would expound to you, both in brief and in detail, a discourse on *bhaddekaratta*, one who has an excellent night.

Thus the Bhagavā spoke. Delighted with what the Bhagavā had said, those bhikkhus received it with gladness.

End of the Bhaddekaratta Sutta,
the first in this vagga.

5. CŪḶAKAMMAVIBHAṄGA SUTTA

The Shorter Discourse Explaining the Force of Acts or Deeds

289. Thus have I heard:

Once the Bhagavā was staying at the Jetavana monastery of Anāthapiṇḍika in Sāvatthī. At that time, young Subha, son of Todeyya, approached the Bhagavā and exchanged greetings with him. After bringing to an end the amiable and courteous greetings, he sat in a suitable place and said to the Bhagavā thus:

"O Gotama, among human beings, although all are human beings some are found to be inferior and some to be superior. What is the cause and what is the reason? O Gotama, some human beings are found to have short lives and some to have long lives, some are found to be sickly and some to be healthy, some are found to be ugly and some to be beautiful, some are found to be of little influence and some to be of great influence, some are found to be of little wealth and some to be of great wealth, some are found to be of inferior lineage and some to be of superior lineage, some are found to be unwise and some to be wise. O Gotama, among human beings, although all are human beings some are found to be inferior and some to be superior. What is the cause and what is the reason?"

"Young man, beings have kamma (act or deed) as their possession, kamma as their inheritance, kamma as their cause, kamma as their relative, kamma as their refuge. It is only kamma that conditions beings either to be inferior or superior." "O Gotama, I do not understand the meaning in detail of these words that the revered Gotama has taught in brief without elaborating. May it please the honourable Gotama to expound the dhamma, so that I could understand in detail the meaning of what the revered Gotama has taught in brief without elaborating."

290. "Young man, in that case, listen well and pay good attention. I shall speak." "Very well, revered Sir," replied young Subha, son of Todeyya. The Bhagavā spoke thus:

Young man, in this world, some person, whether male or female, takes the life of beings, is cruel, has blood-stained hands, is inclined to killing and destroying, lacks compassion for beings. Due to the result-producing actions which that person has performed, on death and dissolution of the body, that person appears in wretched destinations (duggati), in miserable existences (apāya), states of ruin (vinipāta), and realms of continuous suffering (niraya). If that person, on death and dissolution of the body, does not appear in wretched destinations, in miserable existences, states of ruin, and realms of continuous suffering, but is reborn in the world of human beings – that person will be short--lived wherever he or she is born. Young man, taking of life, being cruel, having blood-stained hands, inclination to killing and destroying and lacking compassion for beings constitute conduct that leads to a short life. (1)

Young man, in this world, some person, whether male or female, abandons all thoughts of taking life and abstains from destruction of life, setting aside the stick and sword, ashamed to do evil, and is compassionate and dwells with solicitude for the welfare of all beings. Due to the result-producing actions which that person has performed, on death and dissolution of the body, that person appears in a good destination, the happy world of the devas. If that person, on death and dissolution of the body, does not appear in a good destination, the happy world of the devas, but is reborn in the world of human beings – that person will live long wherever he or she is born. Young man, abandoning all thoughts of taking life, abstaining from destruction of life, setting aside the stick and sword, being ashamed to do evil, and being compassionate and dwelling with solicitude for the welfare of all beings constitute conduct which leads to a long life. (1)

291. Young man, in this world, some person, whether male or female, is given to oppressing beings by beating or by throwing stones or by attacking with sticks or by hacking with weapons. Due to the result-

-producing actions which that person has performed, on death and dissolution of the body, that person appears in wretched destinations, in miserable existences, states of ruin, and realms of continuous suffering. If that person, on death and dissolution of the body, does not appear in wretched destinations, in miserable existences, states of ruin, and realms of continuous suffering, but is reborn in the world of human beings – that person will be sickly wherever he or she is born. Young man, being given to oppressing beings by beating or by throwing stones or by attacking with sticks or by hacking with weapons constitute conduct which leads to sickliness. (2)

Young man, in this world, some person, whether male or female, is not given to oppressing beings by beating or by throwing stones or by attacking with sticks or by hacking with weapons. Due to the result--producing actions which that person has performed, on death and dissolution of the body, that person appears in a good destination, the happy world of the devas. If that person, on death and dissolution of the body, does not appear in a good destination, the happy world of the devas, but is reborn in the world of human beings – that person will be healthy wherever he or she is born. Young man, not being given to oppressing beings by beating or by throwing stones or by attacking with sticks or by hacking with weapons constitute conduct which leads to good health. (2)

292. Young man, in this world, some person, whether male or female, is given to anger and is given to despair. Even when little is said against him, that person becomes ill-tempered, agitated, malevolent and obdurate and shows anger, hatred and annoyance. Due to the result-producing actions which that person has performed, on death and dissolution of the body, that person appears in wretched destinations, in miserable existences, states of ruin, and realms of continuous suffering. If that person, on death and dissolution of the body, does not appear in wretched destinations, in miserable existences, states of ruin, and realms of continuous suffering, but is reborn in the world of human beings – that person will be ugly wherever he or she is born. Young man, being angry, being given to despair, becoming ill-tempered, agitated, malevolent and

obdurate, showing anger, hatred and annoyance even when little is said against him, constitute conduct which leads to ugliness. (3)

Young man, in this world, some person, whether male or female, is not given to anger and is not given to despair. Even when much is said against him, that person does not become ill-tempered, agitated, malevolent and obdurate and does not show anger, hatred and annoyance. Due to the result-producing actions which that person has performed, on death and dissolution of the body that person appears in a good destination, the happy world of the devas. If that person, on death and dissolution of the body, does not appear in a good destination, the happy world of the devas, but is reborn in the world of human beings – that person will be good looking wherever he or she is born. Young man, not being angry, not being given to despair, not becoming ill-tempered, not becoming agitated, not becoming malevolent, not becoming obdurate even when much is said against him, not showing anger, hatred and annoyance constitute conduct which leads to having good looks. (3)

293. Young man, in this world, some person, whether male or female, has an envious mind, is envious, begrudging, and harbours envy about other's receiving material benefits, honour, esteem, veneration and reverence. Due to the result-producing actions which that person has performed, on death and dissolution of the body, that person appears in wretched destinations, in miserable existences, states of ruin, and realms of continuous suffering. If that person, on death and dissolution of the body, does not appear in wretched destinations, in miserable existences, states of ruin, and realms of continuous suffering, but is reborn in the world of human beings – that person will be of little influence wherever he or she is born. Young man, having an envious mind, being envious, begrudging, and harbouring envy about other's receiving material benefits, honour, esteem, veneration and reverence constitute conduct which leads to lack of influence. (4)

Young man, in this world, some person whether male or female, has not an envious mind, is not envious, and not begrudging, and does not harbour envy about other's receiving material benefits, honour, esteem, veneration and reverence. Due to the result-producing actions which that person has performed, on death and dissolution of the body, that person appears in a good destination, the happy world of the devas. If that person, on death and dissolution of the body, does not appear in a good destination, the happy world of the devas, but is reborn in the world of human beings – that person will be of great influence wherever he or she is born. Young man, not having an envious mind, being not envious, not begrudging, and not harbouring envy about other's receiving material benefits, honour, esteem, veneration and reverence constitute conduct which leads to having great influence. (4)

294. Young man, in this world, some person, whether male or female, does not give food, drink, cloth, vehicles, flowers, perfumes, unguents, beds, dwelling places and lamps to samaṇas or brāhmaṇas. Due to the result-producing actions which that person has performed, on death and dissolution of the body, that person appears in wretched destinations, in miserable existences, states of ruin, and realms of continuous suffering. If that person, on death and dissolution of the body, does not appear in wretched destinations, in miserable existences, states of ruin, and realms of continuous suffering, but is reborn in the world of human beings – that person will be poor wherever he or she is born. Young man, not giving food, drink, cloth, vehicles, flowers, perfumes, unguents, beds, dwelling places and lamps to samaṇas or brāhmanas constitute conduct which leads to poverty.(5)

Young man, in this world, some person, whether male or female, gives food, drink, cloth, vehicles, flowers, perfumes, unguents, beds, dwelling places and lamps to samaṇas or brāhmaṇas. Due to the result-producing actions which that person has performed, on death and dissolution of the body, that person appears in a good destination, the happy world of the devas. If that person, on death and dissolution of the body, does not appear in a good distination, the happy world of the devas, but is reborn in the world of human beings – that person will be wealthy wherever he or she is born. Young man, giving food, drink, cloth, vehicles, flowers, perfumes, unguents, beds, dwelling places and lamps to samanas or brahmanas constitute conduct which leads to great wealth. (5)

295. Young man, in this world, some person, whether male or female, is harsh and arrogant – not paying obeisance to those to whom obeisance is due, not welcoming[1] those who should be welcomed, not offering a seat to those who should be offered a seat, not making way for those who should be given way, not respecting those who should be respected, not esteeming those who should be esteemed, not venerating those who should be venerated, not revering those who should be revered. Due to the result-producing actions which that person has performed, on death and dissolution of the body, that person appears in wretched destinations, in miserable existences, states of ruin, and realms of continuous suffering. If that person, on death and dissolution of the body, does not appear in wretched destinations, in miserable existences, states of ruin, and realms of continuous suffering, but is reborn in the world of human beings – that person will be of inferior lineage wherever he or she is born. Young man, being harsh and arrogant, not paying obeisance to those to whom obeisance is due, not welcoming those who should be welcomed, not offering a seat to those who should be offered a seat, not making way for those who should be given way, not respecting those who should be respected, not esteeming those who should be esteemed, not venerating those who should be venerated, not revering those who should be revered constitute conduct which leads to inferior lineage. (6)

Young man, in this world, some person, whether male or female, is not harsh or arrogant – paying obeisance to those to whom obeisance is due, welcoming those who should be welcomed, offering a seat to those who should be offered a seat, making way for those who should be given way, respecting those who should be respected, esteeming those who should be esteemed, venerating those who should be venerated, revering those who should be revered. Due to the

1. welcoming: In the text, the Pāḷi word used is *paccuṭṭheti* which literally means 'rising up from one's seat'.

result-producing actions which that person has performed, on death and dissolution of the body, that person appears in a good destination, the happy world of the devas. If that person, on death and dissolution of the body, does not appear in a good destination, the happy world of the devas, but is reborn in the world of human beings – that person will be of superior lineage wherever he or she is born. Young man, being not harsh or arrogant, paying obeisance to those to whom obeisance is due, welcoming those who should be welcomed, offering a seat to those who should be offered a seat, making way for those who should be given way, respecting those who should be respected, esteeming those who should be esteemed, venerating those who should be venerated, revering those who should be revered constitute conduct which leads to superior lineage. (6)

296. Young man, in this world, some person, whether male or female, is not in the habit of approaching a samaṇa or a brāhmaṇa and asking (thus:) 'What, Sir, is meritoriousness and what is demeritoriousness? What is blamable and what is blameless? What should be resorted to and what should not be resorted to? Doing what will lead to my disadvantage and suffering for a long time? Doing what will lead to my advantage and happiness for a long time?' Due to the result-producing actions which that person has performed, on death and dissolution of the body, that person appears in wretched destinations, in miserable existences, states of ruin, and realms of continuous suffering. If that person, on death and dissolution of the body, does not appear in wretched destinations, in miserable existences, states of ruin, and realms of continuous suffering, but is reborn in the world of human beings – that person will be unwise wherever he or she is born. Young man, not being in the habit of approaching a samana or a brāhmana and asking (thus:) 'What, Sir, is meritoriousness and what is demeritoriousness? What is blamable and what is blameless? What should be resorted to and what should not be resorted to? Doing what will lead to my disadvantage and suffering for a long time? Doing what will lead to my advantage and happiness for a long time?' constitute conduct which leads to lack of wisdom. (7)

Young man, in this world, some person, whether male or female, is in the habit of approaching a samaṇa or a brāhmaṇa and asking (thus:) 'What, sir, is meritoriousness and what is demeritoriousness? What is blamable and what is blameless? What should be resorted to and what should not be resorted to? Doing what will lead to my disadvantage and suffering for a long time? Doing what will lead to my advantage and happiness for a long time?' Due to the result-producing actions which that person has performed, on death and dissolution of the body, that person appears in a good destination, the happy world of the devas. If that person, on death and dissolution of the body, does not appear in a good destination, the happy world of the devas, but is reborn in the world of human beings – that person will be of great wisdom wherever he or she is born. Young man, being in the habit of approaching a samaṇa or a brāhmaṇa and asking (thus:) 'What, Sir, is meritoriousness and demeritoriousness? What is blamable and what is blameless? What should be resorted to and what should not be resorted to? Doing what will lead to my disadvantage and suffering for a long time? Doing what will lead to my advantage and happiness for a long time?' constitute conduct which leads to great wisdom. (7)

297. Young man, thus conduct that leads to a short life is the cause of a short life. Conduct that leads to a long life is the cause of long life. Conduct that leads to sickliness is the cause of sickliness. Conduct that leads to good health is the cause of good health. Conduct that leads ugliness is the cause of ugliness. Conduct that leads to good looks is the cause of having good looks. Conduct that leads to lack of influence is the cause of lack of influence. Conduct that leads to great influence is the cause of having great influence. Conduct that leads to poverty is the cause of poverty. Conduct that leads to great wealth is the cause of great wealth. Conduct that leads to inferior lineage is the cause of inferior lineage. Conduct that leads to superior lineage is the cause of superior lineage. Conduct that leads to lack of wisdom is the cause of lack of wisdom. Conduct that leads to great wisdom is the cause of great wisdom. Young man, beings have kamma (act or deed) as their possession, kamma as their inheritance, kamma as their cause,

kamma as their relative and kamma as their refuge. It is only kamma that conditions beings either to be inferior or superior.

When this had been said, young Subha, son of Todeyya, addressed the Bhagavā thus:

"O Gotama! Excellent (is the dhamma)! O Gotama! Excellent (is the dhamma)! Just as, O Gotama, one turns up what lies upside down, just as one uncovers what is covered, just as one shows the way to another who is lost, just as one holds up a lamp in the darkness for those with eyes to see visible objects, even so have you revealed the dhamma to me in various ways. I take refuge in the revered Gotama, I take refuge in the Dhamma, and I take refuge in the Saṁgha. May the Revered Gotama take me as a lay disciple from now on till the end of my life."

End of the Cūḷakammavibhaṅga Sutta,
the fifth in this vagga.

7. SAḶĀYATANA VIBHAṄGA SUTTA

Discourse on the Analysis of the Six Sense-Bases

304. Thus have I heard:

Once the Bhagavā was staying at the Jetavana monastery of Anāthapiṇḍika in Sāvatthī. At that time the Bhagavā addressed the bhikkhus, saying: "Bhikkhus!" And they answered him: "Venerable Sir!" Then the Bhagavā said thus: "Bhikkhus I shall give you a discourse on the analysis of the six sense-bases. Listen well and pay good attention. I shall speak." "Very well, Venerable Sir," replied the bhikkhus to the Bhagavā. The Bhagavā spoke these words:

The six internal sense-bases should be understood. The six external sense-bases should be understood. The six kinds of Consciousness should be understood. The six kinds of Contact should be understood. The eighteen kinds of application of the mind should be understood. The thirty-six causes that lead beings into and out of the round of existences should be understood. Of these thirty-six, some should be relied on and others should be rejected. An ariya practises mindfulness of three factors. The Teacher, who is an ariya and who practises such mindfulness, is worthy of giving guidance to a group of followers. Of the teachers who tame beings, the Teacher is recognized as the incomparable one in taming those who deserve to be tamed. This is the brief outline of the analysis of the six sense-bases.

305. It has been said, 'The six internal sense-bases should be understood.' With reference to what has this been said? There are these sense-bases: the eye, the ear, the nose, the tongue, the body and the mind. With reference to these, it has been said 'The six internal sense-bases should be understood.' (1)

It has been said, 'The six external sense-bases should be understood'. With reference to what has this been said? There are these sense-bases: visible object, sound, odour, taste, tangible object and mind-object. With reference to these, it has been said 'The six external sense-bases should be understood.' (2)

It has been said, 'The six kinds of Consciousness should be understood.' With reference to what has this been said? There are the eye-consciousness, the ear--consciousness, the nose-consciousness, the tongue--consciousness, the body-consciousness and the mind--consciousness. With reference to these, it has been said, 'The six kinds of Consciousness should be understood.' (3)

It has been said, 'The six kinds of Contact should be understood.' With reference to what has this been said? There are: contact by means of the eye, contact by means of the ear, contact by means of the nose, contact by means of the tongue, contact by means of the body and contact by means of the mind. With reference to these, it has been said, 'The six kinds of Contact should be understood.' (4)

It has been said, 'The eighteen kinds of application of the mind should be understood.' With reference to what has this been said? On seeing a visible object with the eye, one thinks of it as being a pleasant visible object or thinks of it as being an unpleasant visible object or thinks of it as a visible object which is neither pleasant nor unpleasant. On hearing a sound with the ear ...p... On smelling an odour with the nose ...p... On tasting a flavour with the tongue ...p... On touching a tangible object with the body ...p... On cognizing a mind-object with the mind, one thinks of it as being a pleasant mind-object or thinks of it as being an unpleasant mind-object or thinks of it as a mind-object which is neither pleasant nor unpleasant. Thus, there are six kinds of application of the mind associated with what is pleasant, six kinds of application of the mind associated with what is unpleasant and six kinds of application of the mind associated with what is neither pleasant nor unpleasant. With reference to these, it has been said 'The eighteen kinds of application of the mind should be understood.'(5)

306. It has been said, 'The thirty-six causes that lead beings into and out of the round of existences should be understood'. With reference to what has this been said? There are six kinds of pleasant feeling based on sense-pleasures, six kinds of pleasant feeling based on release from sense-pleasures, six kinds of unpleasant feeling based on sense-pleasures, six kinds of unpleasant feeling based on release from sense-pleasures, six kinds of equanimity based on sense-pleasures, six kinds of equanimity based on release from sense-pleasures.

Of these thirty-six, which are the six kinds of pleasant feeling based on sense-pleasures? Regarding visible objects cognizable by eye-consciousness, desirable, delightful, pleasing, heart-warming and relating to sense-pleasures, there arises a pleasant feeling in one who repeatedly contemplates such visible objects on cognizing them, or who repeatedly reflects on such visible objects of the past which have ceased to be, which have disappeared and which he had once cognized. Such pleasant feeling is said to be pleasantness based on sense-pleasures. Regarding sounds cognizable by ear-consciousness ...p... Regarding odours cognizable by nose-consciousness ..... Regarding tastes cognizable by tongue-consciousness ..... Regarding tangible objects cognizable by body-consciousness ..... Regarding mind--objects cognizable by mind-consciousness, desirable, delightful, pleasing, ...p... Such pleasant feeling is said to be pleasant feeling based on sense-pleasures. These are the six kinds of pleasant feeling based on sense--pleasures.

Of these thirty-six, which are the six kinds of pleasant feeling based on release from sense-pleasures? Regarding visible objects, for one who knows that they are impermanent, subject to change, disappearance and dissolution and sees fundamentally and truly with insight-knowledge thus: 'All visible objects, whether of the past or of the present, are impermanent, unsatisfactory and subject to change,' there arises a pleasant feeling in him. Such pleasant feeling is said to be pleasant feeling based on release from sense-pleasures. Regarding sounds ..... Regarding odours ..... Regarding tastes ..... Regarding tangible objects ..... Regarding mind-objects, for one who knows that they are impermanent, subject to change, disappearance and dissolution, and sees fundamentally and truly with insight-knowledge thus: 'All mind-objects, whether of the past or of the present, are impermanent, unsatisfactory and subject to change,' there arises a pleasant feeling in him. Such pleasant feeling is said to be pleasant feeling based on release from sense-pleasures. These are the six kinds of pleasant feeling based on release from sense--pleasures.

307. Of these thirty-six, which are the six kinds of unpleasant feeling based on sense-pleasures? Regarding visible objects cognizable by eye-consciousness ...p... Regarding sounds cognizable by ear-consciousness ...p... Regarding odours cognizable by nose-consciousness ...p... Regarding tastes cognizable by tongue-consciousness ...p... Regarding tangible objects cognizable by body--consciousness ...p... Regarding mind-objects cognizable by mind-consciousness, desirable, delightful, pleasing, heart-warming and relating to sense-pleasures, there arises an unpleasant feeling in one who repeatedly thinks of such mind-objects which he does not cognize, or who repeatedly reflects on such mind-objects of the past which have ceased to be, which have disappeared and which he had not cognized. Such unpleasant feeling is said to be unpleasant feeling based on sense-pleasures. These are the six kinds of unpleasant feeling based on sense-pleasures.

Of these thirty-six, which are the six kinds of unpleasant feeling based on release from sense-pleasures? Regarding visible objects, one knows that they are impermanent, subject to change, disappearance and dissolution, and sees fundamentally and truly with insight-knowledge thus: 'All visible objects, whether of the past or of the present, are impermanent, unsatisfactory and subject to change.' Knowing and seeing thus, he aspires to supreme arahatship in this way: 'The ariyas are now abiding in the attainment of Arahatta Fruition. When will it be possible for me to abide in the attainment of Arahatta Fruition?' In one who aspires thus to supreme arahatship, there arises an unpleasant feeling because of aspiring in such a way. Such unpleasant feeling is said to be unpleasant feeling based on release from sense-pleasures. Regarding sounds ...p... Regarding odours ...p... Regarding tastes ...p... Regarding tangible objects ...p... Regarding mind-objects, one knows that they are impermanent, subject to change, disappearance and dissolution, and sees fundamentally and truly with Insight-knowledge thus: 'All mind-objects, whether of the past or of the present, are impermanent, unsatisfactory and subject to change.' Knowing and seeing thus, he aspires to supreme arahatship in this way: 'The ariyas are now abiding in the attainment of Arahatta Fruition. When will it be possible for me to abide in the attainment of Arahatta Fruition?' In one who aspires thus to supreme arahatship, there arises an unpleasant feeling because of aspiring in such a way. Such unpleasant feeling is said to be unpleasant feeling based on release from sense-pleasures. These are the six kinds of unpleasant feeling based on release from sense-pleasures.

308. Of these thirty-six, which are the six kinds of equanimity based on sense-pleasures? Seeing a visible object with the eye, there arises equanimity in the common worldling who is foolish and confused, and in the common worldling who has not yet overcome the defilements,[1] who has not yet overcome the resultant effects of kamma-actions,[2] who does not see faults (in visible objects) and who is uninstructed. Such equanimity cannot overcome (attachment to) visible objects. Therefore this kind of equanimity is said to be equanimity based on sense-pleasures. Hearing a sound with the ear, ... Smelling an odour with the nose, ... Tasting a flavour with the tongue, ... Touching a tangible object with the body, ... Cognizing a mind-object with the mind, there arises equanimity in the common worldling who is foolish and confused, and in the common worldling who has not yet overcome the resultant effects of kamma-actions, who does not see faults (in mind-objects) and who is uninstructed. Such equanimity cannot overcome (attachment to) mind-objects. Therefore this kind of equanimity is said to be equanimity based on sense-pleasures. These are the six kinds of equanimity based on sense-pleasures.

---

1. defilements: In the text, the Pāli word used is *'odhi'* which literally means 'boundary' or 'limit'. The Commentary explains this as the boundary or limit of defilements.

2. The reference is to one who is still subject to rebirth.

Of these thirty-six, which are the six kinds of equanimity based on release from sense-pleasures? Regarding visible objects, for one who knows that they are impermanent, subject to change, disappearance and dissolution, and sees fundamentally and truly with Insight-knowledge thus: 'All visible objects, whether of the past or of the present, are impermanent, unsatisfactory and subject to change, 'there arises equanimity in him. Such equanimity overcomes (attachment to) visible objects. Therefore such kind of equanimity is said to be equanimity based on release from sense--pleasures. Regarding sounds, ... Regarding odours, ... Regarding tastes, ... Regarding tangible objects, ... Regarding mind-objects, for one who knows that they are impermanent, subject to change, disappearance and dissolution, and sees fundamentally and truly with Insight-knowledge thus: 'All mind-objects, whether of the past or of the present, are impermanent, unsatisfactory and subject to change,' there arises equanimity in him. Such equanimity overcomes (attachment to) mind-objects. Therefore such kind of equanimity is said to be equanimity based on release from sense-pleasures. These are the six kinds of equanimity based on release from sense-pleasures. With reference to these, it has been said 'The thirty-six causes that lead beings into and out of the round of existences should be understood.'

309. It has been said, 'Of these thirty-six, some should be relied on and others should be rejected.' With reference to what has this been said? Bhikkhus, of these thirty-six, relying on and resorting to the six kinds of pleasant feeling based on release from sense--pleasures one should reject and transcend the six kinds of pleasant feeling based on sense-pleasures. In this way are the six kinds of pleasant feeling based on sense--pleasures rejected and transcended.

Bhikkhus, of these thirty-six, relying on and resorting to the six kinds of unpleasant feeling based on release from sense-pleasures, one should reject and transcend the six kinds of unpleasant feeling based on sense-pleasures. In this way are the six kinds of unpleasant feeling based on sense-pleasures rejected and transcended.

Bhikkhus, of these thirty-six, relying on and resorting to the six kinds of equanimity based on release from sense-pleasures, one should reject and transcend the six kinds of equanimity based on sense-pleasures. In this way are the six kinds of equanimity based on sense-pleasures rejected and transcended.

Bhikkhus, of these thirty-six, relying on and resorting to the six kinds of pleasant feeling based on release from sense-pleasures, one should reject and transcend the six kinds of unpleasant feeling based on release from sense-pleasures. In this way are the six kinds of unpleasant feeling based on release from sense-pleasures rejected and transcended.

Bhikkhus, of these thirty-six, relying on and resorting to the six kinds of equanimity based on release from sense-pleasures, one should reject and transcend the six kinds of pleasant feeling based on release from sense-pleasures. In this way are the six kinds of pleasant feeling based on release from sense-pleasures rejected and transcended.

310. Bhikkhus, there are various kinds of equanimity based on various kinds of objects of attention. And there is a single kind of equanimity based on a single object of attention. Bhikkhus, which are the various kinds of equanimity based on various kinds of objects of attention? Bhikkhus, there is the equanimity based on visible objects, there is the equanimity based on sounds, there is the equanimity based on odours, there is the equanimity based on tastes, there is the equanimity based on tangible objects. Bhikkhus, these are the various kinds of equanimity based on various kinds of objects of attention.

Bhikkhus, which is the single kind of equanimity based on a single object of attention? Bhikkhus, there is the equanimity based on the Jhāna of Infinity of Space, or the equanimity based on the Jhāna of Infinity of Consciousness, or the equanimity based on the Jhāna of Nothingness, or the equanimity based on the Jhāna of Neither Consciousness Nor Non-Consciousness. Bhikkhus, this kind of equanimity is the single kind of equanimity based on a single object of attention.

Bhikkhus, of these two, relying on and resorting to the single kind of equanimity based on a single object of attention, one should reject and transcend the various kinds of equanimity based on various kinds of objects of attention. In this way are the various kinds of equanimity based on various kinds of objects of attention rejected and transcended.

Bhikkhus, relying on and resorting to vipassanā insight *(atammayatā)*, one should reject and transcend the single kind of equanimity based on a single object of attention. In this way is the single kind of equanimity based on a single object of attention rejected and transcended. With reference to this, it has been said, 'Of these thirty-six, some should be relied on and others should be rejected.'

311. It has been said, 'An ariya practises mindfulness of three factors. The Teacher, who is an ariya and who practises such mindfulness, is worthy of giving guidance to a group of followers.' With reference to what has this been said? Bhikkhus, in this world, the Teacher, who is always compassionate and solicitous of the welfare of beings, taught the disciples out of compassion, thus: 'This practice is for your welfare. This practice is for your happiness'. The Teacher's disciples do not listen, do not pay attention or try to understand. They disregard the Teacher's exhortation. Bhikkhus, in such a circumstance, the Tathāgata is not unhappy and does not experience unhappiness. The Tathāgata remains in mindfulness and clear comprehension without any displeasure. Bhikkhus, this is said to be mindfulness of the first factor. An ariya practises such mindfulness. The Teacher, who is an ariya and who practises such mindfulness, is worthy of giving guidance to a group of followers.

And again, bhikkhus, the Teacher, who is always compassionate and solicitous of the welfare of beings, taught the disciples out of compassion thus: 'This practice is for your welfare. This practice is for your happiness.' Some of the Teacher's disciples do not listen, do not pay attention, or try to understand. They disregard the Teacher's exhortation. Some of the Teacher's disciples listen, pay attention and try to understand. They do not disregard the Teacher's exhortation. Bhikkhus, in such a circumstance, the

Tathāgata is not unhappy and does not experience unhappiness. Neither is he happy nor does he experience happiness. Avoiding both unhappiness and happiness, the Tathāgata remains in mindfulness and clear comprehension. Bhikkhus, this is said to be mindfulness of the second factor. An ariya practises such mindfulness. The Teacher, who is an ariya and who practises such mindfulness, is worthy of giving guidance to a group of followers.

And again, bhikkhus, the Teacher, who is always compassionate and solicitous of the welfare of beings, taught the disciples out of compassion thus: 'This practice is for your welfare. This practice is for your happiness.' The Teacher's disciples listen, pay attention and try to understand. They do not disregard the Teacher's exhortation. Bhikkhus, in such a circumstance, the Tathāgata is happy and enjoys happiness. But the Tathāgata remains in mindfulness and clear comprehension without attachment. Bhikkhus, this is said to be mindfulness of the third factor. An ariya practises such mindfulness. The Teacher, who is an ariya and who practises such mindfulness, is worthy of giving guidance to a group of followers. With reference to these, it has been said, 'An ariya practises mindfulness of three factors. The Teacher, who is an ariya and who practises such mindfulness, is worthy of giving guidance to a group of followers.'

312. It has been said, 'Of the teachers who tame beings, the Teacher is recognized as the incomparable one in taming those who deserve to be tamed.' With reference to what has this been said? Bhikkhus, the trained elephant that has been trained by the elephant-trainer runs only in one direction, either east or west or north or south. Bhikkhus, the trained horse that has been trained by the horse-trainer runs only in one direction, either east or west or north or south. Bhikkhus, the trained bullock that has been trained by the bullock-trainer runs only in one direction, either east or west or north or south. Indeed, bhikkhus, the instructed person who has been tamed by the Homage--Worthy, Perfectly Self-Enlightened Tathāgata runs in the eight directions. Contemplating corporeal objects, one enters the rūpa jhāna (absorption in the fine material

sphere).This (temporary release from defilements) is one Direction. Not paying attention to internal objects, one contemplates external objects. This (release) is the second Direction. One applies oneself to the brightness and clarity (subha) of the object of contemplation. This (release) is the third Direction. By concentrating on the concept 'Space is Infinite' one achieves and remains in Ākāsānañcāyatana jhāna, where all forms of consciousness that turn on corporeality (rūpasaññā) have been completely transcended, all forms of consciousness arising out of contact between the senses and their objects (paṭighasaññā) have vanished, and other forms of consciousness, many and varied (nānattasaññā), are not paid attention to. This (release) is the fourth Direction. By concentrating on the concept 'Consciousness is Infinite' one achieves and remains in Viññāṇañcāyatana jhāna, having totally gone beyond the jhāna of the Infinity of Space. This (release) is the fifth Direction. By concentrating on the concept 'Nothing is there' one achieves and remains in the Ākiñcaññāyatana jhāna, having totally gone beyond the jhāna of the Infinity of Consciousness. This (release) is the sixth Direction. One achieves and remains in the Nevasaññānāsaññāyatana jhāna, the jhāna of Neither Consciousness Nor Non--Consciousness, having totally gone beyond the jhāna of Nothingness. This (release) is the seventh Direction. One achieves and remains in the sustained attainment of Cessation, Nirodha-samāpatti, in which all forms of consciousness cease, having totally gone beyond the jhāna of Neither Consciousness Nor Non-Consciousness. This (release) is the eighth Direction.[3] Bhikkhus, the instructed person who has been tamed by the Homage--Worthy, Perfectly Self-Enlightened, runs in these eight directions. With reference to this, it has been said, 'Of the teachers who tame beings, the Teacher is recognized as the Incomparable One in taming those who deserve to be tamed.'

---

3. Direction: The eight directions are metaphors for the eight *vimokkhas*. *Vimokkha* means release from hindrances and defilements. But freedom or release through jhāna is not identical with the emancipation of an arahat as it is still possible to fall from the jhāna state.

Thus spoke the Bhagavā. Those bhikkhus, delighted, rejoiced in what the Bhagavā had said.

End of the Saḷāyatanavibhaṅga Sutta, the seventh in this vagga.

9. ARAṆAVIBHAṄGA SUTTA

Discourse on Analysis of Being Free from Fault

323. Thus have I heard:

Once the Bhagavā was staying at the Jetavana monastery of Anāthapiṇḍika in Sāvatthī. At that time the Bhagavā addressed the bhikkhus, saying: "Bhikkhus!" And they answered him: "Venerable Sir!" Then the Bhagavā said these words: "Bhikkhus, I shall give you a discourse on the Analysis of Freedom from Fault. Listen and pay good attention. I shall speak."

Enjoyment of sense-pleasures, which is vulgar, which is the practice of householders and common worldlings, which is not the practice of the ariyas and which is unbeneficial, should not be indulged in. Self-mortification, which is painful, which is not the practice of the ariyas and which is unbeneficial, should not be practised. Indeed, bhikkhus, avoiding these two extremes, there is the Middle Way, which is clearly perceived by the Tathāgata, which makes for higher vision, for insight, so as to achieve calm, special apperception (of the Four Ariya Truths), enlightenment and peace (Nibbāna). Flattery should be known; disparagement should also be known. Knowing flattery and disparagement, in the exposition of the dhamma, one should neither flatter nor disparage others; one should speak purely objectively. Happiness should be known as blameless or otherwise. Knowing it, one should seek happiness in one's self. One should not speak ill of others in their absence nor denigrate them in their presence. One should speak unhurriedly and not hastily. One should not stick to local dialect and one should not depart from conventional usage. This is the brief outline of the Analysis of Freedom from Fault.

324. It has been said, 'Enjoyment of sense--pleasures, which is vulgar, which is the practice of householders and common worldlings, which is not the practice of the ariyas and which is unbeneficial, should not be indulged in. Self-mortification, which is painful, which is not the practice of the ariyas and which is unbeneficial, should not be practised.' With reference to what has this been said? Indulging with delight in sense-pleasures is vulgar, is the practice of householders and common worldlings, is not the practice of the ariyas and is unbeneficial. It is accompanied by suffering, oppressiveness, despair and agony, and is a wrong practice. Non-engagement in indulgence with delight in sense-pleasures which is vulgar, which is the practice of householders and common worldlings, which is not the practice of the ariyas and which is unbeneficial, is not accompanied by suffering, oppressiveness, despair and agony, and is a right practice. The practice of self-mortification, which is painful, which is not the practice of the ariyas and which is unbeneficial, is accompanied by suffering, oppressiveness, despair and agony, and is a wrong practice. Non-engagement in the practice of self-mortification which is painful, which is not the practice of the ariyas and which is undeneficial, is not accompanied by suffering, oppressiveness, despair and agony, and is a right practice. With reference to this, it has been said, 'Enjoyment of sense-pleasures, which is vulgar, which is the practice of householders and common worldlings, which is not the practice of the ariyas and which is unbeneficial, should not be indulged in.'

325. It has been said, 'Avoiding these two extremes, there is the Middle Way which is clearly perceived by the Tathāgata, which makes for higher vision, for insight, so as to achieve calm, special apperception (of the Four Ariya Truths), enlightenment and peace (Nibbāna).' With reference to what has this been said? There is the Ariya Path of Eight Constituents: Right View, Right Thinking, Right Speech, Right Action, Right Livelihood, Right Effort, Right Mindfulness, Right Concentration. With reference to this, it has been said, 'Avoiding these two extremes, there is the Middle Way, which is clearly perceived by the Tathāgata, which makes for higher vision, for

insight, so as to achieve calm, special apperception (of the Four Ariya Truths), enlightenment and peace (Nibbāna).

326. It has been said, 'Flattery should be known; disparagement should also be known. Knowing flattery and disparagement, in the exposition of the dhamma, one should neither flatter nor disparage others; one should speak purely objectively.' With reference to what has this been said? Bhikkhus, speaking in what way amounts to flattering and disparaging others and amounts to not speaking purely objectively? All those who engage in indulgence with delight in sense-pleasures which is vulgar, which is the practice of householders and common worldlings, which is not the practice of the ariyas and which is unbeneficial, experience suffering, oppressiveness, despair and agony; they are following a wrong practice. Saying thus amounts to disparaging some persons.

All those who do not engage in indulgence with delight in sense-pleasures which is vulgar, which is the practice of householders and common worldlings, which is not the practice of the ariyas and which is unbeneficial, do not experience suffering, oppressiveness, despair and agony; they are following a right practice. Saying thus amounts to flattering some persons.

All those who engage in the practice of self-mortification, which is painful, which is not the practice of the ariyas and which is unbeneficial, experience suffering, oppressiveness, despair and agony; they are following a wrong practice. Saying thus amounts to disparaging some persons.

All those who do not engage in the practice of self-mortification, which is painful, which is not the practice of the ariyas and which is unbeneficial, do not experience suffering, oppressiveness, despair and agony; they are following a right practice. Saying thus amounts to flattering some persons.

All those who have not yet cut off the fetters binding one to the round of existences experience suffering, oppressiveness, despair and agony; they are following a wrong practice. Saying thus amounts to disparaging some persons.

All those who have cut off the fetters binding one to the round of existences do not experience suffering, oppressiveness, despair and agony; they are following a right practice. Saying thus amounts to flattering some persons. Bhikkhus, thus comes about flattering and disparaging others, and not speaking purely objectively.

327. Bhikkhus, speaking in what way amounts to not flattering and not disparaging others and amounts to speaking purely objectively? Not saying: 'All those who engage in indulgence with delight in sense-pleasures which is vulgar, which is the practice of householders and common worldlings, which is not the practice of the ariyas and which is unbeneficial, experience suffering, oppressiveness, despair and agony; they are following a wrong practice', and saying thus: 'Indulging with delight in sense-pleasures is, indeed, accompanied by suffering, oppressiveness, despair and agony, and is a wrong practice,' is said to be speaking purely objectively.

Not saying: 'All those who do not engage in indulgence with delight in sense-pleasures which is vulgar, which is the practice of householders and common worldlings, which is not the practice of the ariyas and which is unbeneficial, do not experience suffering, oppressiveness, despair and agony; they are following a right practice, and saying thus: 'Non-engagement in indulgence with delight in sense-pleasures is, indeed, not accompanied by suffering, oppressiveness, despair and agony, and is a right practice,' is said to be speaking purely objectively.

Not saying: 'All those who engage in the practice of self-mortification, which is painful, which is not the practice of the ariyas and which is unbeneficial, experience suffering, oppressiveness, despair and agony; they are following a wrong practice,' and saying thus: 'The practice of self-mortification is accompanied by suffering, oppressiveness, despair and agony, and is a wrong practice', is said to be speaking purely objectively.

Not saying: 'All those who do not engage in the practice of self-mortification, which is painful, which is not the practice of the ariyas and which is unbeneficial, do not experience suffering, oppressiveness, despair and agony; they are following a right practice,' and saying thus: 'Non-engagement in the practice of self-mortification is not accompanied by suffering, oppressiveness, despair and agony, and is a right practice', is said to be speaking purely objectively.

Not saying: 'All those who have not yet cut off the fetters binding one to the round of existences experience suffering, oppressiveness, despair and agony; they are following a wrong practice,' and saying thus: 'Indeed, if the fetters binding one to the round of existences have not been cut off, existence also has not been cut off,' is said to be speaking purely objectively.

Not saying: 'All those who have cut off the fetters binding one to the round of existences, do not experience suffering, oppressiveness, despair and agony; they are following a right practice,' and saying thus: 'Indeed, if the fetters binding one to the round of existences have been cut off, existence also has been cut off,' is said to be speaking purely objectively. Indeed, bhikkhus, thus comes about not flattering and not disparaging others but speaking purely objectively. With reference to this, it has been said 'Flattery should be known; disparagement should also be known. Knowing flattery and disparagement, one should neither flatter nor disparage others; one should speak purely objectively.'

328. It has been said, 'Happiness should be known as blameless or otherwise. Knowing it, one should seek happiness in one's self.' With reference to what has this been said? Bhikkhus, there are five (kinds of) sense-pleasures. And what are the five? They are: visible object which is cognizable by eye-consciousness, which is desirable, delightful, pleasing, alluring, accompanied by sensual pleasure and enticing; sound which is cognizable by ear-consciousness, ...p...; odour which is cognizable by nose-consciousness, ...p..., taste which is cognizable by tongue-consciousness, ...p...; tangible object which is cognizable by body-consciousness, which is desirable, delightful, pleasing, alluring, accompanied by sensual pleasure and enticing. Bhikkhus, these are the five (kinds of) sense-pleasures. Bhikhus,

indeed, happiness and pleasantness arise dependent on these five sense-pleasures. This kind of happiness is said to be happiness arising from sense-pleasures, happiness that is like excrement, happiness of common worldlings, and happiness of those who are not ariyas. I teach (thus:) "This kind of happiness should not be taken up, should not be developed and should not be repeatedly cultivated and should be feared."

Bhikkhus, in this Teaching, being detached from sensuality and demeritorious factors, the bhikkhu achieves and remains in the first jhāna which has vitakka (initial application of the mind), vicāra (sustained application of the mind), and which has pīti (delightful satisfaction) and sukha (bliss) born of detachment from the nīvaraṇas (hindrances). Having got rid of vitakka and vicāra, he achieves and remains in the second jhāna, with internal tranquillity, with enhancement of one-pointedness of mind, devoid of vitakka and vicāra, but with pīti and sukha born of concentration. Being detached from pīti as well, he dwells in equanimity ...p... the third jhāna ...p... he achieves and remains in the fourth jhāna.

This kind of happiness is said to be happiness arising out of release from sense-pleasure, happiness arising out of detachment from sense-pleasure, happiness arising out of calm achieved through extinction of hindrances (nīvaraṇas), happiness arising out of Enlightenment through Magga Insight. I teach (thus:) "This kind of happiness should be taken up, should be developed, should be repeatedly cultivated and should not be feared." With reference to this, it has been said, 'Happiness should be known as blameless or otherwise. Knowing it, one should seek happiness in one's self.'

329. It has been said, 'One should not speak ill of others in their absence nor denigrate others in their presence.' With reference to what has this been said? Bhikkhus, of these two, speaking ill of others in their absence, if known to be false, not true and unbeneficial, should not be engaged in. Speaking ill of others in their absence, if known to be true, right but unbeneficial, should be avoided. In speaking ill of others in their absence, even if known to be true, right, and also beneficial, one should know the time to speak such words.

Bhikkhus, of these two, denigrating others in their presence, if known to be false, not true and unbeneficial, should not be engaged in. Denigrating others in their presence, if known to be true, right but unbeneficial, should be avoided. In denigrating others in their presence, even if known to be true, right and also beneficial, one should know the time to speak such words. With reference to this, it has been said, 'One should not speak ill of others in their absence nor denigrate others in their presence.'

330. It has been said, 'One should speak unhurriedly and not hastily.' With reference to what has this been said? Bhikkhus, of these two, for one who speaks hastily, there is bodily fatigue, mental discomfort, impairment of voice, soreness of throat, and his words are indistinct and unintelligible. Of these two, for one who speaks unhurriedly, there is no bodily fatigue, no mental discomfort, no impairment of voice, no soreness of throat, and his words are distinct and intelligible. With reference to this, it has been said, 'One should speak unhurriedly and not hastily.'

331. It has been said, 'One should not stick to local dialect, and one should not depart from general usage.' With reference to what has this been said? Bhikkhus, speaking in what way amounts to sticking to local dialect and departing from conventional usage? Bhikkhus, in this matter, in certain localities, this very bowl is known as 'pāti', or as 'patta', or as 'vitta' or, as 'sarāva' or as 'dhāropa' or as 'poṇa' or as 'pisīlava'. In this way, this same thing is known variously in various localities. Based on the knowledge of one's own usage, one thinks wrongly as 'This alone is true; anything else is false,' and speaks accordingly. Bhikkhus, indeed, speaking in this way amounts to sticking to local dialect and departing from general usage.

332. Bhikkhus, speaking in what way amounts to not sticking to local dialect and not departing from general usage? Bhikkhus, in this matter, in certain localities, this very bowl is known as 'pāti', or as 'patta', or as 'vitta', or as sarāva, or as 'dhāropa', or as 'poṇa', or as 'pisīlava.' In this way, this very bowl

is known variously in various localities. Not sticking to one's own dialect, and knowing thus: 'These revered ones call this very bowl in this way,' one calls it according to their usage. Bhikkhus, indeed, speaking in this way amounts to not sticking to local dialect and not departing from general usage. With reference to this, it has been said, 'One should not stick to local dialect, and one should not depart from general usage.'

333. Bhikkhus, the indulgence with delight in sense-pleasures is vulgar, is the practice of householders and common worldlings, is not the practice of the ariyas and is unbeneficial. It is accompanied by suffering, oppressiveness, despair and agony, and is a wrong practice. For that reason, it is a practice associated with fault. Bhikkhus, non-engagement in that indulgence with delight in sense-pleasures which is vulgar, which is the practice of householders and common worldlings, which is not the practice of the ariyas and which is unbeneficial, is not accompanied by suffering, oppressiveness, despair and agony, and is a right practice. For that reason, it is a practice free from fault.

334. Bhikkhus, the practice of self-mortification, which is painful, which is not the practice of the ariyas and which is unbeneficial, is accompanied by suffering, oppressiveness, despair and agony, and is a wrong practice. For that reason, it is a practice associated with fault. Bhikkhus, non-engagement in the practice of self-mortification, which is painful, which is not the practice of the ariyas and which is unbeneficial, is not accompanied by suffering, oppressiveness, despair and agony, and is a right practice. For that reason, it is a practice free from fault.

335. Bhikkhus, the Middle Way, which is clearly perceived by the Tathāgata, which makes for higher vision, for insight, so as to achieve calm, special apperception (of the Four Ariya Truths), enlightenment and peace (Nibbāna), is not accompanied by suffering, oppressiveness, despair and agony, and is a right practice. For that reason, it is a practice free from fault.

336. Bhikkhus, in the exposition of the dhamma, flattering and disparaging others and not speaking purely objectively is accompanied by suffering, oppressiveness, despair and agony, and is a wrong practice. For that reason it is a practice associated with fault. Bhikkhus, in the exposition of the dhamma, not flattering and disparaging others, and speaking purely objectively is not accompanied by suffering, oppressiveness, despair and agony, and is a right practice. For that reason, it is a practice free from fault.

337. Bhikkhus, of the two kinds of happiness, happiness arising from sense-pleasure, happiness that is like excrement, happiness of common worldlings, and happiness of those who are not ariyas is accompanied by suffering, oppressiveness, despair and agony, and (enjoyment of it) is a wrong practice. For that reason, this kind of happiness is associated with fault. Bhikkhus, of the two kinds of happiness, happiness arising out of release from sense-pleasure, happiness arising out of detachment from sense-pleasure, happiness arising out of calm achieved through extinction of hindrances (nīvaraṇas), happiness arising out of Enlightenment through Magga Insight is not accompanied by suffering, oppressiveness, despair and agony and (enjoyment of it) is a right practice. For that reason, this kind of happiness is free from fault.

338. Bhikkhus, that speaking ill of others in their absence which is false, not true and unbeneficial, is accompanied by suffering, oppressiveness, despair and agony, and is a wrong practice. For that reason, it is a practice associated with fault. Bhikkhus, that speaking ill of others in their absence which is true, right but unbeneficial is accompanied by suffering, oppressiveness, despair and agony, and is a wrong practice. For that reason, it is a practice associated with fault. Bhikkhus, that speaking ill of others in their absence with is true, right and also beneficial is not accompanied by suffering, oppressiveness, despair and agony, and is a right practice. For that reason, it is a practice free from fault.

339. Bhikkhus, the denigration of others in their presence which is false, not true and unbeneficial, is

accompanied by suffering, oppressiveness, despair and agony, and is a wrong practice. For that reason, it is a practice associated with fault. Bhikkhus, the denigration of others in their presence which is true, right but unbeneficial is accompanied by suffering, oppressiveness, despair and agony, and is a wrong practice. For that reason, it is a oractice associated with fault. Bhikkhus, the denigratio.. of others in their presence which is true, right and also beneficial is not accompanied by suffering, oppressiveness, despair and agony, and is a right practice. For that reason, it is a practice free from fault.

340. Bhikkhus, in speaking, speaking hastily is accompanied by suffering, appressiveness, despair and agony, and is a wrong practice. For that reason, it is associated with fault. Bhikkhus, in speaking, speaking unhurriedly is not accompanied by suffering, appressiveness, despair and agony, and is a right practice. For that reason, it is a practice free from fault.

341. Bhikkhus, in use of words, sticking to local dialect and departing from general usage is accompained by suffering, oppressiveness, despair and agony, and is a wrong practice. For that reason, it is a practice asso·iated with fault. Bhikkhus, in use of words, not sticking to local dialect and not departing from general usage is not accompanied by suffering, oppressiveness, despair and agony, and is a right practice. For that reason, it is a practice free from fault.

Bhikkhus, therefore, the factors associated with fault should be known; and the factors free from fault should be known. Knowing the factors associated with fault, and knowing the factors free from fault, one should follow the practice which is free from fault. Bhikkhus, indeed, this is what you should do. Bhikkhus, Subhūti, a worthy person, follows the practice which is free from fault.[1]

---

1. The Venerable Subhūti Thera was designated by the Buddha as pre-eminent in respect of living free from fault. Subhūti Thera exercised absorption in goodwill (mettā jhāna) towards all living beings before receiving any offering. For that reason he was also designated by the Buddha as pre-eminent among those worthy of receiving offerings.

Thus spoke the Bhagavā. Delighted, the bhikkhus rejoiced in what the Bhagavā had said.

End of the Araṇavibhaṅga Sutta, the ninth in this vagga.

10. DHĀTUVIBHAṄGA SUTTA

Discourse on the Analysis of the Elements

342. Thus have I heard:

Once the Bhagavā, while wandering through the country of Māgadha, arrived at Rājagaha. There the Bhagavā approached the potter named Bhaggava, and said to him thus: "Bhaggava, if it is not burdensome for you, I would like to spend the night at your place." "Venerable Sir, it is not burdensome for me. But there is a bhikkhu who is already staying in this place. If that bhikkhu consents, your reverence may stay as you please."

At that time a worthy man by the name of Pukkusāti who, having gone forth from the household life into the homeless life of a recluse out of devotion to and faith in the Bhagavā, was already staying in that place of the potter. The Bhagavā approached the Venerable Pukkusāti and said to him, "Bhikkhu, if it is not burdensome for you, I would like to spend the night in this place." "Friend, this place of the potter is quite spacious. Your reverence may stay as you please".

The Bhagavā then entered the potter's place, and spreading a grass-mat in one place, sat down cross-legged; keeping his body erect, he set up mindfulness, orientating it towards the object of concentration. The Bhagavā spent most of the night sitting in meditation. The Venerable Pukkusāti also spent most of the night sitting in meditation.[1]

---

1. The night is divided into three parts, of which the Buddha spent two and a half parts in sustained absorption in the Fruition attainment. The Venerable Pukkusāti spent the same length of time in sustained absorption in the fourth jhāna through mindfulness of breathing. (The Commentary).

It then occurred to the Bhagavā thus: 'This worthy man assumes a body-posture that inspires respect.[2] It would be well if I were to ask him some questions. The Bhagavā then asked the Venerable Pukkusāti thus: "Bhikkhu, out of devotion to whom, did you become a bhikkhu? Who is your teacher? In whose teaching do you profess your faith?" "Friend, there is the samaṇa Gotama who was a Sakyan prince, who had gone forth as a recluse from the Sakyan clan. The good fame and reputation of that Exalted Gotama spread far and wide thus: 'Thus indeed is the Bhagavā, who is worthy of special veneration; he truly comprehends the dhammas by his own intellect and insight; he possesses penetrative knowledge and perfect course of practice; he speaks only what is beneficial and true; he knows all the three lokas (worlds); he is incomparable in taming those who deserve to be tamed; he is the Teacher of devas and men; he is the Enlightened One, knowing and teaching the Four Ariya Truths; he is the most exalted'. Out of devotion to that Exalted One I became a bhikkhu. That Exalted One is my teacher and I profess my faith in the teaching of that Exalted One."

"Bhikkhu, that Bhagavā, who is worthy of special veneration and who truly comprehends all dhammas by his own intellect and insight, where is he staying now?" "Friend, there is the city called Sāvatthī in the north. That Bhagavā, who is worthy of special veneration and who truly comprehends all dhammas by his own intellect and insight, is now staying there." "Bhikkhu, have you ever seen that Exalted One? Would you know him if you should see him?" "Friend, I have never seen that Exalted One and I wouldn't know him if I should see him."[3]

It then occurred to the Bhagavā thus: 'Indeed, this worthy man has become a bhikkhu out of devotion

2. This refers to the sitting posture. Of the four postures of the body in meditation, namely, standing, sitting, lying and walking, the sitting posture is the one that inspires the highest esteem. (The Commentary).

3. Normally the Buddha's glory was such that every beholder would have no difficulty in recognizing the Buddha. In this instance the Buddha with his power had veiled his identity and assumed the appearance of an ordinary bhikkhu going on an alms-round. Hence the inability to recognize the Buddha by Pukkusāti. (The Commentary).

to me. It would be well if I were to deliver a discourse to him'. The Bhagavā then said to the Venerable Pukkusāti, "Bhikkhu, I shall deliver a discourse to you. Listen and pay good attention. I shall speak." "Very well, friend," replied the Venerable Pukkusāti to the Bhagavā. The Bhagavā then spoke these words:

343. Bhikkhu, man has six elements (dhātus)[4], has six sense-bases on which contact depends, eighteen kinds of application of the mind, and four firm foundations. For one who is set on these four firm foundations, there is no outflow of defilements such as conceit. If there is no outflow of defilements such as conceit, one is said to be a tranquil arahat. One should not neglect vipassanā insight; one should safeguard the truth, should cultivate renunciation (of the substrata of existence) and should practise to achieve calm (through extinction of defilements). This is a brief outline of the Analysis of the Elements.

344. It has been said, "Bhikkhu, man has six elements". With reference to what has this been said? (Bhikkhu, there are these six elements:) the element of solidity, the element of fluidity and cohesion, the element of heat, the element of motion, the element of space, the element of consciousness. With reference to this, it has been said, "Bhikkhu, man has six elements".

345. It has been said, "Bhikkhu, man has six sense-bases on which contact depends". With reference to what has this been said? There are these sense-bases on which contact depends: eye-base, ear-base, nose-base, tongue-base, body-base, mind-base. With reference to this, it has been said, "Bhikkhu, man has six sense-bases on which contact depends".

346. It has been said, "Bhikkhu, man has eighteen kinds of application of the mind". With reference to what has this been said? On seeing a visible object with

---

4. The Buddha began his discourse to Pukkusāti with the six elements, dispensing with the fifteen saraṇa dhammas (relating to good conduct and behaviour or practices), which have to be taken up before vipassanā meditation. The Buddha did so because he knew that Pukkusāti had already attained the fourth jhāna.

the eye, one takes it in his mind as being a pleasant visible object, or takes it in his mind as being an unpleasant visible object, or takes it in his mind as a visible object which is neither pleasant nor unpleasant. On hearing a sound with the ear ...p... On smelling an odour with the nose ...p... On tasting a flavour with the tongue ...p... On contacting a tangible object with the body ...p... On cognizing a mind-object with the mind, one takes it in his mind as being a pleasant mind--object or takes it in his mind as being an unpleasant mind-object, or takes it in his mind as a mind-object which is neither pleasant nor unpleasant. Thus, there are six kinds of application of the mind associated with what is pleasant, six kinds of application of the mind associated with what is unpleasant and six kinds of application of the mind associated with what is neither pleasant nor unpleasant. With reference to this, it has been said, "Bhikkhu, man has eighteen kinds of application of the mind".

347. It has been said, "Bhikkhu, man has four firm foundations". With reference to what has this been said? There are these four firm foundations: Arahatta Fruition knowledge, truth, renunciation (of the substrata of existence), and calm (through extinction of defilements). With reference to this it has been said, "Bhikkhu, man has four firm foundations".

348. It has been said, "One should not neglect vipassanā insight; one should safeguard the truth, should cultivate renunciation (of the substrata of existence) and should practise to achieve calm (through extinction of defilements)." With reference to what has this been said? Bhikkhu, how is vipassanā Insight not neglected? Bhikkhu, there are these six elements (dhātus): the pathavī element, (the element of solidity), the āpo element (the element of fluidity and cohesion), the tejo element(the element of heat), the vāyo element (the element of motion), the ākāsa element (the element of space), the viññāna element (the element of consciousness).

349. Bhikkhu, what is the pathavī element? There is the pathavī element in oneself, just as there is external pathavī element. Bhikkhu! What is the pathavī

element in oneself? What is in oneself, pertains to oneself, and is hard, solid and clung to (by craving and wrong view) is pathavī element in oneself. And what is it? It is the hair of the head, the hair of the body, nails, teeth, skin, flesh, sinews, bones, marrow, kidneys, heart, liver, membranes, spleen, lungs, large intestine, small intestine, (contents of the) stomach, faeces and whatever else is in oneself, pertains to oneself, and is hard, solid and clung to. These, bhikkhu, are called the pathavī element in oneself.

The pathavī element in oneself and the external pathavī element are both merely the element of pathavī.

That (pathavī element) should be seen fundamentally and truly, with right understanding, thus: "This is not mine; this is not 'I'; this is not my atta, Self". Having thus seen this (pathavī element) fundamentally and truly, with right understanding, one gets disgusted with (the pathavī element) and one's mind becomes free of attachment to the pathavī element.

350. Bhikkhu, what is the āpo element, the element of fluidity and cohesion? There is āpo element in oneself, just as there is external āpo element.

And what, bhikkhu, is the āpo element in oneself? What is in oneself, pertains to oneself, and is fluid or has the property of fluidity and is clung to (by craving and wrong view) is āpo element in oneself. And what is it? It is bile, phlegm, pus, blood, sweat, fat, tears, serum, saliva, mucus, synovial fluid, urine and whatever else is in oneself, pertains to oneself, and is fluid or has the property of fluidity and is clung to. Bhikkhu! These are called the āpo element in oneself.

The āpo element in oneself and the external āpo element are both merely the element of āpo. That (āpo element) should be seen fundamentally and truly, with right understanding, thus: "This is not mine; this is not 'I'; this is not my atta, Self." Having thus seen this (āpo element) fundamentally and truly, with right understanding, one gets disgusted with the āpo element and one's mind becomes free of attachment to the āpo element.

351. Bhikkhu, what is the tejo element, the element of heat and cold? There is tejo element in oneself, just as there is external tejo element.

And what, bhikkhu, is the tejo element in oneself? What is in oneself, pertains to oneself, and is hot or cold or has the property of heat and cold, and is clung to (by craving and wrong view) is tejo element in oneself. And what is it? It is the element of heat and cold that generates warmth, that causes decay, that burns up, that digests whatever is eaten, drunk, chewed or tasted, as well as whatever else is in oneself, pertains to oneself, and is hot or cold or has the property of heat and cold and is clung to. Bhikkhu! This is called the tejo element in oneself.

The tejo element in oneself and the external tejo element are both merely the element of tejo. That (tejo element) should be seen fundamentally and truly, with right understanding, thus: "This is not mine; this is not 'I'; this is not my atta, Self." Having thus seen this (tejo element) fundamentally and truly, with right understanding, one gets disgusted with the tejo element and one's mind becomes free of attachment to the tejo element.

352. Bhikkhu, what is the vāyo element, the element of motion? There is vāyo element in oneself, just as there is external vāyo element.

And what, bhikkhu, is the vāyo element in oneself? What is in oneself, pertains to oneself, and is air or has the property of air, and is clung to (by craving and wrong view) is vāyo element in oneself. And what is it? It is air (lit., winds) moving upwards (in the body), air moving downwards (in the body), air in the abdomen, air in the intestines, air moving through all organs of the body, air breathed in, air breathed out, and whatever else is in oneself, pertains to oneself, and is air or has the property of air, and is clung to. Bhikkhu! This is called the vāyo element in oneself.

The vāyo element in oneself and the external vāyo element are both merely the element of vāyo. That (vāyo element) should be seen fundamentally and truly, with right understanding, thus: "This is not mine; this is not 'I'; this is not my atta, Self." Having thus seen this (vāyo element) fundamentally and truly, with right understanding, one gets disgusted with the vāyo element and one's mind becomes free of attachment to the vāyo element.

353. Bhikkhu, what is the ākāsa element, the element of space? The ākāsa element can be in oneself and can be external. And what, bhikkhu, is the ākāsa element in oneself? What is in oneself, pertains to oneself, and is space or has the property of space and is clung to, namely, the aural opening, the nasal opening, the oral opening, that (opening) which takes in what is eaten, drunk, chewed or savoured, that (cavity) which retains what is eaten, drunk, chewed or savoured, that (opening) through which what is eaten, drunk, chewed or savoured leaves downwards, as well as whatever else is in oneself, pertains to oneself, and is space or has the property of space, or is voidness or has the property of voidness, or is hollowness or has the property of hollowness, or is apart from flesh or blood and is in the body as an object of clinging, bhikkhu, is called the ākāsa element in oneself.

Indeed, the ākāsa element in oneself and the external ākāsa element are both merely the element of ākāsa.

That (ākāsa element) should be seen fundamentally and truly, with right understanding, thus: "This is not mine; this is not 'I'; this is not my atta, Self." Having thus seen this (ākāsa element) fundamentally and truly, with right understanding, one gets disgusted with the ākāsa element and one's mind becomes free of attachment to the ākāsa element.

354. Apart from these, there only remains consciousness that is perfectly pure and bright. What does this consciousness cognize? It cognizes pleasantness; it cognizes unpleasantness; it cognizes what is neither pleasant nor unpleasant. Bhikkhu, pleasant sensation arises dependent on contact that is the cause of pleasant sensation. When experiencing pleasant sensation, one knows that pleasant sensation is experienced. One knows that when contact which is the cause of pleasant sensation ceases, pleasant sensation which is appropriate to that contact and which has arisen dependent on that contact also ceases and becomes extinct.

355. Bhikkhu, unpleasant sensation arises dependent on contact that is the cause of unpleasant sensation. When experiencing unpleasant sensation, one knows that unpleasant sensation is experienced. One knows that when contact which is the cause of unpleasant sensation ceases, unpleasant sensation which is appropriate to that contact and which has arisen dependent on that contact also ceases and becomes extinct.

356. Bhikkhu, sensation which is neither pleasant nor unpleasant arises dependent on contact that is the cause of sensation which is neither pleasant nor unpleasant. When experiencing sensation which is neither pleasant nor unpleasant, one knows that the sensation which is neither pleasant nor unpleasant is experienced. One knows that when contact, which is the cause of neither pleasant nor unpleasant sensation ceases, the neither pleasant nor unpleasant sensation which is appropriate to that contact and which has arisen dependent on that contact also ceases and becomes extinct.

357. For example, bhikkhu, when two pieces of firewood are brought together and rubbed against each other, heat is generated and fire is produced. When these two pieces of firewood are set apart in different places, the heat that is caused by the friction of the two pieces of firewood ceases and becomes extinct. Similarly, bhikkhu, pleasant sensation arises dependent on contact that is the cause of pleasant sensation. When experiencing pleasant sensation, one knows that pleasant sensation is experienced. One knows that when contact which is the cause of pleasant sensation ceases, pleasant sensation which is appropriate to that contact and which has arisen dependent on that contact also ceases and becomes extinct.

358. Bhikkhu, unpleasant sensation arises dependent on contact that is the cause of unpleasant sensation. When experiencing unpleasant sensation, one knows that unpleasant sensation is experienced. One knows that when contact which is the cause of unpleasant sensation ceases, unpleasant sensation which is appropriate to that contact and which has arisen dependent on that contact also ceases and becomes extinct.

359. Bhikkhu, sensation which is neither pleasant nor unpleasant arises dependent on contact that is the cause of sensation which is neither pleasant nor unpleasant. When experiencing sensation which is neither pleasant nor unpleasant, one knows that the sensation which is neither pleasant nor unpleasant is experienced. One knows that when contact which is the cause of neither pleasant nor unpleasant sensation ceases, the neither pleasant nor unpleasant sensation which is appropriate to that contact and which has arisen dependent on that contact also ceases and becomes extinct.

360. Apart from these, there only remains equanimity[5] that is perfectly pure and bright and is also malleable, ready for application and resplendent. Suppose, bhikkhu, a skilled goldsmith or his apprentice were to make a furnace. When the furnace has been made, he might kindle a fire at the mouth of the furnace. Having done so, he might take the gold with a pair of tongs and put it into the crucible. At times, he might blow (the flame) on to that gold; at times, he might sprinkle water on it; at times, he might examine it. When that gold has been well purified, perfectly purified, removed of impurities, and is free from dross, it also becomes malleable, ready for application and resplendent. It may then be made into whatever kind of ornament, whether a ribbon, an earring, a necklace, a gold-garland or any other kind of ornament that he might wish to make. In the same way, bhikkhu, there only remains equanimity which is of the same nature as this gold—equanimity that is perfectly pure and bright, and is also malleable, ready for application and resplendent.

361. That person knows thus: "If I were to direct this equanimity, which is perfectly pure and bright, towards the jhāna of Infinity of Space (ākāsānañcāyatana jhāna) so as to achieve it and if I were to cultivate a mind appropriate to that jhāna, this equanimity of mine being dependent on and attached to that jhāna would last for a long time.

"If I were to direct this equanimity, which is perfectly pure and bright, towards the jhāna of Infinity

5. Equanimity of the fourth jhāna is meant here. (the Commentary).

of Consciousness (viññāṇañcāyatana jhāna) so as to achieve it and if I were to cultivate a mind appropriate to that jhāna, this equanimity of mine being dependent on and attached to that jhāna would last for a long time.

"If I were to direct this equanimity which is perfectly pure and bright, towards the jhāna of Nothingness (ākiñcaññāyatana jhāna) so as to achieve it and if I were to cultivate a mind appropriate to that jhāna, this equanimity of mine being dependent on and attached to that jhāna would last for a long time.

"If I were to direct this equanimity, which is perfectly pure and bright, towards the jhāna of Neither Consciousness Nor Non-Consciousness (nevasaññānā-saññāyatana jhāna) so as to achieve it and if I were to cultivate a mind appropriate to that jhāna, this equanimity of mine being dependent on and attached to that jhāna would last for a long time!"[6]

362. That person knows thus: "If I were to direct this equanimity, which is perfectly pure and bright, towards the jhāna of Infinity of Space and even if I were to cultivate a mind appropriate to that jhāna, yet this jhāna is conditioned. If I were to direct this equanimity, which is perfectly pure and bright, towards the jhāna of Infinity of Consciousness and even if I were to cultivate a mind appropriate to that jhāna, yet this jhāna is conditioned. If I were to direct this equanimity, which is perfectly pure and bright, towards the jhāna of Nothingness and even if I were to cultivate a mind appropriate to that jhāna, yet this jhāna is conditioned. If I were to direct this equanimity, which is perfectly pure and bright, towards the jhāna of Neither Consciousness Nor Non-Consciousness and even if I were to cultivate a mind appropriate to that jhāna, yet this jhāna is conditioned".

---

6. Those who achieve these arūpa jhānas will be reborn in the arūpa brahmā realms where life-span is immensely long. Despite the immense longevity of life in those realms, existence therein is impermanent and conditioned. Those brahmās who pass away without attainment of any magga may be reborn either in the deva realms or in the realm of human beings. After passing away in those realms, there is the possibility of their being reborn in the abodes of woe. Therefore the Buddha taught Pukkusāti that these arūpa jhānas are conditioned, lest he remained attached to them.

That person does not strive or act either for the development or for the decline of those jhānas. One who does not strive or act either for the development or for the decline of those jhānas, does not cling to anything in the world. If there is no clinging, there is no attachment. One who is free from attachment, will realize parinibbāna in this very life. He knows: "Rebirth is ended; the Noble Practice of Purity has been accomplished; what needed to be done (for the attainment of Magga Insight) has been done; nothing else remains to be done (for such attainment)."

363. When that person experiences a pleasant sensation, he knows that that sensation is impermanent; he knows that it should not be clung to; he knows that it should not be delighted in. When experiencing an unpleasant sensation, he knows that that sensation is impermanent; he knows that it should not be clung to; he knows that it should not be delighted in. When experiencing a sensation which is neither pleasant nor unpleasant, he knows that that sensation is impermanent; he knows that it should not be clung to; he knows that it should not be delighted in.

364. When that person experiences a pleasant sensation, he experiences that sensation without association with any defilement (such as attachment). When experiencing an unpleasant sensation, he experiences that sensation without association with any defilement (such as anger). When experiencing a sensation which is neither pleasant nor unpleasant, he experiences that sensation without association with any defilement (such as ignorance of the truth). When that person experiences a sensation (at one of the five sense-doors) pertaining only to the body, he knows that he is experiencing a sensation pertaining only to the body; when experiencing a sensation (at the mind-door) pertaining only to life, he knows that he is experiencing a sensation pertaining only to life. He knows that on death and dissolution of the body and after the dissolution of the mental aggregates, all sensations experienced in this body, none of which are to be cherished, will become extinguished.

365. For example, bhikkhu, depending on oil and wick, the oil lamp burns. On the exhaustion of oil and wick and on there being no replenishment and no more cause to burn, the lamp is extinguished. In the same way, bhikkhu, when experiencing a sensation pertaining only to the body, he knows that he is experiencing a sensation pertaining only to the body; when experiencing a sensation pertaining only to life, he knows that he is experiencing a sensation pertaining only to life. He knows that on death and dissolution of the body and after the dissolution of the mental aggregates, all sensations experienced in this body, none of which are to be cherished, will become extinguished. Therefore the bhikkhu who is endowed with such knowledge is established on the supreme foundation which is arahatta fruition knowledge. Bhikkhu, this knowledge which arises on the cessation of all dukkha is indeed the supreme ariyan knowledge.

366. The Arahatta Fruition Knowledge of the arahat is established in the Ultimate Truth of Nibbāna and is not subject to dissolution. Bhikkhu, the dhamma that is subject to dissolution is false. The dhamma that is not subject to dissolution is Nibbāna and is true. Therefore the bhikkhu who is endowed with such truth is established on the supreme foundation which is the Truth. Bhikkhu, this Nibbāna which is not subject to dissolution is indeed the supreme Ariyan Truth.

367. Indeed, in the past before he had attained any magga, there was in him well established substrata of existence[7] which were clung to with craving. He has now relinquished those substrata of existence, has cut them off at the roots, has made them like the stump of a palm tree and has rendered them incapable of

---

7. substrata of existence: *upadhi*: where suffering exists, or that which tends to cause suffering. It consists of four kinds:
   (1) Khandhā upadhi, the five aggregates where the suffering of old age, sickness, etc., exist,
   (2) Kāma upadhi, the five sense-pleasures where all kinds of suffering arise.
   (3) Abhisaṅkhāra upadhi, meritorious and demeritorious kamma-actions which tend to cause suffering.
   (4) Kilesā upadhi, the defilements which tend to cause suffering.

coming into existence, so that they are unable to arise in the future. Therefore, the bhikkhu who is thus endowed is established on the supreme foundation which is the Renunciation (of the substrata of existence). Bhikkhu, this relinquishment of all substrata of existence is indeed the supreme Ariyan Renunciation.

368. Indeed, in the past before he had attained any magga, there was in him covetousness (abhijjhā), desire (chanda) and intense attachment (sārāga). He has relinquished them, has cut them off at the roots, has made them like the stump of a palm tree and has rendered them incapable of coming into existence, so that they are unable to arise in the future.

Indeed, in the past before he had attained any magga, there was in him enmity (āghāta), ill will (byāpāda) and intense hatred (sampadosa). He has relinquished them, has cut them off at the roots, has made them like the stump of a palm tree and has rendered them incapable of coming into existence, so that they are unable to arise in the future.

Indeed, in the past before he had attained any magga, there was in him ignorance (avijjā) and bewilderment (moha). He has relinquished them, has cut them off at the roots, has made them like the stump of a palm tree and has rendered them incapable of coming into existence, so that they are unable to arise in the future. Therefore the bhikkhu who is thus endowed is established on the supreme foundation of calm (through extinction of defilements). Bhikkhu, this calming of attachment, hatred and bewilderment is indeed the supreme Ariyan Calm. With reference to this, it has been said, "One should not neglect vipassanā insight; one should safeguard the Truth; one should cultivate renunciation (of the substrata of existence); and one should practise to achieve calm (through extinction of defilements)."

369. It has been said, "For one who is set on these four firm foundations, there is no outflow of defilements such as conceit. If there is no outflow of defilements such as conceit, one is said to be a tranquil Arahat". With reference to what, has this been said? Bhikkhu, 'I am' is a wrong conception. 'This is I' is a wrong conception. 'I will exist in the future'

'is a wrong conception. 'I will not exist in the future' is a wrong conception. 'I will have corporeality in the future' is a wrong conception. 'I will have no corporeality in the future' is a wrong conception. 'I will have consciousness in the future' is a wrong conception. 'I will have no consciousness in the future' is a wrong conception. 'I will have neither consciousness nor non consciousness in the future 'is a wrong conception. Bhikkhu, wrong view is a disease, is an abscess, is a thorny spike.

Bhikkhu, one who has passed beyond all these wrong conceptions is said to be the tranquil arahat. Bhikkhu, for a tranquil arahat, there is no more rebirth, no more ageing, no more death, no more dissolution, no more attachment. Indeed, bhikkhu, in him there is no more cause for rebirth. For one who is not subject to rebirth, how can there be ageing? For one who is not subject to ageing, how can there be death? For one who is not subject to death, how can there be dissolution? For one who is not subject to dissolution (i.e., an arahat), what is there to be attached to? With reference to this, it has been said, "For one who is set on these four firm foundations, there is no outflow of defilements such as conceit. If there is no outflow of defilements such as conceit, one is said to be an arahat, the Calmed One." Bhikkhu, bear in mind this analysis of six elements which I have taught you in brief.

370. Then, the Venerable Pukkusāti reflected thus: 'It is the Teacher who has come to me; it is the Sugata who has come to me; it is the Perfectly Self-Enlightened One who has come to me'. He then rose from his seat, rearragned his robe so as to cover his left shoulder, placed his head at the Bhagavā's feet and said these words to the Bhagavā. "Venerable Sir, I have committed a misdeed, being foolish, bewildered and unwise. I have thought it proper to address the Bhagavā as 'friend'. Venerable Sir, may the Bhagavā accept this admission of my guilt so that I may restrain myself in the future". Bhikkhu, indeed you have committed a misdeed, being foolish, bewildered and unwise. You have thought it proper to address me as 'friend'. But now, since you have realized your own

guilt and admitted it to make amends, we accept your admission. Bhikkhu, realizing one's guilt, making amends and abstaining from such misdeed in the future means enhancement in my Teaching.

"Venerable Sir, may I in the presence of the Bhagavā receive full admission into the Order?" "Bhikkhu, have you got an alms-bowl and robes?" "Venerable Sir, I do not have an alms-bowl and robes as yet." "Bhikkhu the Tathāgatas do not give full admission into the Order to one who does not have an alms-bowl and robes." When this has been said, the Venerable Pukkusāti, pleased and delighted with what the Bhagavā said, rose from his seat, made obeisance to the Bhagavā and, keeping him on his right, departed in search of an alms-bowl and robes.

Then the Venerable Pukkusāti who has gone in search of alms-bowl and robes was killed by a frenzied cow. Several bhikkhus then approached the Bhagavā and, having made obeisance to him, sat in a suitable place. Having seated, those bhikkhus addressed the Bhagavā thus: "Venerable Sir, that worthy man by the name of Pukkusāti who has been given a brief discourse by the Bhagavā is now dead. What is his destination? What is his present existence?"

Bhikkhus, Pukkusāti, the worthy man, was wise. He had attained the Anāgāmi Fruition which is conducive to the attainment of Arahatta Magga. He caused me no trouble for(his) attainment of Arahatta Magga. Bhikkhus, Pukkusāti, the worthy man, through the total destruction of the five fetters that lead to (rebirth in) the lower planes (of sensual existence), has a spontaneous birth (in a Suddhāvāsa Brahmā realm) and not being liable to return from that realm, he will realize parinibbāna there.

Delighted, those bhikkhus rejoiced in what the Bhagavā had said.

End of the Dhātuvibhaṅga Sutta,
the tenth in this vagga.

12. DAKKHIṆĀVIBHAṄGA SUTTA

Discourse on the Analysis of Kinds of Offerings

376. Thus have I heard:

Once the Bhagavā was residing at the Nigrodhārāma monastery in Kapilavatthu in the country of the Sakyans. On that occasion, Mahā Pajāpati Gotamī, bringing a new pair of robes with her, approached the Bhagavā, made obeisance to him, and sat in a suitable place. Having seated, she addressed the Bhagavā thus: "Venerable Sir, I have spun (the thread) and have woven by myself this pair of new robes, intending it for the Bhagavā. Venerable Sir, may the Bhagavā, out of compassion, accept this pair of new robes of mine". When so requested, the Bhagavā said to Mahā Pajāpati Gotamī thus: "Gotamī, offer it to the Order of bhikkhus. By offering it to the Order, you would have venerated me as well as the Order."

For the second time Mahā Pajāpati Gotamī addressed the Bhagavā thus: "Venerable Sir, I have spun (the thread) and have woven by myself this pair of new robes, intending it for the Bhagavā. Venerable Sir, may the Bhagavā, out of compassion, accept this pair of new robes of mine." For the second time the Bhagavā also said to Mahā Pajāpati Gotamī thus: "Gotamī, offer it to the Order. By offering it to the Order, you would have venerated me as well as the Order." For the third time Mahā Pajāpati Gotamī addressed the Bhagavā thus: "Venerable Sir, I have spun (the thread) and have woven by myself this pair of new robes, intending it for the Bhagavā. Venerable Sir, may the Bhagavā, out of compassion, accept this pair of new robes of mine." For the third time the Bhagavā also said to Mahā Pajāpati Gotamī thus: "Gotamī, offer it to the Order. By offering it to the Order, you would have venerated me as well as the Order."

377. Upon this, the Venerable Ānanda addressed the Bhagavā thus: "Venerable Sir, may the Bhagavā accept Mahā Pajāpati Gotamī's new pair of robes. Venerable Sir, Mahā Pajāpati Gotamī has done much for the Bhagavā; she has been your foster mother, she brought you up, she fed you and gave you her milk. She suckled you after your mother passed away. Venerable Sir, the Bhagavā has also done much for Mahā Pajāpati Gotamī. Venerable Sir, on account of the Bhagavā, Mahā Pajāpati Gotamī has taken refuge in the Buddha, has taken refuge in the Dhamma and has taken refuge in the Saṁgha. Venerable Sir, on account of the Bhagavā, Mahā Pajāpati Gotamī has abstained from killing, has abstained from taking what is not given, has abstained from sexual misconduct, has abstained from telling lies, has abstained from taking intoxicants. Venerable Sir, on account of the Bhagavā, Mahā Pajāpati Gotamī has unshakable perfect faith in the Buddha, has unshakable perfect faith in the Dhamma, has unshakable perfect faith in the Saṁgha, and is endowed with Sīla (moral virtues) cherished by the ariyas. Venerable Sir, on account of the Bhagavā, Mahā Pajāpati Gotamī has no doubts regarding dukkha, no doubts regarding the origin of dukkha, no doubts regarding the cessation of dukkha, no doubts regarding the path leading to the cessation of dukkha. Venerable Sir, the Bhagavā has also done much for Mahā Pajāpati Gotamī."

378. Ānanda, what you have said is true. Ānanda, the disciple, on account of the teacher, takes refuge in the Buddha, in the Dhamma and in the Saṁgha. Ānanda, I do not teach that it is the best way of showing gratitude for that disciple to pay respect to that teacher, to welcome him, to make obeisance to him with joined palms raised (to the forehead), to offer him such requisites as robes, food, shelter and medicine for use in illness.

Ānanda, the disciple, on account of the teacher, abstains from killing, abstains from taking what is not given, abstains from sexual misconduct, abstains from telling lies, abstains from taking intoxicants. Ānanda, I do not teach that it is the best way of showing gratitude for that disciple to pay respect to that teacher, to welcome him, to make obeisance to him with joined palms raised (to the forehead), to offer him such requisites as robes, food, shelter, and medicine for use in illness.

Ānanda, the disciple, on account of the teacher, has unshakable perfect faith in the Buddha, ... in the Dhamma ..... in the Saṁgha, and is endowed with sīla cherished by the ariyas. Ānanda, I do not teach that it is the best way of showing gratitude for that disciple to pay respect to that teacher, to welcome him, to make obeisance to him with joined palms raised (to the forehead), to offer him such requisites as robes, food, shelter and medicine for use in illness.

Ānanda, the disciple, on account of the teacher, has no doubts regarding dukkha; no doubts regarding the origin of dukkha, no doubts regarding the cessation of dukkha, no doubts regarding the path leading to the cessation of dukkha. Ānanda, I do not teach that it is the best way of showing gratitude for that disciple to pay respect to that teacher, to welcome him, to make obeisance to him with joined palms raised (to the forehead), to offer him such requisites as robes, food, shelter and medicine for use in illness.

379. Ānanda, there are offerings made to fourteen kinds of individual beings. What are the fourteen? An offering made to a Tathāgata who is worthy of special veneration and who is Perfectly Self-Enlightened is the first kind of offering made to an individual. An offering made to a Paccekabuddha[1] is the second kind of offering made to an individual. An offering made to an arahat disciple of the Tathāgata is the third kind of offering made to an individual. An offering made to one who is practising to attain Arahatta Fruition (i.e. one who has attained Arahatta Magga) is the fourth kind of offering made to an individual. An offering made to one who is an Anāgāmī is the fifth kind of offering made to an individual. An offering made to one who is practising to attain Anāgāmi Fruition (i.e. one who has attained Anāgāmi

1. Paccekabuddha: One who, like the Buddha, is Self-enlightened in the Four Ariya Truths and has uprooted all the kilesas. However, he does not expound this dhamma to others. Paccekabuddhas appear during the absence of the Buddha sāsana or Teaching.

Magga) is the sixth kind of offering made to an individual. An offering made to one who is a Sakadāgāmī is the seventh kind of offering made to an individual. An offering made to one who is practising to attain Sakadāgāmi Fruition (i.e. one who has attained Sakadāgāmi Magga) is the eighth kind of offering made to an individual. An offering made to one who is a Sotāpanna is the ninth kind of offering made to an individual. An offering made to one who is practising to attain Sotāpatti Fruition (i.e. one who has attained Sotāpatti Magga) is the tenth kind of offering made to an individual. An offering made in a period when the Buddha's Teaching is absent, to one who lives detached from sensual pleasures[2] is the eleventh kind of offering made to an individual. An offering made to a common worldling who is endowed with morality is the twelfth kind of offering made to an individual. An offering made to a common worldling who is without morality is the thirteenth kind of offering made to an individual. An offering made to an animal is the fourteenth kind of offering made to an individual being.

Ānanda, of these fourteen kinds of offering, an offering made to an animal would result in a hundred-fold benefit. An offering made to a common worldling who is without morality would result in a thousandfold benefit. An offering made to a common worldling who is endowed with morality would result in a hundred-thousand-fold benefit. An offering made in a period when the Buddha's Teaching is absent to one who lives detached from sensual pleasures would result in benefit multiplied by a thousand crores. An offering made to one who is practising to attain Sotāpatti Fruition would result in benefit which is immeasurable and limitless. There is no need to say how much more would be the benefit that accrues from an offering made to a Sotāpanna. There is no need to say how much more would be the benefit that accrues from an offering made to one who is practising to attain Sakadāgāmi Fruition. There is no need to say how much more would be the benefit that accrues from an offering made to

2. one who lives ..... pleasures: This refers to one who believes in the resultant effects of volitional actions and who is detached from sensual pleasures through attainment of supernormal powers.

a Sakadāgāmī. There is no need to say how much more would be the benefit that accrues from an offering made to one who is practising to attain Anāgāmi Fruition. There is no need to say how much more would be the benefit that accrues from an offering made to an Anāgāmī. There is no need to say how much more would be the benefit that accrues from an offering made to one who is practising to attain Arahatta Fruition. There is no need to say how much more would be the benefit that accrues from an offering made to an arahat. There is no need to say how much more would be the benefit that accrues from an offering made to a Paccekabuddha. There is no need to say how much more would be the benefit that accrues from an offering made to a Tathāgata who is worthy of special veneration and who is Perfectly Self-Enlightened.

380. Ānanda, there are these seven kinds of offering made to the Order. What are the seven? An offering made to the Order, headed by the Buddha containing both bhikkhus and bhikkhunīs is the first kind of offering made to the Order. An offering made to the Order, containing both bhikkhus and bhikkhunīs after the passing away (parinibbāna) of the Tathāgata is the second kind of offering made to the Order. An offering made to the Order consisting of bhikkhus only is the third kind of offering made to the Order. An offering made to the Order consisting of bhikkhunīs only is the fourth kind of offering made to the Order. An offering made to the Order with the request, 'May the Order assign such and such a number of bhikkhus and bhikkhunīs to receive my offering,' is the fifth kind of offering made to the Order. An offering made to the Order with the request, 'May the Order assign such and such a number of bhikkhus to receive my offering,' is the sixth kind of offering made to the Order. An offering made to the order with the request, 'May the Order assign such and such a number of bhikkhunīs to receive my offering' is the seventh kind of offering made to the Order.

Ānanda, in the future, there will be those who are samaṇas only in name and who only have a piece of robe round the neck, who are devoid of morality and whose habits are immoral. An offering may be made to such persons, who are devoid of morality, with the intention of making offering to the Order (of bhikkhus endowed with morality). Ānanda, I teach that even in such a case also the benefit which accrues from an offering is immeasurable and limitless. Ānanda, by no means do I teach that the benefit which accrues from an offering made to an individual is greater than that of one made to the Order.

381. Ānanda, there are these four kinds of purity of offering. What are the four? Ānanda, there is the offering in which the donor is pure but the recipient is not. Ānanda, there is the offering in which the recipient of the offering is pure, but the donor is not. Ānanda, there is the offering in which neither the donor nor the recipient is pure. Ānanda, there is the offering in which the donor as well as the recipient is pure.

Ānanda, which is the kind of offering in which the donor is pure but the recipient is not? Ānanda, in this matter, the donor is endowed with morality and has good habits; the recipient is devoid of morality and has immoral habits. Ānanda, such kind of offering is one in which the donor is pure, but the recipient is not.

Ānanda, which is the kind of offering in which the recipient of the offering is pure but the donor is not? Ānanda, in this matter, the donor is devoid of morality and has immoral habits; the recipient is endowed with morality and has good habits. Ānanda, such kind of offering is one in which the recipient of the offering is pure but the donor is not.

Ānanda, which is the kind of offering in which neither the donor nor the recipient is pure? Ānanda, in this matter, the donor as well as the recipient is devoid of morality and has immoral habits. Ānanda, such kind of offering is one in which neither the donor nor the recipient is pure.

Ānanda, which is the kind of offering in which the donor as well as the recipient is pure? Ānanda, in this matter, the donor as well as the recipient is endowed with morality and have good habits. Ānanda, such kind of offering is one in which the donor as well as the recipient is pure. Ānanda, these are the four kinds of purity of offering.

The Bhagavā delivered this discourse. After having said this, the Sugata, the Teacher, further said thus:

382. A certain person endowed with morality makes an offering of a lawfully acquired object to a person without morality, with purity of mind and very much believing in the great consequences of kamma--actions. That kind of offering is one which is pure in respect of the one who makes the offering.

A certain person without morality makes an offering of an unlawfully acquired object to a person who is endowed with morality, without purity of mind and without believing in the great consequences of kamma-actions. That kind of offering is one which is pure in respect of the recipient of the offering.

A certain person without morality makes an offering of an unlawfully acquired object to a person without morality, without purity of mind and without believing in the great consequences of kamma-actions. I do not teach that that kind of offering results in great benefit.

A certain person endowed with morality makes an offering of a lawfully acquired object to a person also endowed with morality, with purity of mind and very much believing in the great consequences of kamma-actions. I teach that that kind of offering indeed results in great benefit.

A certain person who is free from attachment makes an offering of a lawfully acquired object to a person who is also free from attachment, with purity of mind and very much believing in the great consequences of kamma-actions. I teach that that kind of offering is indeed the greatest amongst offerings of material requisites.

End of the Dakkhiṇāvibhanga Sutta,
the twelfth in this vagga.

Namo tassa bhagavato arahato sammāsambuddhassa

(v) SAḶĀYATANA VAGGA

1. Anāthapiṇḍikovāda Sutta
3. Puṇṇovada Sutta
4. Nandakovāda Sutta
6. Chachakka Sutta
7. Mahāsaḷāyatanika Sutta
10. Indriyabhāvanā Sutta

1. ANĀTHAPIṆḌIKOVĀDA SUTTA

Exhortation to Anāthapiṇḍika

383. Thus have I heard:

Once the Bhagavā was staying at the Jetavana monastery of Anāthapiṇḍika in Sāvatthī. At that time, Anāthapiṇḍika the householder was sick, in pain and gravely ill. Then Anāthapiṇḍika the householder sent for an attendant and said to him, "Come, O man, go to the Bhagavā and pay homage with your head at his feet, carrying my words. Say to him, 'Venerable Sir, Anāthapiṇḍika the householder is sick, in pain and gravely ill. He pays homage with his head at the feet of the Bhagavā '. And also go to the Venerable Sāriputta and pay homage with your head at his feet, carrying my words. Say to him, 'Venerable Sir, Anāthapiṇḍika the householder is sick, in pain and gravely ill. He pays homage with his head at the feet of the Venerable Sāriputta,' and also say thus: 'Venerable Sir. May the Venerable Sāriputta, out of compassion, come to the house of Anāthapiṇḍika '."

"Very well, sir," replied the attendant to Anāthapiṇḍika the householder, and went to the Bhagavā. Paying homage to the Bhagavā and sitting in a suitable place, that attendant said to the Bhagavā, "Venerable Sir, Anāthapiṇḍika the householder is sick, in pain and gravely ill. He pays homage with his head at the feet of the Bhagavā." He then went to the Venerable Sāriputta, paid homage to him and sat in a suitable place. Having taken his seat, that attendant said to the Venerable Sāriputta thus: "Venerable Sir, Anāthapiṇḍika the householder is sick, in pain and gravely ill. He pays homage with his head at the feet of the Venerable Sāriputta and also says thus: 'May the Venerable Sāriputta, out of compassion, come to the house of Anāthapiṇḍika the householder'." The

Venerable Sāriputta signified his acceptance by remaining silent.

384. Then, the Venerable Sāriputta rearranged the robes he was wearing and, carrying his alms-bowl and great robe, went to the house of Anāthapiṇḍika the householder accompanied by the Venerable Ānanda; and there he sat down on the prepared seat. Thus seated, the Venerable Sāriputta asked Anāthapiṇḍika the householder thus: "Householder, are you feeling well? Are you feeling better? Is your pain decreasing and not increasing? Does it appear to be decreasing and not increasing?"

"Venerable Sāriputta, I am not feeling well. I am not feeling better. My severe pain is increasing; it is not decreasing. It appears to be increasing and not decreasing.

"Venerable Sāriputta, as if a strong man were striking the top of the head with a sharp iron spike, violent winds are assailing the inside of the top of my head. Venerable Sāriputta, I am not feeling well. I am not feeling better. My severe pain is increasing; it is not decreasing. It appears to be increasing and not decreasing.

"Venerable Sāriputta, as if the head were being bound by a strong man with a strong leather thong, I am experiencing a very severe headache. Venerable Sāriputta, I am not feeling well. I am not feeling better. My severe pain is increasing; it is not decreasing. It appears to be increasing and not decreasing.

"Venerable Sāriputta, as if a skilled butcher or his assistant were cutting through the stomach with a sharp butcher's knife, violent winds are cutting through my stomach. Venerable Sāriputta, I am not feeling well. I am not feeling better. My severe pain is increasing; it is not decreasing. It appears to be increasing and not decreasing.

"Venerable Sāriputta, as if two strong men, grasping each arm of a very weak man, were grilling the latter on a pit of live coals, my body is burning with intense heat. Venerable Sāriputta, I am not feeling well. I am not feeling better. My severe pain is increasing; it is not decreasing. It appears to be increasing and not decreasing."

385. Householder, for that reason you should practise thus: 'I will have no attachment for the eye; then, the consciousness which is dependent on the eye will not arise in me.' Householder, you should practise in this way.

Householder, for that reason you should practise thus: 'I will have no attachment for the ear; then, the consciousness which is dependent on the ear will not arise in me.' Householder, you should practise in this way.

Householder, for that reason you should practise thus: 'I will have no attachment for the nose; then, the consciousness which is dependent on the nose will not arise in me.' Householder, you should practise in this way.

Householder, for that reason you should practise thus: 'I will have no attachment for the tongue; then, the consciousness which is dependent on the tongue will not arise in me.' Householder, you should practise in this way.

Householder, for that reason you should practise thus: 'I will have no attachment for the body; then, the consciousness which is dependent on the body will not arise in me.' Householder, you should practise in this way.

Householder, for that reason you should practise thus: 'I will have no attachment for the mind; then, the consciousness which is dependent on the mind will not arise in me.' Householder, you should practise in this way. (1)

Householder, for that reason you should practise thus: 'I will have no attachment for any visible object; then, the consciousness which is dependent on the visible object will not arise in me.' Householder, you should practise in this way.

Householder, for that reason you should practise thus: 'I will have no attachment for sound ...p... 'I will have no attachment for odour ...p... 'I will have no attachment for taste ...p... 'I will have no attachment for any tangible object ...p... 'I will have no attachment for any mind-object; then, the consciousness which is dependent on the mind-object will not arise in me.'

Householder, you should practise in this way. (2)

Householder, for that reason you should practise thus: 'I will have no attachment for eye-consciousness; then, the consciousness which is dependent on eye-consciousness will not arise in me.' Householder, you should practise in this way.

Householder, for that reason you should practise thus: 'I will have no attachment for ear-consciousness ...p... 'I will have no attachment for nose-consciousness ...p... 'I will have no attachment for tongue-consciousness ...p... 'I will have no attachment for body-consciousness ...p... 'I will have no attachment for mind-consciousness; then, the consciousness which is dependent on mind-consciousness, will not arise in me'. Householder, you should practise in this way. (3)

Householder, for that reason you should practise thus: 'I will have no attachment for eye-contact; then, the consciousness which is dependent on eye-contact will not arise in me.' Householder, you should practise in this way. Householder, for that reason you should practise thus: 'I will have no attachment for ear-contact ...p... 'I will have no attachment for nose-contact ...p... 'I will have no attachment for tongue-contact ...p... 'I will have no attachment for body-contact ...p... 'I will have no attachment for mind-contact; then, the consciousness which is dependent on mind-contact will not arise in me.' Householder, you should practise in this way. (4)

Householder, for that reason you should practise thus: 'I will have no attachment for sensation arising out of eye-contact; then, the consciousness which is dependent on sensation arising out of eye-contact will not arise in me.' Householder, you should practise in this way.

Householder, for that reason you should practise thus: 'I will have no attachment for sensation arising out of ear-contact ...p... 'I will have no attachment for sensation arising out of nose-contact ...p... 'I will have no attachment for sensation arising out of tongue-contact ...p... 'I will have no attachment for sensation arising out of body-contact ...p... 'I will have no attachment for sensation arising out of mind-contact; then, the consciousness which is dependent on sensation arising out of mind-contact will not arise in me.' Householder, you should practise in this way. (5)

386. Householder, for that reason you should practise thus: 'I will have no attachment for the element of solidity; then, the consciousness which is dependent on the element of solidity will not arise in me.' Householder, you should practise in this way.

Householder, for that reason you should practise thus: 'I will have no attachment for the element of fluidity and cohesion ...p... 'I will have no attachment for the element of heat ...p...' I will have no attachment for the element of motion ...p... 'I will have no attachment for the element of space ...p... 'I will have no attachment for the element of consciousness; then, the consciousness which is dependent on the element of consciousness will not arise in me.' Householder, you should practise in this way. (6)

Householder, for that reason you should practise thus: 'I will have no attachment for corporeality; then, the consciousness which is dependent on corporeality will not arise in me.' Householder, you should practise in this way.

Householder, for that reason you should practise thus: 'I will have no attachment for sensation ...p... 'I will have no attachment for perception ...p... 'I will have no attachment for volitional activities ...p... 'I will have no attachment for consciousness; then, the consciousness which is dependent on consciousness will not arise in me.' Householder, you should practise in this way. (7)

Householder, for that reason you should practise thus: 'I will have no attachment for the jhāna of Infinity of Space; then, the consciousness which is dependent on the jhāna of Infinity of Space will not arise in me.' Householder, you should practise in this way.

Householder, for that reason you should practise thus: 'I will have no attachment for the jhāna of Infinity of Consciousness ...p... 'I will have no attachment for the jhāna of Nothingness ...p... 'I will have no attachment for the jhāna of Neither-consciousness Nor--Non-consciousness; then, the consciousness which is dependent on the jhāna of Neither-consciousness Nor--Non-consciousness will not arise in me.' Householder, you should practise in this way. (8)

Householder, for that reason you should practise thus: 'I will have no attachment for the present world;[1] then, the consciousness which is dependent on the present world will not arise in me.' Householder, you should practise in this way.

Householder, for that reason you should practise thus: 'I will have no attachment for other worlds;[2] then, the consciousness which is dependent on other worlds will not arise in me.' Householder, you should practise in this way.

Householder, for that reason you should practise thus: 'I will have no attachment for what has been seen or heard or touched or known, or attained, or sought and repeatedly sought or has been intently thought of; then, the consciousness which is dependent on it will not arise in me.' Householder, you should practise in this way. (9)

387. When this had been said, Anāthapiṇḍika the householder wept, with tears streaming. Then the Venerable Ānanda said to Anāthapiṇḍika the householder: "Householder, are you attached to your possessions? Householder, are you disheartened?" "Venerable Ānanda, I am not attached to my possessions. Nor am I disheartened. I have indeed for a long time attended upon the Bhagavā. I have also attended upon the bhikkhus who are worthy of respect. But I have not heard such words of the dhamma before." "Householder, the laity who wear white clothes cannot understand clearly this word of the dhamma. Householder, this word of the dhamma can only be understood by bhikkhus." "Venerable Sāriputta, I beg of you. Let this word of the dhamma be made clear to the laity who wear white clothes. Venerable Sir, there are worthy men whose

1. present world: what is taught here in detachment from one's possessions such as abode, food and raiments.

2. other worlds means other than the human world: e.g. the deva world where also one should not long for mansion and raiments.

understanding is not clouded by the dust of defilements. They are wanting in the dhamma for not having heard the dhamma. There are likely to be people who will be able to understand the dhamma."

After thus exhorting Anāthapiṇḍika the householder, the Venerable Sāriputta and the Venerable Ānanda rose from their seats and departed. Not long after the departure of the Venerable Sāriputta and the Venerable Ānanda, Anāthapiṇḍika the householder expired. He was reborn in the Tusitā deva realm. Then soon after the middle watch of the night, the deva Anāthapiṇḍika of extremely attractive appearance approached the Bhagavā (at the Jetavana monastery), illuminating the entire Jetavana monastery. He made obeisance to the Bhagavā and stood at a suitable place. Thus standing, the deva Anāthapiṇḍika then addressed the Bhagavā with the following verses:

"This Jetavana monastery is frequented by many bhikkhus. It is where King of the Dhamma, the Bhagavā, resides. (That is why) it gives rise to delightful satisfaction in me. It is through action,[3] knowledge, dhamma and virtuous living based on morality that beings are purified; they are not purified through lineage or wealth.[4]

"That is why the wise person, seeking his own advantage, should contemplate the dhamma[5] with right perception. Contemplating in this way, that person is purified by realizing the Four Ariya Truths.

"A certain bhikkhu reaches the other shore (that is Nibbāna). In this respect he is equal to Sāriputta. But, Sāriputta with his knowledge, morality and calm is the noblest among those bhikkhus who reach the other shore (that is Nibbāna)."

---

3. action: kamma: According to the Commentary, this means volitional activities associated with magga (maggacetanā).

4 What is meant here is that purity is gained by means of the Ariya Path of Eight Constituents. According to the Commentary, Knowledge (vijjā) stands for Right View and Right Thinking. Dhamma stands for Right Effort, Right Mindfulness and Right Concentration. Morality (sīla) stands for Right Speech, Right Action and Right Livelihood.

5. dhamma: Here it means the five *khandha* aggregates.

The deva Anāthapiṇḍika spoke these words. The Teacher was pleased. Thereupon the deva Anāthapiṇḍika, thinking, 'The Teacher is pleased with these words of mine,' made obeisance to the Bhagavā and vanished.

388. Then, when the night had passed, the Bhagavā addressed the bhikkhus thus: "Bhikkhus, soon after the middle watch of the night a certain deva of extremely attractive appearance approached me, illuminating the entire Jetavana monastery. That deva made obeisance to me and stood at a suitable place. Thus standing, he addressed me with the following verses:

"This Jetavana monastery is frequented by many bhikkhus. It is where King of the Dhamma, the Bhagavā, resides. (That is why) it gives rise to delightful satisfaction in me. It is through action, knowledge, dhamma, and virtuous living based on morality that beings are purified; they are not purified through lineage or wealth.

"That is why the wise person, seeking his own advantage and welfare, should contemplate the dhamma with right contemplation. Contemplating in this way, that person is purified by realizing the Four Ariya Truths.

"A certain bhikkhu reaches the other shore (that is Nibbāna). In this respect he is equal to Sāriputta. But Sāriputta with his knowledge, morality and calm is the noblest among those bhikkhus who reach the other shore (that is Nibbāna)."

Bhikkhus, that deva said these words. Then, thinking 'The Teacher is pleased with these words of mine,' the deva made obeisance to me and vanished.

When this was said, the Venerable Ānanda addressed the Bhagavā thus: "Venerable Sir, that deva must have been the deva Anāthapiṇḍika. Venerable Sir, Anāthapiṇḍika the householder greatly adored the Venerable Sāriputta." Well said, Ānanda, well said. Ānanda, what you think is true. Ānanda, that deva is indeed the deva Anāthapiṇḍika.

Thus spoke the Bhagavā. Delighted, the Venerable Ānanda rejoiced at what the Bhagavā had said.

End of the Anāthapiṇḍikovāda Sutta,
the first in this vagga.

3. PUṆṆOVĀDA SUTTA

Discourse to Puṇṇa

395. Thus have I heard:

Once the Bhagavā was staying at the Jetavana monastery of Anāthapiṇḍika in Sāvatthī. One evening, the Venerable Puṇṇa, rising from his solitary meditation, approached the Bhagavā, made obeisance and sat at a suitable place. Thus seated, he said these words to the Bhagavā: "Venerable Sir, I beg of you. May the Bhagavā favour me with a brief exhortation. After listening to the Bhagavā's exhortation, I would seek solitary seclusion and remain directing my mind (towards Nibbāna) with mindfulness and diligence." "Puṇṇa, if so, listen and pay good attention. I shall speak." "Very well, Venerable Sir", replied the Venerable Puṇṇa to the Bhagavā. The Bhagavā then gave this discourse.

Puṇṇa, there is the visible object cognizable by eye-consciousness, which is desirable, delightful, pleasing, alluring, associated with sensual pleasure and enticing. If the bhikkhu takes delight in that visible object, speaks about it with joy and gets absorbed in it, clinging arises in him who takes delight in that visible object, speaks about it with joy and gets absorbed in it. Puṇṇa, I teach that because of the arising of clinging, dukkha arises.

Puṇṇa, there is the sound cognizable by ear--consciousness ...p... the smell cognizable by nose--consciousness ...p... the taste cognizable by tongue--consciousness ...p... the tangible object cognizable by body-consciousness ...p... the mind-object cognizable by mind-consciousness, which is desirable, delightful, pleasing, alluring, associated with sensual pleasure and enticing. If the bhikkhu takes delight in that mind--object, speaks about it with joy and gets absorbed in it, clinging arises in him who takes delight in that mind-object, speaks about it with joy and gets absorbed in it. Puṇṇa, I teach that because of the arising of clinging, dukkha arises.

Puṇṇa, there is the visible object cognizable by eye-consciousness, desirable, delightful, pleasing, alluring, associated with sensual pleasure and enticing. If the bhikkhu does not take delight in that visible object, does not speak about it with joy and does not get absorbed in it, clinging ceases in him who does not take delight in that visible object, does not speak about it with joy and does not get absorbed in it. Puṇṇa, I teach that because of the cessation of clinging, dukkha ceases.

Puṇṇa, there is the sound cognizable by ear--consciousness ...p... the smell cognizable by nose--consciousness ...p... the taste cognizable by tongue--consciousness ...p... the tangible object cognizable by body-consciousness ...p... the mind-object cognizable by mind-consciousness, desirable, delightful, pleasing, alluring, associated with sensual pleasure and enticing. If the bhikkhu does not take delight in that mind--object, does not speak about it with joy and does not get absorbed in it, clinging ceases in him who does not take delight in that mind-object, does not speak about it with joy and does not get absorbed in it. Puṇṇa, I teach that because of the cessation of clinging, dukkha ceases.

"Puṇṇa, having received this exhortation in brief from me, in which locality do you intend to reside?" "Venerable Sir, having received this exhortation in brief from the Bhagavā, I intend to reside in the countryside known as Sunāparanta."

396. "Puṇṇa, the people of Sunāparanta are brutal. Puṇṇa, the people of Sunāparanta use rough and abusive words. Puṇṇa, suppose the people of Sunāparanta were to abuse and threaten you. In that case, Puṇṇa, how would you feel?" "Venerable Sir, suppose the people of Sunāparanta were to abuse and threaten me. In that case, I would feel thus: 'These people of Sunāparanta have not yet assaulted me physically. These people of Sunāparanta are not so bad; these people of Sunāparanta really are not so bad.' O Bhagavā, this is

how I would feel on being thus abused and threatened. O Sugata, this is how I would feel on being thus abused and threatened."

"Puṇṇa, suppose the people of Sunāparanta were to assault you physically. In that case, Puṇṇa, how would you feel?" "Venerable Sir, suppose the people of Sunāparanta were to assault me physically. In that case, I would feel thus: 'These people of Sunāparanta have not yet stoned me. These people of Sunāparanta are not so bad; these people of Sunāparanta really are not so bad.' O Bhagavā, this is how I would feel on being thus assaulted physically. O Sugata, this is how I would feel on being thus assaulted physically."

"Puṇṇa, suppose the people of Sunāparanta were to stone you. In that case, Puṇṇa, how would you feel?" "Venerable Sir, suppose the people of Sunāparanta were to stone me. In that case, I would feel thus: 'These people of Sunāparanta have not yet beaten me with a stick. These people of Sunāparanta are not so bad; these people of Sunāparanta really are not so bad.' O Bhagavā, this is how I would feel on being thus stoned. O Sugata, this is how I would feel on being thus stoned."

"Puṇṇa, suppose the people of Sunāparanta were to beat you with a stick. In that case, how would you feel?" "Venerable Sir, suppose the people of Sunāparanta were to beat me with a stick. In that case, I would feel thus: 'These people of Sunāparanta have not yet cut me with a sword. These people of Sunāparanta are not so bad; these people of Sunāparanta really are not so bad.' O Bhagavā, this is how I would feel on being thus beaten with a stick. O Sugata, this is how I would feel on being thus beaten with a stick."

"Puṇṇa, suppose the people of Sunāparanta were to cut you with a sword. In that case, Puṇṇa, how would you feel?" "Venerable Sir, suppose the people of Sunāparanta were to cut me with a sword. In that case, I would feel thus: 'These people of Sunāparanta have not yet tried to kill me with a sharp sword. These people of Sunāparanta are not so bad; these people of Sunāparanta really are not so bad.' O Bhagavā, this is how I would feel on being thus cut with a sword. O Sugata, this is how I would feel on being thus cut with a sword."

"Puṇṇa, suppose the people of Sunāparanta wer to try to kill you with a sharp sword. In that case Puṇṇa, how would you feel?" "Venerable Sir, suppos the people of Sunāparanta were to try to kill me wit a sharp sword. In that case, I would feel thus: 'Ther are disciples of the Bhagavā who, being weary of an ashamed of, and being disgusted with the body and wit life, are looking for lethal weapons to kill themselves but I have got the lethal weapons without having t look for it. O Bhagavā, this is how I would feel on thu being threatened with death by a sharp sword. O Sugat this is how I would feel on thus being threatened wit death by a sharp sword."

"Puṇṇa, it is well, it is well. Puṇṇa, being endowed with such complete forbearance (which eradicates and calms all ill will) you will be able tc live in Sunāparanta countryside. O Puṇṇa, you may go when you wish."

397. Thereupon, pleased and delighted with what the Bhagavā said, the Venerable Puṇṇa rose from his seat and made obeisance to the Bhagavā. Having departed from his presence, he tidied up the monastic building and carrying his alms-bowl and great robe, left for Sunāparanta countryside. Travelling stage by stage, he finally arrived at Sunāparanta countryside. The Venerable Puṇṇa took up his residence there. Then, the Venerable Puṇṇa taught the dhamma to five hundred male and five hundred female lay disciples during that vassa (rains-retreat). During that same vassa the Venerable Puṇṇa attained the threefold knowledge[1] and subsequently passed away realizing parinibbāna.

Then, many bhikkhus approached the Bhagavā and, having paid homage to him, sat at an appropriate place. Thus seated, those bhikkhus addressed the Bhagavā thus: "Venerable Sir, the worthy man by the name of Puṇṇa was given a brief discourse by the Bhagavā. That worthy man has now passed away. What is his destination? What is his present existence?" Bhikkhus, Puṇṇa the worthy man was wise. He had

---

1. the threefold knowledge: recollection of past existences, Insight into the destination of beings, recognition of emancipation through extinction of (āsavas).

practised in accordance with the dhamma which is conducive to the attainment of Arahatta Magga. He caused me no trouble for (his) attainment of Arahatta Magga. Bhikkhus, the worthy man Puṇṇa has passed away realizing parinibbāna.

Thus spoke the Bhagavā. Delighted, those bhikkhus rejoiced in what the Bhagavā had said.

End of the Puṇṇovāda Sutta, the third in this vagga.

4. NANDAKOVĀDA SUTTA

Discourse Containing Nandaka's Exhortation

398. Thus have I heard:

Once the Bhagavā was staying at the Jetavana monastery of Anāthapiṇḍika in Sāvatthī. At that time Mahā Pajāpati Gotamī approached the Bhagavā together with five hundred bhikkhunīs, made obeisance to him and, standing at a suitable place, addressed him thus: "Venerable Sir, may the Bhagavā instruct the bhikkhunīs. Venerable Sir, may the Bhagavā admonish the bhikkhunīs. Venerable Sir, may the Bhagavā discourse on the dhamma to the bhikkhunīs."

At that time, the senior bhikkhus took turns to instruct the bhikkhunīs. But, the Venerable Nandaka had no wish to take his turn to instruct the bhikkhunīs. The Bhagavā then asked the Venerable Ānanda: "Ānanda, whose turn is it today to instruct the bhikkhunīs?" "Venerable Sir, all the senior bhikkhus have taken their turn to instruct the bhikkhunīs. Venerable Sir, this Venerable Nandaka has no wish to take his turn to instruct the bhikkhunīs."[1]

The Bhagavā then sent for the Venerable Nandaka and said to him, "Nandaka, instruct the bhikkhunīs. Nandaka admonish the bhikkhunīs. You, who have given up unwholesome deeds, discourse on the dhamma to the bhikkhunīs." "Very well, Venerable Sir" replied the Venerable Nandaka to the Bhagavā. Then in

---

1. The Venerable Nandaka's reluctance to discourse on the Dhamma to the five hundred bhikkhunīs was based on his knowledge of past existences (Pubbenivāsānussati ñāṇa) that these bhikkhunīs had been his consorts in past existences. He was afraid that if somebody else who possessed similar knowledge saw him surrounded by these bhikkhunīs, he might be misunderstood as being still attached to his former consorts. (The Commentary)

the early morning he suitably rearranged his robes and carrying alms-bowl and great robe entered Sāvatthī on his daily round for alms. After going round for alms in Sāvatthī and after having had the meal he left the place and went alone to the monastery of Rājakārāma. The bhikkhunīs seeing the Venerable Nandaka coming in the distance prepared a seat for him and placed water for washing his feet. The Venerable Nandaka sat on the prepared seat and washed his feet. Those bhikkhunīs also made obeisance to the Venerable Nandaka and sat at a suitable place. The Venerable Nandaka then addressed the bhikkhunīs thus:" Sisters, this discourse will be in the form of questions. When so questioned, if you know, you should say that you know. If you do not know, you should say that you do not know. If anyone should have any uncertainty or perplexity regarding the question, you should ask me thus: 'Venerable Sir, what is this word? What is the meaning of this word?'" "Venerable Sir, we are delighted and satisfied with the Venerable Nandaka's words of invitation for us to ask questions."

399. "Sisters, what do you think of this? Is the eye permanent or impermanent?" "Impermanent, Venerable Sir," "That which is impermanent, is it painful or pleasant?" "Painful, Venerable Sir." "Is it proper to consider what is impermanent, painful and subject to change, as: 'This is mine; this is I; this is my Self (atta)'?" "Indeed no, Venerable Sir." "Sisters, what do you think of this? Is the ear permanent or impermanent?" "Impermanent, Venerable Sir." "...p... Is the nose permanent or impermanent?" "Impermanent, Venerable Sir." "...p... Is the tongue permanent or impermanent?" "Impermanent, Venerable Sir." "...p... Is the body permanent or impermanent?" "Impermanent, Venerable Sir." "...p... Is mind permanent or impermanent?" "Impermanent, Venerable Sir." "That which is impermanent, is it painful or pleasant?" "Painful, Venerable Sir." "Is it proper to consider what is impermanent, painful and subject to change, as: 'This is mine; this is I; this is my Self (atta)'?" "Indeed no, Venerable Sir." "Why is that so?" "Venerable Sir, it is because we have already seen fundamentally and truly with right understanding thus: 'These six internal sense-bases are impermanent'." "Sisters, well said, well said. Sisters, indeed an ariya disciple

sees things fundamentally and truly with right understanding in the same way."

400. "Sisters, what do you think of this? Are visible objects permanent or impermanent?" "Impermanent, Venerable Sir." "That which is impermanent, is it painful or pleasant?" "Painful, Venerable Sir." "Is it proper to consider what is impermanent, painful and subject to change, as: 'This is mine; this is I; this is my Self (atta)'?" "Indeed, no, Venerable Sir." "Sisters, what do you think of this? Are sounds permanent or impermanent?" "Impermanent, Venerable Sir." "...p... Are odours permanent or impermanent?" "Impermanent, Venerable Sir." "...p... Are flavours permanent or impermanent?" "Impermanent, Venerable Sir." "...p... Are tangible objects permanent or impermanent?" "Impermanent, Venerable Sir." "...p... Are mind-objects permanent or impermanent?" "Impermanent, Venerable Sir." "That which is impermanent, is it painful or pleasant?" "Painful, Venerable Sir." "Is it proper to consider what is impermanent, painful and subject to change, as: 'This is mine; this is I; this is my Self (atta)'?" "Indeed no, Venerable Sir." "Why is that so?" "Venerable Sir, it is because we have already seen fundamentally and truly with right understanding thus: 'These six external sense-bases are impermanent.'" "Sisters, well said, well said. Sisters, indeed an ariya disciple sees things fundamentally and truly with right understanding in the same way."

401. "Sisters, what do you think of this? Is eye--consciousness permanent or impermanent?" "Impermenant, Venerable Sir." "That which is impermanent, is it painful or pleasant?" "Painful, Venerable Sir." "Is it proper to consider what is impermanent, painful and subject to change, as: 'This is mine; this is I; this is my Self (atta)'?" "Indeed, no, Venerable Sir." "Sisters, what do you think of this? Is ear--consciousness permanent or impermanent?" "Impermanent, Venerable Sir." "...p... Is nose-consciousness permanent or impermanent?" "Impermanent, Venerable Sir." "...p... Is tongue-consciousness permanent or impermanent?" "Impermanent, Venerable Sir." "...p... Is body-consciousness permanent or impermanent?" "Impermanent, Venerable Sir." "...p... Is mind-consciousness permanent or impermanent?" "Impermanent,

Venerable Sir." "That which is impermanent, is it painful or pleasant?" "Painful, Venerable Sir." "Is it proper to consider what is impermanent, painful and subject to change as: 'This is mine; this is I; this is my Self (atta)'?" "Indeed, no, Venerable Sir." "Why is that so?" "Venerable Sir, it is because we have already seen fundamentally and truly with right understanding thus: 'These six kinds of consciousness are impermanent.'" "Sisters, well said, well said. Sisters, indeed an ariya disciple sees things fundamentally and truly with right understanding in the same way."

402. "For example, sisters, the oil in the oil--lamp that is burning is impermanent and is subject to change. The wick is also impermanent and is subject to change. The flame is also impermanent and is subject to change. The radiance is also impermanent and is subject to change. Sisters, suppose someone were to say thus: 'The oil in the oil-lamp that is burning is impermanent and is subject to change. The wick is also impermanent and is subject to change. The flame is also impermanent and is subject to change. But the radiance of this oil-lamp is permanent, stable and enduring and is not subject to change.' Sisters, would he be saying what is true?" "No, indeed, Venerable Sir, he would not." "Why is that so?" "Venerable Sir, the oil in the oil-lamp that is burning is impermanent and is subject to change. The wick is also impermanent and is subject to change. The flame is also impermanent and is subject to change. What more can be said of the radiance? It must also be impermanent and subject to change."

"Similarly, sisters, suppose someone were to say thus: 'These six internal sense-bases are impermanent. Dependent on these six internal sense-bases, pleasant sensation or unpleasant sensation or the sensation that is neither pleasant nor unpleasant is experienced. That sensation is permanent, stable and enduring and is not subject to change.' Sisters, would he be saying what is true?" "No, indeed, Venerable Sir." "Why is that so?" "Venerable Sir, it is because dependent on such and such a cause, such and such a kind of sensation arises. With the cessation of such and such a cause, such and such a kind of sensation ceases." "Sisters, well said, well said. Sisters, an ariya disciple sees things fundamentally and truly with right understanding in the same way."

403. "For example, sisters, the root of a big standing tree with heart-wood is impermanent and is subject to change. The trunk is also impermanent and is subject to change. The branches and the leaves are also impermanent and are subject to change. The shade of that tree is also impermanent and is subject to change."

"Sisters, suppose someone were to say thus: 'The root of the big standing tree with heart-wood is impermanent and is subject to change. The trunk is also impermanent and is subject to change. The branches and the leaves are also impermanent and are subject to change. But the shade of that tree is permanent, stable, enduring and is not subject to change.' Sisters, would he be saying what is true?" "No, indeed, Venerable Sir." "Why is that so?" "Venerable Sir, the root of that big standing tree with heart-wood is impermanent and is subject to change. The trunk is also impermanent and is subject to change. The branches and the leaves are also impermanent and are subject to change. What more can be said of the shade of that tree? It must also be impermanent and subject to change."

"Similarly, sisters, suppose someone were to say thus: 'These six external sense-bases are impermanent. Dependent on these six external sense-bases, pleasant sensation or unpleasant sensation or the sensation that is neither pleasant nor unpleasant is experienced. That sensation is permanent, stable and enduring and is not subject to change.' Sisters, would he be saying what is true?" "No, indeed, Venerable Sir." "Why is it so?" "Venerable Sir, it is because dependent on such and such a cause, such and such a kind of sensation arises. With the cessation of such and such a cause, such and such a kind of sensation ceases." "Sisters, well said, well said. Sisters, indeed, an ariya disciple sees things fundamentally and truly with right understanding in the same way."

404. "For example, sisters, a skilled butcher or his assistant, after killing a cow, cuts with a sharp butcher's knife, without damaging the flesh or the skin. In so doing, he severs, hacks, cuts and cuts out with a

sharp butcher's knife, only the intervening membranes, the nerves and the sinews between flesh and skin. After severing, hacking, cutting and cutting out thus, he severs the skin and covers the cow with this skin and says: 'This cow is one united with this skin as before.' Sisters, would he be saying what is true?" "No, indeed, Venerable Sir." "Why is that so?" "Venerable Sir, a skilled butcher or his assistant, after killing a cow, cuts with a sharp butcher's knife, without damaging the flesh or the skin. In so doing, he severs, hacks, cuts and cuts out with a sharp butcher's knife, only the intervening membranes, the nerves and the sinews between flesh and skin. After severing, hacking, cutting and cutting out thus, he severs the skin and covers the cow with this skin and says: 'This cow is one united with this skin as before.' Though he may say so, that cow is no longer one united with the skin."

Sisters, I cite this example to let you know the meaning. In this example, what is going to be said is the meaning. Sisters, 'the flesh' is the name of the six internal sense-bases. Sisters, 'the skin' is the name of the six external sense-bases. 'The intervening membranes, nerves and sinews' are the name of pleasureable attachment. Sisters, 'the sharp butcher's knife' is the name of the Ariya Magga Knowledge which severs, hacks, cuts and cuts out the defilements, the fetters and the bonds.

405. Sisters, these are the seven Factors of Enlightenment. Cultivating and repeatedly practising these seven Factors of Enlightenment, the bhikkhu, by means of abhiññā, special apperception, personally and in this very life, realizes, attains to and remains in the emancipation of mind (cetovimutti) and in the emancipation by insight (paññāvimutti), free of āsavas (defilements that befuddle the mind) through their destruction. What are the seven Factors of Enlightenment? Sisters, in this Teaching, the bhikkhu cultivates the enlightenment-factor of mindfulness that is directed to detachment from defilements, freedom from attachment, cessation of defilements, and that promotes and develops the uprooting of defilements and speedy attainment of Nibbāna. He cultivates the enlightenment-factor of investigative knowledge of phenomena ...p... He cultivates the enlightenment-factor of effort ...p...

He cultivates the enlightenment-factor of delightful satisfaction ...p... He cultivates the enlightenment-factor of serenity ...p... He cultivates the enlightenment-factor of concentration ...p... He cultivates the enlightenment-factor of equanimity that is directed to detachment from defilements, freedom from attachment, cessation of defilements, and that promotes and develops the uprooting of defilements and speedy attainment of Nibbāna. Sisters, these are the seven Factors of Enlightenment. Cultivating and repeatedly practising these seven factors of enlightenment, the bhikkhu, by means of abhiññā, personally and in this very life, realizes, attains to and remains in the emancipation of mind and in the emancipation by insight, free of āsavas through their destruction.

406. The Venerable Nandaka, after thus instructing the bhikkhunīs, permitted them to depart from his presence by saying: "Sisters, it is time for you to leave." Thereupon the bhikkhunīs, pleased and delighted with the Venerable Nandaka's instruction, rose from their seats, made obeisance to the Venerable Nandaka. Then they approached the Bhagavā, made obeisance to him and stood at an appropriate place. To the bhikkhunīs standing thus, the Bhagavā said, "Bhikkhunīs, it is time for you to leave." Thereupon, the bhikkhunīs made obeisance to the Bhagavā and departed. Then, not long after the departure of the bhikkhunīs, the Bhagavā addressed the bhikkhus thus: "For example, bhikkhus, on the Sabbath day, the fourteenth day of the lunar month, there is no uncertainty or perplexity on the part of many people as to whether the moon is full or not quite full. In fact, the moon is not quite full then. Bhikkhus, in the same way, those bhikkhunīs were delighted with the Venerable Nandaka's discourse but their aspirations have not yet been completely fulfilled."

407. The Bhagavā then said to the Venerable Nandaka: "Nandaka, for the reason stated above you had better go and instruct those bhikkhunīs again tomorrow with the same instruction." "Very well, Venerable Sir," the Venerable Nandaka replied to the Bhagavā. The next morning, when the night had passed, the Venerable Nandaka rearranged his robes, and carrying alms-bowl and great robe entered Sāvatthī

for alms-food. After going round in Sāvatthī on his daily round for alms, and after having had the meal, he left the place and went alone to the monastery of Rājakārāma. The Bhikkhunīs, seeing the Venerable Nandaka coming in the distance, prepared a seat for him and placed water for washing his feet. The Venerable Nandaka sat on the prepared seat and washed his feet. Those bhikkhunīs also made obeisance to the Venerable Nandaka and sat at a suitable place. The Venerable Nandaka then addressed the bhikkhunīs thus: "Sisters, this discourse will be in the form of questions. When so questioned, if you know, you should say that you know. If you do not know, you should say that you do not know. If anyone should have any uncertainty or perplexity regarding the question, you should ask me thus: 'Venerable Sir, what is this word? What is the meaning of this word?'" "Venerable Sir, we are delighted and satisfied with the Venerable Nandaka's invitation for us to ask questions."

408. "Sisters, what do you think of this? Is the eye permanent or impermanent?" "Impermanent, Venerable Sir." "That which is impermanent, is it painful or pleasant?" "Painful, Venerable Sir." "Is it proper to consider what is impermanent, painful and subject to change, as: 'This is mine; this is I; this is my Self (atta)'?" "Indeed, no, Venerable Sir." "Sisters, what do you think of this? Is the ear permanent or impermanent?" "Impermanent, Venerable Sir." "...p... Is the nose permanent or impermanent?" "Impermanent, Venerable Sir." "...p... Is the tongue permanent or impermanent?" "Impermanent, Venerable Sir." "...p... Is the body permanent or impermanent?" "Impermanent, Venerable Sir." "...p... Is the mind permanent or impermanent?" "Impermanent, Venerable Sir." "That which is impermanent, is it painful or pleasant?" "Painful, Venerable Sir." "Is it proper to consider what is impermanent, painful and subject to change, as: 'This is mine; this is I; this is my Self (atta)'?" "Indeed, no, Venerable Sir." "Why is that so?" "Venerable Sir, it is because we have already seen fundamentally and truly with right understanding thus: 'These six internal sense-bases are impermanent'." "Sisters, well said, well said. Sisters, indeed an ariya disciple sees things fundamentally and truly with right understanding in the same way."

409. "Sisters, what do you think of this? Are visible objects permanent or impermanent?" "Impermanent, Venerable Sir." "That which is impermanent, is it painful or pleasant?" "Painful, Venerable Sir." "Is it proper to consider what is impermanent, painful and subject to change, as: 'This is mine; this is I; this is my Self (atta)'?" "Indeed, no, Venerable Sir." "Sisters, what do you think of this? Are sounds permanent or impermanent?" "Impermanent, Venerable Sir." "...p... Are odours permanent or impermanent?" "Impermanent, Venerable Sir." "...p... Are flavours permanent or impermanent?" "Impermanent, Venerable Sir""...p... Are tangible objects permanent or impermanent?" "Impermanent, Venerable Sir." "...p... Are cognizable objects permanent or impermanent?" "Impermanent, Venerable Sir." "That which is impermanent, is it painful or pleasant?" "Painful, Venerable Sir." "Is it proper to consider what is impermanent, painful and subject to change, as: 'This is mine; this is I; this is my Self (atta)'?" "Indeed, no, Venerable Sir." "Why is that so?" "Venerable Sir, it is because we have already seen fundamentally and truly with right understanding thus: 'These six external sense-bases are impermanent.'" "Sisters, well said, well said. Sisters, indeed an ariya disciple sees things fundamentally and truly with right understanding in the same way."

410. "Sisters, what do you think of this? Is eye-consciousness permanent or impermanent?" "Impermanents, Venerable Sir." "That which is impermanent, is it painful or pleasant?" "Painful, Venerable Sir." "Is it proper to consider what is impermanent, painful and subject to change, as: 'This is mine; this is I; this is my Self (atta)'?" "Indeed, no, Venerable Sir." "Sisters, what do you think of this? Is ear--consciousness permanent or impermanent?" "Impermanent, Venerable Sir." "...p... Is nose-consciousness permanent or impermanent?" "Impermanent, Venerable Sir." "...p... Is tongue-consciousness permanent or impermanent?" "Impermanent, Venerable Sir." "...p... Is body-consciousness permanent or impermanent?" "Impermanent, Venerable Sir." "...p... Is mind--consciousness permanent or impermanent?" "Impermanent, Venerable Sir." "That which is impermanent, is it painful or pleasant?" "Painful, Venerable Sir." "Is it

proper to consider what is impermanent, painful and subject to change, as: 'This is mine; this is I; this is my Self (atta)'?" "Indeed, no, Venerable Sir." "Why is that so?" "Venerable Sir, it is because we have already seen fundamentally and truly with right understanding thus: 'These six kinds of consciousness are impermanent.'" "Sisters, well said, well said. Sisters, indeed an ariya disciple sees things fundamentally and truly with right understanding in the same way."

411. "For example, sisters, the oil in the oil--lamp that is burning is impermanent and is subject to change. The wick is also impermanent and is subject to change. The flame is also impermanent and is subject to change. The radiance is also impermanent and is subject to change. Sisters, suppose someone were to say thus: 'The oil in the oil-lamp that is burning is impermanent and is subject to change. The wick is also impermanent and is subject to change. The flame is also impermanent and is subject to change. But the radiance of this oil-lamp is permanent, stable and enduring and is not subject to change.' Sisters, would he be saying what is true?" "No, indeed, Venerable Sir." "Why is that so?" "Venerable Sir, the oil in the oil--lamp that is burning is impermanent and is subject to change. The wick is also impermanent and is subject to change. The flame is also impermanent and is subject to change. What more can be said of the radiance? It must also be impermanent and subject to change."

"Similarly, sisters, suppose someone were to say thus: 'These six internal sense-bases are impermanent. Dependent on these six internal sense-bases, pleasant sensation or unpleasant sensation or the sensation that is neither pleasant nor unpleasant is experienced. That sensation is permanent, stable and enduring and is not subject to change.' Sisters, would he be saying what is true?" "No, Indeed, Venerable Sir." "Why is that so?" "Venerable Sir, it is because dependent on such and such a cause, such and such a kind of sensation arises. With the cessation of such and such a cause, such and such kind of sensation ceases." "Sisters, well said, well said. Sisters, an ariya disciple sees things fundamentally and truly with right understanding in the same way."

412. "For example, sisters, the root of a big standing tree with heart-wood is impermanent and is subject to change. The trunk is also impermanent and is subject to change. The branches and the leaves are also impermanent and are subject to change. The shade of that tree is also impermanent and is subject to change.

"Sisters, suppose someone were to say thus: 'The root of the big standing tree with heart-wood is impermanent and is subject to change. The trunk is also impermanent and is subject to change. The branches and the leaves are also impermanent and are subject to change. But the shade of that tree is permanent, stable, enduring and is not subject to change.' Sisters, would he be saying what is true? "No, indeed, Venerable Sir." "Why is that so?" "Venerable Sir, the root of that big standing tree with heart-wood is impermanent and is subject to change. The trunk is also impermanent and is subject to change. The branches and the leaves are also impermanent and are subject to change. What more can be said of the shade of that tree? It must also be impermanent and subject to change."

"Similarly, sisters, suppose someone were to say thus: 'These six external sense-bases are impermanent. Dependent on these six external sense-bases, pleasant sensation or unpleasant sensation or the sensation that is neither pleasant nor unpleasant is experienced. That sensation is permanent, stable and enduring and is not subject to change.' Sisters, would he be saying what is true? "No, indeed, Venerable Sir.""Why is that so?" 'Venerable Sir, it is because dependent on such and such a cause, such and such a kind of sensation arises. With the cessation of such and such a cause, such and such a kind of sensation ceases." "Sisters, well said, well said. Sisters, indeed an ariya disciple sees things fundamentally and truly with right understanding in the same way."

413. "For example, sisters, a skilled butcher or his assistant, after killing a cow, cuts with a sharp butcher's knife, without damaging the flesh or the skin. In so doing, he severs, hacks, cuts and cuts out with a sharp butcher's knife, only the intervening membranes, the nerves and the sinews between flesh and skin. After

severing hacking, cutting and cutting cut thus, he severs the skin and covers the cow with this skin and says: 'This cow is one united with the skin as before.' Sisters, would he be saying what is true?" "No, indeed, Venerable Sir." "Why is that so?" "Venerable Sir, a skilled butcher or his assistant, after killing a cow, cuts with a sharp butcher's knife, without damaging the flesh or the skin. In so doing, he severs, hacks, cuts and cuts out with a sharp butcher's knife, only the intervening membranes, the nerves and the sinews between flesh and skin. After severing, hacking, cutting and cutting out thus, he severs the skin and covers the cow with this skin and says: 'This cow is one united with this skin as before.' Though he may say so, that cow is no longer one united with the skin."

Sisters, I cite this example to let you know the meaning. In this example, what is going to be said is the meaning. Sisters,' the flesh' is the name of the six internal sense-bases. Sisters, 'the skin' is the name of the six external sense-bases. 'The intervening membranes, the nerves and the sinews' are the name of pleasurable attachment. Sisters, 'the sharp butcher's knife' is the name of the Ariya Magga Knowledge which severs, hacks, cuts and cuts out the defilements, the fetters and the bonds.

414. Sisters, these are the seven Factors of Enlightenment. Cultivating and repeatedly practising these seven Factors of Enlightenment the bhikkhu, by means of abhiññā, special apperception, personally and in this very life, realizes, attains to and remains in the emancipation of mind (cetovimutti) and in the emancipation by insight (paññāvimutti), free of āsavas (defilements befuddling the mind) through their destruction. What are the seven Factors of Enlightenment? Sisters, in this Teaching, the bhikkhu cultivates the enlightenment-factor of mindfulness that is directed to detachment (viveka) from defilements, freedom from attachment (virāga), cessation (nirodha) of defilements, and that promotes and develops the uprooting of defilements and speedy attainment of Nibbāna (vossagga). He cultivates the enlightenment-factor of investigative knowledge of phenomena ...p... He cultivates the enlightenment-factor of effort ...p... He cultivates the enlightenment-factor of delightful

satisfaction ...p... He cultivates the enlightenment--factor of serenity ...p... He cultivates the enlightenment-factor of concentration ...p... He cultivates the enlightenment-factor of equanimity that is directed to detachment from defilements, freedom from attachment, cessation of defilements, and that promotes and develops the uprooting of defilements and speedy attainment of Nibbāna. Sisters, these are the seven Factors of Enlightenment. Cultivating and repeatedly practising these seven Factors of Enlightenment, the bhikkhu, by means of abhiññā, personally and in this very life, realizes, attains to and remains in the emancipation of mind and in the emancipation by insight, free of āsavas through their destruction.

415. The Venerable Nandaka, after thus instructing the bhikkhunīs, permitted them to depart from his presence by saying: "Sisters, it is time for you to leave." Thereupon the bhikkhunīs, pleased and delighted with the Venerable Nandaka's instruction, rose from their seats, made obeisance to the Venerable Nandaka. Then they approached the Bhagavā, made obeisance to him and stood at an appropriate place. To the bhikkhunīs standing thus, the Bhagavā said: "Bhikkhunīs, it is time for you to leave." Thereupon, the bhikkhunīs made obeisance to the Bhagavā and departed. Then, not long after the departure of the bhikkhunīs, the Bhagavā addressed the bhikkhus thus: "For example, bhikkhus, on the sabbath day, the fifteenth day of the lunar month, there is no uncertainty or perplexity on the part of many people as to whether the moon is full or not quite full. In fact, the moon is full then. Bhikkhus, in the same way, those bhikkhunīs were not only delighted with the Venerable Nandaka's discourse but their aspirations have also been completely fulfilled. Bhikkhus, of these five hundred bhikkhunīs, those who are the lowest (in attaining Insight) are now Sotāpannas, Stream-Winners. They are not liable to fall into realms of misery and suffering and are assured of a good destination and of attaining (the three higher levels of Insight, culminating in) Enlightenment.

Thus spoke the Bhagavā. Delighted, the bhikkhus rejoiced in what the Bhagavā had said.

End of the Nandakovāda Sutta,
the fourth in this vagga.

6. CHACHAKKA SUTTA

Discourse on Six Groups of Six

420. Thus have I heard:

Once the Bhagavā was staying at the Jetavana monastery of Anāthapiṇḍika in Sāvatthī. On that occasion the Bhagavā addressed the bhikkhus, saying: "Bhikkhus!" The bhikkhus replied to the Bhagavā: "Venerable Sir!" The Bhagavā spoke thus: "Bhikkhus, I am going to expound to you the dhamma which is excellent in the beginning, excellent in the middle and excellent in the end, which is complete in meaning and phrasing. I shall set out the Noble Life of Purity which is utterly perfect and pure. I shall give you a discourse on the Six Groups of Six. Listen and pay good attention. I shall speak." "Very well, Venerable Sir," replied the bhikkhus to the Bhagavā. The Bhagavā then spoke these words:

The six internal sense-bases should be understood.[1] The six external sense-bases should be understood. The six kinds of consciousness should be understood. The six kinds of Contact should be understood. The six kinds of Sensation should be understood. The six kinds of Craving should be understood.

421. It has been said, 'The six internal sense--bases should be understood.' With reference to what has this been said? There are these sense-bases: the eye, the ear, the nose, the tongue, the body and the mind. With reference to these, it has been said 'The six internal sense-bases should be understood.' This is the first Group of Six. (1)

---

1. 'should be understood' means should be understood with vipassanā and Magga Insight.

It has been said 'The six external sense-bases should be understood.' With reference to what has this been said? There are these sense-bases: visible object, sound, odour, taste, tangible object and mind-object. With reference to these, it has been said, 'The six external sense-bases should be understood.' This is the second Group of Six. (2)

It has been said, 'The six kinds of consciousness should be understood.' With reference to what has this been said? Dependent on eye and visible object, eye--consciousness arises. Dependent on ear and sound, ear-consciousness arises. Dependent on nose and odour, nose-consciousness arises. Dependent on tongue and taste, tongue-consciousness arises. Dependent on body and tangible object, body-consciousness arises. Dependent on mind and mind-object, mind-consciousness arises. With reference to these, it has been said, 'The six kinds of consciousness should be understood.' This is the third Group of Six. (3)

It has been said, 'The six kinds of Contact should be understood.' With reference to what has this been said? Dependent on eye and visible object, eye--consciousness arises. The coming together of these three is Contact. Dependent on ear and sound, ear--consciousness arises. The coming together of these three is Contact. Dependent on nose and odour, nose--consciousness arises. The coming together of these three is Contact. Dependent on tongue and taste, tongue-consciousness arises. The coming together of these three is Contact. Dependent on body and tangible object, body-consciousness arises. The coming together of these three is Contact. Dependent on mind and mind-object, mind-consciousness arises. The coming together of these three is Contact. With reference to these, it has been said, 'The six kinds of Contact should be understood.' This is the fourth Group of Six. (4)

It has been said, 'The six kinds of Sensation should be understood.' With reference to what has this been said? Dependent on eye and visible object, eye--consciousness arises. The coming together of these three is Contact. Dependent on Contact, Sensation arises. Dependent on ear and sound, ear-consciousness arises. The coming together of these three is Contact.

Dependent on Contact, Sensation arises. Dependent on nose and odour, nose-consciousness arises. The coming together of these three is Contact. Dependent on Contact, Sensation arises. Dependent on tongue and taste, tongue-consciousness arises. The coming together of these three is Contact. Dependent on Contact, Sensation arises. Dependent on body and tangible object, body-consciousness arises. The coming together of these three is Contact. Dependent on Contact, Sensation arises. Dependent on mind and mind-object, mind-consciousness arises. The coming together of these three is Contact. Dependent on Contact, Sensation arises. With reference to these, it has been said, 'The six kinds of Sensation should be understood.' This is the fifth Group of Six. (5)

It has been said, 'The six kinds of Craving should be understood.' With reference to what has this been said? Dependent on eye and visible object, eye--consciousness arises. The coming together of these three is Contact. Dependent on Contact, Sensation arises; dependent on Sensation, Craving arises. Dependent on ear and sound, ear-consciousness arises. ...p... Dependent on nose and odour, nose-consciousness arises ...p... Dependent on tongue and taste, tongue--consciousness arises ...p... Dependent on body and tangible object, body-consciousness arises ...p... Dependent on mind and mind-object, mind-consciousness arises. The coming together of these three is Contact. Dependent on Contact, Sensation arises; dependent on Sensation, Craving arises. With reference to these, it has been said, 'The six kinds of Craving should be understood.' This is the Sixth Group of Six. (6)

422. If someone were to say, 'The eye is Self (atta)', that statement would be improper. The arising and disintegrating of the eye is evident. The arising and disintegrating of a certain phenomenon is evident. If that phenomenon is said to be Self (atta), it would amount to saying, 'My Self both arises and disintegrates. Therefore, if someone were to say 'The eye is Self', that statement would be improper. Thus, the eye is non-Self.

If someone were to say, 'Visible object is Self', that statement would be improper. The arising and disintegrating of visible object is evident. The arising and disintegrating of a certain phenomenon is evident. If that phenomenon is said to be Self, it would amount to saying, 'My Self both arises and disintegrates'. Therefore, if someone were to say, 'Visible object is Self', that statement would be improper. Thus the eye is non-Self; visible object is non-Self.

If someone were to say, 'Eye-consciousness is Self', that statement would be improper. The arising and disintegrating of eye-consciousness is evident. The arising and disintegrating of a certain phenomenon is evident. If that phenomenon is said to be Self, it would amount to saying, 'My Self both arises and disintegrates Therefore, if someone were to say, 'Eye-consciousness is Self', that statement would be improper. Thus the eye is non-Self; visible object is non-Self; eye--consciousness is non-Self.

If someone were to say, 'Eye-contact is Self', that statement would be improper. The arising and disintegrating of eye-contact is evident. The arising and disintegrating of a certain phenomenon is evident. If that phenomenon is said to be Self, it would amount to saying, 'My Self both arises and disintegrates.' Therefore, if someone were to say, 'Eye-contact is Self', that statement would be improper. Thus the eye is non-Self; the visible object is non-Self; eye-consciousness is non-Self; eye-contact is non-Self.

If someone were to say, 'Sensation is Self', that statement would be improper. The arising and disintegrating of sensation is evident. The arising and disintegrating of a certain phenomenon is evident. If that phenomenon is said to be Self, it would amount to saying, 'My Self both arises and disintegrates.' Therefore, if someone were to say, 'Sensation is Self', that statement would be improper. Thus the eye is non-Self; visible object is non-Self; eye-consciousness is non-Self; eye-contact is non-Self; sensation is non-Self.

If someone were to say, 'Craving is Self', that statement would be improper. The arising and disintegrating of Craving is evident. The arising and disintegrating of a certain phenomenon is evident. If that phenomenon is said to be Self, it would amount to saying, 'My Self both arises and disintegrates.' Therefore, if someone were to say, 'Craving is Self', that statement would be improper. Thus the eye is non-Self; visible object is non-Self; eye-consciousness is non-Self; eye-contact is non-Self; sensation is non-Self; Craving is non-Self.

423. If someone were to say, 'The ear is Self' ...p... If someone were to say, 'The nose is Self', ...p... If someone were to say, 'The tongue is Self', ...p... If someone were to say, 'The body is Self', ...p... if someone were to say, 'The mind is Self', that statement would be improper. The arising and disintegrating of mind is evident. The arising and disintegrating of a certain phenomenon is evident. If that phenomenon is said to be Self, it would amount to saying, 'My Self both arises and disintegrates.' Therefore, if someone were to say, 'The mind is Self', that statement would be improper. Thus the mind is non-Self.

If someone were to say, 'mind-object is Self', that statement would be improper. The arising and disintegrating of mind-object is evident. The arising and disintegrating of a certain phenomenon is evident. If that phenomenon is said to be Self, it would amount to saying, 'My Self both arises and disintegrates.' Therefore if someone were to say, 'Mind-object is Self,' that statement would be improper. Thus the mind is non-Self; mind-object is non-Self.

If someone were to say, 'Mind-consciousness is Self,' that statement would be improper. The arising and disintegrating of mind-consciousness is evident. The arising and disintegrating of a certain phenomenon is evident. If that phenomenon is said to be Self, it would amount to saying, 'My Self both arises and disintegrates. Therefore, if someone were to say, 'Mind-consciousness is Self,' that statement would be improper. Thus the mind is non-Self; mind-object is non-Self; mind-consciousness is non-Self.

If someone were to say, 'Mind-contact is Self,' that statement would be improper. The arising and disintegrating of mind-contact is evident. The arising and disintegrating of a certain phenomenon is evident. If that phenomenon is said to be Self, it would amount to saying, 'My Self both arises and disintegrates.'

Therefore, if someone were to say, 'Mind-contact is Self,' that statement would be improper. Thus the mind is non-Self; mind-object is non-Self; mind-consciousness is non-Self; mind-contact is non-Self.

If someone were to say, 'Sensation is Self', that statement would be improper. The arising and disintegrating of sensation is evident. The arising and disintegrating of a certain phenomenon is evident. If that phenomenon is said to be Self, it would amount to saying, 'My Self both arises and disintegrates.' Therefore, if someone were to say, 'Sensation is Self,' that statement would be improper. Thus the mind is non-Self, mind-object is non-Self; mind-consciousness is non-Self; mind-contact is non-Self; sensation is non-Self.

If someone were to say, 'Craving is self,' that statement would be improper. The arising and disintegrating of Craving is evident. The arising and disintegrating of a certain phenomenon is evident. If that phenomenon is said to be Self, it would amount to saying, 'My Self both arises and disintegrates.' Therefore, if someone were to say, 'Craving is Self,' that statement would be improper. Thus the mind is non-Self; mind-object is non-Self; mind-consciousness is non-Self; mind-contact is non-Self; sensation is non-Self; craving is non-Self.

424. Bhikkhus, this is the Path leading to the arising of *sakkāyadiṭṭhi*, the illusion of Self -- Eye is considered as: 'This is mine; this is I; this is my Self (atta).' Visible object is considered as: 'This is mine; this is I; this is my Self.' Eye-consciousness is considered as: 'This is mine; this is I; this is my Self.' Eye-contact is considered as: 'This is mine; 'this is I; this is my Self'. Sensation is considered as: 'This is mine; this is I; this is my Self.' Craving is considered as: 'This is mine; this is I; this is my Self.' Ear is considered as: 'This is mine; this is I; this is my Self.' ...p... Nose is considered as: ' This is mine; this is I; this is my Self.' ..p... Tongue is considered as: 'This is mine; this is I; this is my Self.' ...p... Body is considered as: 'This is mine; this is I; this is my Self.' Mind is considered as: 'This is mine; this is I; this is my Self.' Mind-object is considered as: 'This is mine;

this is I; this is my Self.' Mind-consciousness is considered as: 'This is mine; this is I; this is my Self.' Mind-contact is considered as: 'This is mine; this is I; this is my Self.' Sensation is considered as: 'This is mine; this is I; this is my Self.' Craving is considered as: 'This is mine; this is I; this is my Self.'

Bhikkhus, this is the Path leading to the cessation of *sakkāyadiṭṭhi*, the illusion of Self -- The eye is considered as: 'This is not mine; this is not I; this is not my Self (atta).' Visible object is considered as: 'This is not mine; this is not I; this is not my Self.' Eye-consciousness is considered as: 'This is not mine; this is not I; this is not my Self.' Eye-contact is considered as: 'This is not mine; this is not I; this is not my Self.' Sensation is considered as: 'This is not mine; this is not I; this is not my Self.' Craving is considered as: 'This is not mine; this is not I; this is not my Self.' The ear is considered as: 'This is not mine; this is not I; this is not my Self.' ...p... The nose is considered as: 'This is not mine; this is not I; this is not my Self.' ...p... The tongue is considered as: 'This is not mine; this is not I; this is not my Self.' ...p... The body is considered as: 'This is not mine; this is not I; this is not my Self.' The mind is considered as: 'This is not mine; this is not I; this is not my Self.' Mind-object is considered as: 'This is not mine; this is not I; this is not my Self.' Mind--consciousness is considered as: 'This is not mine; this is not I: this is not my Self.' Mind-contact is considered as: 'This is not mine; this is not I; this is not my Self.' Sensation is considered as: 'This is not mine; this is not I; this is not my Self.' Craving is considered as: 'This is not mine; this is not I; this is not my Self.'

425. Bhikkhus, dependent on eye and visible object, eye-consciousness arises: The coming together of these three is contact. Dependent on contact, pleasant sensation, or unpleasant sensation, or a sensation that is neither pleasant nor unpleasant arises (in one). When experiencing a pleasant sensation, that person revels in that sensation, speaks about it with joy and gets absorbed in it. Latent attachment (rāgānusaya) lies dormant in him. When experienceing an unpleasant sensation, that person grieves, mourns,

laments, beats his breast, weeps and becomes bewildered. Latent animosity (paṭighānusaya) lies dormant in him. When experiencing a sensation that is neither pleasant nor unpleasant, that person does not understand fundamentally and truly the origin of that sensation, its cessation, its pleasantness, its faults and the (way of) escape from attachment to it. Latent ignorance (avijjānusaya) lies dormant in him. Bhikkhus, indeed there is no reason or possibility for that person to make an end of the cycle of dukkha in this very life, without getting rid of latent attachment regarding pleasant sensation, without stamping out latent animosity regarding unpleasant sensation, without uprooting latent ignorance regarding sensation that is neither pleasant nor unpleasant, without getting rid of ignorance (avijjā) and without letting knowledge (vijjā) arise.

Bhikkhus, dependent on ear and sound, ear-consciousness arises ...p... Bhikkhus, dependent on nose and odour, nose-consciousness arises ...p... Bhikkhus, dependent on tongue and taste, tongue-consciousness arises ...p... Bhikkhus, dependent on body and tangible object, body-consciousness arises ...p... Bhikkhus, dependent on mind and mind-object, mind-consciousness arises. The coming together of these three is Contact. Dependent on Contact, pleasant sensation, or unpleasant sensation, or a sensation that is neither pleasant nor unpleasant arises (in one). When experiencing a pleasant sensation, that person revels in that sensation, speaks about it with joy and gets absorbed in it. Latent attachment lies dormant in him. When experiencing unpleasant sensation, that person grieves, mourns, laments, beats his breast and becomes bewildered. Latent animosity lies dormant in him. When experiencing a sensation that is neither pleasant nor unpleasant, he does not understand fundamentally and truly the origin of that sensation, its cessation, its pleasantness, its faults and the (way of) escape from attachment to it. Latent ignorance lies dormant in him. Bhikkhus, indeed there is no reason or possibility for that person to make an end of the cycle of dukkha in this very life, without getting rid of latent attachment regarding pleasant sensation, without stamping out latent animosity regarding unpleasant sensation, without uprooting latent ignorance regarding sensation that is neither pleasant nor unpleasant, without getting rid of ignorance and without letting knowledge arise.

426. Bhikkhus, dependent on eye and visible object, eye-consciousness arises. The coming together of these three is Contact. Dependent on Contact, pleasant sensation, or unpleasant sensation, or a sensation that is neither pleasant nor unpleasant arises (in one). When experiencing a pleasant sensation, that person does not revel in that sensation, does not speak about it with joy and does not get absorbed in it. Latent attachment does not lie dormant in him. When experiencing an unpleasant sensation, that person does not grieve, does not mourn, does not lament, does not beat his breast, does not weep and does not become bewildered. Latent animosity does not lie dormant in him. When experiencing a sensation that is neither pleasant nor unpleasant, he understands fundamentally and truly the origin of that sensation, its cessation, its pleasantness, its faults and the (way of) escape from attachment to it. Latent ignorance does not lie dormant in him. Bhikkhus, indeed there is the possibility for that person to make an end of the cycle of dukkha in this very life, by getting rid of latent attachment regarding pleasant sensation, by stamping out latent animosity regarding unpleasant sensation, by uprooting latent ignorance regarding sensation that is neither pleasant nor unpleasant, by getting rid of ignorance and by letting knowledge arise.

Bhikkhus, dependent on ear and sound, ear--consciousness arises ...p... Bhikkhus, dependent on nose and odour, nose-consciousness arises...p... Bhikkhus, dependent on tongue and taste, tongue-consciousness arises ...p... Bhikkhus, dependent on body and tangible object, body-consciousness arises ...p... Bhikkhus, dependent on mind and mind-object, mind-consciousness arises. The coming together of these three is Contact. Dependent on Contact, pleasant sensation or unpleasant sensation, or a sensation that is neither pleasant nor unpleasant arises (in one). When experiencing a pleasant sensation, that person does not revel in that sensation, does not speak about it with joy and does not get absorbed in it. Latent attachment does not lie dormant in him. When experiencing an unpleasant sensation, that person does not grieve, does not mourn, does not lament, does not beat his breast, does not weep and does not become bewildered. Latent animosity does not lie dormant in him. When experiencing a sensation that is neither pleasant nor unpleasant, he understands fundamentally and truly the origin of that sensation, its cessation, its pleasantness, its faults and the (way of) escape from attachment to it. Latent ignorance does not lie dormant in him. Bhikkhus, indeed, there is the possibility for that person to make an end of the cycle of dukkha in this very life, by getting rid of latent attachment regarding pleasant sensation, by stamping out latent animosity regarding unpleasant sensation, by uprooting latent ignorance regarding sensation that is neither pleasant nor unpleasant, by getting rid of ignorance and by letting knowledge arise.

427. Bhikkhus, the instructed ariya disciple who sees thus gets disgusted with the eye, gets disgusted with visible object, gets disgusted with eye-consciousness, gets disgusted with eye-contact, gets disgusted with sensation and gets disgusted with craving. He gets disgusted with the ear, gets disgusted with sound ...p... He gets disgusted with the nose, gets disgusted with odour...p... He gets disgusted with the tongue, gets disgusted with taste ...p... He gets disgusted with the body, gets disgusted with tangible object ...p... He gets disgusted with the mind, gets disgusted with mind--object, gets disgusted with mind-consciousness, gets disgusted with mind-contact, gets disgusted with sensation and gets disgusted with craving. On being disgusted (thus), he is free from attachment. On being free from attachment, he is liberated. On being liberated, knowledge of liberation arises. He knows clearly: 'Rebirth is no more; fulfilled is the Noble Practice of Purity; done is all there is to be done (to realize magga); there is nothing more to do (for such realization).'

Thus spoke the Bhagavā; and those bhikkhus, delighted, rejoiced in the words of the Bhagavā. When this plain discourse (without verses) was delivered, the minds of sixty bhikkhus were freed from attachment to any object and were liberated from āsavas.

End of the Chachakka Sutta,
the sixth in this vagga.

7. MAHĀSAḶĀYATANIKA SUTTA

Discourse Based on the All-encompassing Six Sense-bases

428. Thus have I heard:

Once the Bhagavā was staying at the Jetavana monastery of Anāthapiṇḍika in Sāvatthī. At that time the Bhagavā addressed the bhikkhus saying: "Bhikkhus!" The bhikkhus replied to the Bhagavā: "Venerable Sir!" The Bhagavā spoke thus: "Bhikkhus, I am going to give a discourse based on the all-encompassing six sense--bases. Listen and pay good attention. I shall speak." "Very well, Venerable Sir," replied the bhikkhus to the Bhagavā. The Bhagavā then spoke these words:

429. Bhikkhus, not knowing and not seeing the eye as it really is, not knowing and not seeing visible object as it really is, not knowing and not seeing eye--consciousness as it really is, not knowing and not seeing eye-contact as it really is, and not knowing and not seeing, as it really is, the pleasant sensation or the unpleasant sensation or the sensation that is neither pleasant nor unpleasant, which arises dependent on eye--contact, one has strong attachment for the eye, strong attachment for visible object, strong attachment for eye-consciousness, strong attachment for eye-contact and strong attachment for the pleasant sensation or for the unpleasant sensation or for the sensation that is neither pleasant nor unpleasant, which arises dependent on eye-contact.

In the person who is strongly attached to them, who is tied to them, who is overwhelmed by bewilderment and who sees them as being pleasant, there will be in the future recurience of the five aggregates which are the objects of Clinging. In him who has Craving which gives rise to fresh rebirth, which is accompanied by pleasure and attachment, which finds great delight in this or that sense-object or existence, there is the increase of that Craving. In him there is also increase of physical distress and increase of mental distress, increase of physical torment and increase of mental torment, increase of physical torture and increase of mental torture. That person experiences physical suffering and mental suffering.

Bhikkhus, not knowing and not seeing the ear as it really is, ...p... Bhikkhus, not knowing and not seeing the nose as it really is, ...p... Bhikkhus, not knowing and not seeing the tongue as it really is, ...p... Bhikkhus, not knowing and not seeing the body as it really is ...p... Bhikkhus, not knowing and not seeing the mind as it really is, not knowing and not seeing mind-object as it really is, not knowing and not seeing mind-consciousness as it really is, not knowing and not seeing mind-contact as it really is, and not knowing and not seeing, as it really is, the pleasant sensation or the unpleasant sensation or the sensation that is neither pleasant nor unpleasant, which arises dependent on mind-contact, one has strong attachment for the mind, strong attachment for mind-objects, strong attachment for mind-consciousness, strong attachment for mind-contact and strong attachment for the pleasant sensation or the unpleasant sensation or the sensation that is neither pleasant nor unpleasant, which arises dependent on mind-contact.

In the person who is strongly attached to them, who is tied to them, who is overwhelmed by bewilderment and who sees them as being pleasant, there will be in the future recurrence of the five aggregates which are the objects of Clinging. In him who has Craving which gives rise to fresh rebirth, which is accompanied by pleasure and attachment, which finds great delight in this or that sense-object or existence, there is the increase of that Craving. In him there is the increase of physical distress and increase of mental distress, the increase of physical torment and increase of mental torment, the increase of physical torture and increase of mental torture. That person experiences physical suffering and mental suffering.

430. Bhikkhus, knowing and seeing the eye as it really is, knowing and seeing visible object as it really is, knowing and seeing eye-consciousness as it really is, knowing and seeing eye-contact as it really is, and knowing and seeing, as it really is, the pleasant sensation or the unpleasant sensation or the sensation that is neither pleasant nor unpleasant, which arises dependent on eye-contact, one has no attachment for the eye, no attachment for visible object, no attachment for eye-consciousness, no attachment for eye-contact and no attachment for the pleasant sensation or the unpleasant sensation or the sensation that is neither pleasant nor unpleasant, which arises dependent on eye-contact.

In the person who is not attached to them, who is not tied to them, who is not overwhelmed by bewilderment and who sees them as being full of faults, there will be in the future no recurrence of the five aggregates which are the objects of Clinging. In him who has no Craving which gives rise to fresh rebirth, which is accompanied by pleasure and attachment, which finds great delight in this or that sense-object or existence, there is the disappearance of that Craving. In him there is disappearance of physical distress and disappearance of mental distress, disappearance of physical torment and disappearance of mental torment, disappearance of physical torture and disappearance of mental torture. That person experiences physical comfort and mental ease.

431. The view of such a person is Right View. The thinking of such a person is Right Thinking. The effort of such a person is Right Effort. The mindfulness of such a person is Right Mindfulness. The concentration of such a person is Right Concentration. That person's bodily action, verbal action and his way of living have been pure from the beginning. Thus, the cultivation of the Ariya Path of Eight Constituents of that person is completed.

In him, who has thus cultivated Ariya Path of Eight Constituents, cultivation of the Four Methods of Steadfast Mindfulness (satipaṭṭhāna) is also completed, cultivation of the Four Supreme Efforts(sammappadhāna) is also completed, cultivation of the Four Bases of

Psychic Potency (iddhipāda) is also completed, cultivation of the Five Faculties (indriya) is also completed, cultivation of the Five Powers (bala) is also completed and cultivation of the Seven Factors of Enlightenment (bojjhaṅga) is also completed.

In such a person the two factors of Concentration and vipassanā Insight jointly occur. He knows accurately through Magga Insight (abhiññā) the factors that should be known accurately through Magga Insight (abhiññā). He abandons through Magga Insight the factors that should be abandoned through Magga Insight. He cultivates through Magga Insight the factors that should be cultivated through Magga Insight. He realizes through Magga Insight the factors that should be realized through Magga Insight.

Bhikkhus, what are the factors that should be known accurately through Magga Insight? They are said to be the five aggregates which are the objects of Clinging. They are: the aggregate of corporeality which is the object of Clinging, the aggregate of sensation which is the object of Clinging, the aggregate of perception which is the object of Clinging, the aggregate of volitional activities which is the object of Clinging and the aggregate of consciousness which is the object of Clinging. These are the factors that should be known accurately through Magga Insight.

Bhikkhus, what are the factors that should be abandoned through Magga Insight? They are: ignorance (avijjā) and Craving for existence (bhavataṇhā). They are the factors that should be abandoned through Magga Insight.

Bhikkhus, what are the factors that should be cultivated through Magga Insight? They are: concentration and Vipassanā Insight. These are the factors that should be cultivated through Magga Insight.

Bhikkhus, what are the factors that should be realized through Magga Insight (abhiññā)? They are: Arahatta Magga (vijjā)[1] and Arahatta Fruition (vimutti).

---

1. Arahatta Magga (vijjā): realizing Magga Insight through Magga Insight means knowing through Magga Insight the mind and the mental concomitants which are associated with Magga Insight.

These are the factors that should be realized through Magga Insight.

432. Bhikkhus, knowing and seeing the ear as it really is ...p... Bhikkhus, knowing and seeing the nose as it really is ...p... Bhikkhus, knowing and seeing the tongue as it really is ...p... Bhikkhus, knowing and seeing the body as it really is ...p... Bhikkhus, knowing and seeing the mind as it really is, and knowing and seeing mind-object as it really is, knowing and seeing mind-consciousness as it really is, knowing and seeing mind-contact as it really is and knowing and seeing, as it really is, the pleasant sensation, or the unpleasant sensation, or the sensation that is neither pleasant nor unpleasant, which arises dependent on mind-contact, one has no attachment for the mind, no attachment for mind-object, no attachment for mind-consciousness, no attachment for mind-contact and no attachment for pleasant sensation or for unpleasant sensation or for sensation that is neither pleasant nor unpleasant, which arises dependent on mind-contact.

In the person who is not attached to them, who is not tied to them, who is not overwhelmed by bewilderment and who sees them as being full of faults, there will be in the future no recurrence of the five aggregates which are the objects of Clinging. In him who has no Craving which gives rise to fresh rebirth, which is accompanied by pleasure and attachment, which finds great delight in this or that sense-object or existence, there is the disappearance of that Craving. In him there is disappearance of physical distress and disappearance of mental distress, disappearance of physical torment and disappearance of mental torment, disappearance of physical torture and disappearance of mental torture. That person experiences physical comfort and mental ease.

433. The view of such a person is Right View. The thinking of such a person is Right Thinking. The effort of such a person is Right Effort. The mindfulness of such a person is Right Mindfulness. The concentration of such a person is Right Concentration. That person's bodily action and verbal action and his way of living have been pure from the beginning. Thus

the cultivation of the Ariya Path of Eight Constituents of that person is completed.

In him, who has thus cultivated the Ariya Path of Eight Constituents, cultivation of the Four Methods of Steadfast Mindfulness is also completed, cultivation of the Four Supreme Efforts is also completed, cultivation of the Four Bases of Psychic Potency is also completed, cultivation of the Five Faculties is also completed, cultivation of the Five Powers is also completed and cultivation of the Seven Factors of Enlightenment is also completed.

In such a person the two factors of concentration and vipassanā Insight jointly occur. He knows accurately through Magga Insight (abhiññā) the factors that should be known accurately through Magga Insight. He abandons through Magga Insight the factors that should be abandoned through Magga Insight. He cultivates through Magga Insight the factors that should be cultivated through Magga Insight. He realizes through Magga Insight the factors that should be realized through Magga Insight.

Bhikkhus, what are the factors that should be known accurately through Magga Insight? They are said to be the five aggregates which are the objects of Clinging. They are the aggregate of corporeality which is the object of Clinging, the aggregate of sensation which is the object of Clinging, the aggregate of perception which is the object of Clinging, the aggregate of volitional activities which is the object of Clinging and the aggregate of Consciousness which is the object of Clinging. These are the factors that should be known accurately through Magga Insight.

Bhikkhus, what are the factors that should be abandoned through Magga Insight? They are: ignorance (avijjā) and craving for existence (bhavataṇhā). These are the factors that should be abandoned through Magga Insight.

Bhikkhus, what are the factors that should be cultivated through Magga Insight? They are: concentration and Vipassanā Insight. These are the factors that should be cultivated through Magga Insight.

Bhikkhus, what are the factors that should be realized through Magga Insight? They are: Arahatta Magga (vijjā) and Arahatta Fruition (vimutti). These are the factors that should be realized through Magga Insight.

Thus spoke Bhagavā; those bhikkhus, delighted, rejoiced at what the Bhagavā had said.

End of the Mahāsaḷāyatanika Sutta, the seventh in this vagga.

10. INDRIYABHĀVANĀ SUTTA

Discourse on Cultivation of the Faculties

453. Thus have I heard:

Once the Bhagavā was staying in the Suveḷu Grove near Gajaṅgalā market-town. At that time young Uttara, a pupil of the brahmin Pārāsiviya came to the Bhagavā and exchanged greetings with him. Bringing to an end the courteous and amiable greetings, he sat at a suitable place. The Bhagavā then said to young Uttara, pupil of the brahmin Pārāsiviya thus: "Uttara, does the brahmin Pārāsiviya teach his pupils the cultivation of the faculties?" "O Gotama, the brahmin Pārāsiviya teaches the cultivation of the faculties to his pupils." "Uttara, how does the brahmin Pārāsiviya teach the cultivation of the faculties to his pupils?" "O Gotama, in this world, a visible object should not be looked at with the eye. A sound should not be listened to with the ear. O Gotama, thus does the brahmin Pārāsiviya teach the cultivation of the faculties to his pupils." "Uttara, if that be so, according to the words of the brahmin Pārāsiviya, one who is blind must have cultivated the faculties, one who is deaf must have cultivated the faculties. Uttara, indeed one who is blind does not see a visible object with the eye; one who is deaf does not hear a sound with the ear." On this being said, young Uttara, pupil of the brahmin Pārāsiviya, sat silent, confused, with drooping shoulders and bent head, downcast and incapable of making an answer.

Then the Bhagavā realizing that young Uttara, pupil of the brahmin Pārāsiviya, had become silent, confused, with drooping shoulders and bent head, downcast and incapable of making an answer, said to the Venerable Ānanda, "Ānanda, the brahmin Pārāsiviya teaches his pupils the cultivation of the faculties in one way. Ānanda, in the Teaching of the ariyas the incomparable cultivation of the faculties is quite different." "Bhagavā, this is the time for you to teach. Sugata, this is the time for you to teach. If the Bhagavā would expound on the incomparable cultivation of the faculties, the bhikkhus, hearing it from the Bhagavā, will bear it in mind." "If that be so, Ānanda listen and pay good attention. I shall speak." "Very well Venerable Sir," replied the Venerable Ānanda to the Bhagavā. And the Bhagavā said this:

454. Ānanda, how is the incomparable cultivation of the faculties taught in the Teaching of the ariyas? Ānanda, in this Teaching, in the bhikkhu who sees a visible object with the eye, pleasure arises or displeasure arises or neither-pleasure-nor-displeasure arises. That bhikkhu knows thus: 'Indeed, in me this pleasure has arisen, this displeasure has arisen, this neither--pleasure-nor-displeasure has arisen. In fact, this (pleasure or displeasure or neither-pleasure-nor-displeasure) is conditioned, gross and causally produced. The equanimity of vipassanā insight is serene and sublime.' In that bhikkhu who knows thus, the pleasure that has arisen or the displeasure that has arisen or the neither-pleasure-nor-displeasure that has arisen ceases; but the equanimity of vipassanā insight remains firm. For example, Ānanda, just as a man with good eyes opens his closed eyes or closes his open eyes, so also, Ānanda, the pleasure that has arisen or the displeasure that has arisen or the neither-pleasure-nor--displeasure that has arisen ceases in him with similar speed, with similar swiftness, with similar ease; but the equanimity of vipassanā insight remains firm. Ānanda, in the Teaching of the ariyas this is said to be the incomparable cultivation of the faculties with regard to visibble object cognizable by eye-consciousness.

455. And again, Ānanda, in the bhikkhu who hears a sound with the ear, pleasure arises or displeasure arises or neither-pleasure-nor-displeasure arises. That bhikkhu knows thus: 'Indeed, in me this pleasure has arisen, this displeasure has arisen, this neither--pleasure-nor-displeasure has arisen. In fact, this (pleasure, or displeasure, or neither-pleasure-nor--displeasure) is conditioned, gross and causally produced.

The equanimity of vipassanā insight is serene and sublime.' In that bhikkhu who knows thus, the pleasure that has arisen or the displeasure that has arisen or the neither-pleasure-nor-displeasure that has arisen ceases; and the equanimity of vipassanā insight remains firm. For example, Ānanda, just as a strong man flicks his fingers effortlessly, so also, Ānanda, the pleasure that has arisen or the displeasure that has arisen or the neither-pleasure-nor-displeasure that has arisen ceases in him with similar speed, with similar swiftness, with similar ease; but the equanimity of vipassanā insight remains firm. Ānanda, in the Teaching of the ariyas this is said to be the incomparable cultivation of the faculties with regard to sound cognizable by ear--consciousness.

456. And again, Ānanda, in the bhikkhu who smells an odour with the nose, pleasure arises or displeasure arises or neither-pleasure-nor-displeasure arises. That bhikkhu knows thus: 'Indeed, in me this pleasure has arisen, this displeasure has arisen, this neither-pleasure-nor-displeasure has arisen. In fact, this (pleasure, or displeasure, or neither-pleasure-nor--displeasure) is conditioned, g.oss and causally produced. The equanimity of vipassanā insight is serene and sublime.' In that bhikkhu who knows thus, the pleasure that has arisen or the displeasure that has arisen or the neither-pleasure-nor-displeasure that has arisen ceases; but the equanimity of vipassanā insight remains firm. For example, Ānanda, just as drops of water falling from a lotus leaf that is slightly inclined cannot remain on it, so also, Ānanda, the pleasure that has arisen or the displeasure that has arisen or the neither-pleasure-nor-displeasure that has arisen ceases in him with similar speed, with similar swiftness, with similar ease; but the equanimity of vipassanā insight remains firm. Ānanda, in the Teaching of the ariyas this is said to be the incomparable cultivation of the faculties with regard to odour cognizable by nose--consciousness.

457. And again, Ānanda, in the bhikkhu who tastes a flavour with the tongue, pleasure arises or displeasure arises or neither-pleasure-nor-displeasure arises. That bhikkhu knows thus: 'Indeed, in me this

pleasure has arisen, this displeasure has arisen, this neither-pleasure-nor-displeasure has arisen. In fact, this (pleasure, or displeasure, or neither-pleasure-nor--displeasure) is conditioned, gross and causally produced. The equanimity of vipassanā insight is serene and sublime.' In that bhikkhu who knows thus, the pleasure that has arisen or the displeasure that has arisen or the neither-pleasure-nor-displeasure that has arisen ceases; but the equanimity of vipassanā insight remains frim. For example, Ānanda, just as a strong man collects saliva on the tip of his tongue and spits out effortlessly, so also, Ānanda, the pleasure that has arisen or the displeasure that has arisen or the neither--pleasure-nor-displeasure that has arisen ceases in him with similar speed, with similar swiftness, with similar ease; but the equanimity of vipassanā insight remains firm. Ānanda, in the Teaching of the ariyas this is said to be the incomparable cultivation of the faculties with regard to flavour cognizable by tongue--consciousness.

458. And again, Ānanda, in the bhikkhu who contacts a tangible object with the body, pleasure arises or displeasure arises or neither-pleasure-nor--displeasure arises. That bhikkhu knows thus: 'Indeed, in me this pleasure has arisen, this displeasure has arisen, this neither-pleasure-nor-displeasure has arisen. In fact, this (pleasure, or displeasure or neither--pleasure-nor-displeasure) is conditioned, gross and causally produced. The equanimity of vipassanā insight is serene and sublime.' In that bhikkhu who knows thus, the pleasure that has arisen or the displeasure that has arisen or the neither-pleasure-nor-displeasure that has arisen ceases; but the equanimity of vipassanā insight remains firm. For example, Ānanda, just as a strong man stretches out his bent arm or bends his stretched arm, so also, Ānanda, the pleasure that has arisen or the displeasure that has arisen or the neither-pleasure--nor-displeasure that has arisen ceases in him with similar speed, with similar swiftness, with similar ease; but the equanimity of vipassanā insight remains firm. Ānanda, in the Teaching of the ariyas this is said to be the incomparable cultivation of the faculties with regard to tangible object cognizable by body--consciousness.

459. And again, Ānanda, in the bhikkhu who cognizes a mind-object with the mind, pleasure arises or displeasure arises or neither-pleasure-nor-displeasure arises. That bhikkhu knows thus: 'Indeed, in me this pleasure has arisen, this displeasure has arisen, this neither-pleasure-nor-displeasure has arisen. In fact, this (pleasure, or displeasure, or neither-pleasure-nor--displeasure) is conditioned, gross and causally produced. The equanimity of vipassanā insight is serene and sublime.' In that bhikkhu who knows thus, the pleasure that has arisen or the displeasure that has arisen or the neither-pleasure-nor-displeasure that has arisen ceases; but the equanimity of vipassanā insight remains firm. Suppose, Ānanda, a strong man lets fall two or three drops of water on a cauldron that has been heated the whole day. Ānanda, just as the evaporation and drying up of the drops of water is faster than their fall, so also, Ānanda, the pleasure that has arisen or the displeasure that has arisen or the neither--pleasure-nor-displeasure that has arisen ceases in him with similar speed, with similar swiftness, with similar ease; but the equanimity of vipassanā insight remains firm. Ānanda, in this Teaching of the ariyas this is said to be the incomparable cultivation of the faculties with regard to mind-objects cognizable by mind-consciousness.

460. Ānanda, what is the practice of a *sekha*[1] (one still training himself)? In this Teaching, Ānanda, in the bhikkhu who sees visible object with the eye, pleasure arises or displeasure arises or neither-pleasure--nor-displeasure arises. That bhikkhu is weary of, ashamed of, and is disgusted with the pleasure that has arisen or the displeasure that has arisen or the neither--pleasure-nor-displeasure that has arisen. In the bhikkhu who hears a sound with the ear ...p... In the bhikkhu who smells an odour with the nose ...p... In the bhikkhu who tastes a flavour with the tongue ...p... In the bhikkhu who contacts a tangible object with the body ...p... In the bhikkhu who cognizes a mind-object with the mind, pleasure arises or displeasure arises or neither-

1. *sekha*: one who is still in the process of practising the Teaching, not yet having attained Arahatta Fruition.

-pleasure-nor-displeasure arises. That bhikkhu is weary of, ashamed of, and disgusted with the pleasure that has arisen or the displeasure that has arisen or the neither-pleasure-nor-displeasure that has arisen. Ānanda, this is the practice of a sekha.

461. Ānanda, what is the practice of an ariya who has completed the cultivation of the faculties? In this Teaching, Ānanda, in the bhikkhu who sees a visible object with the eye, pleasure arises or displeasure arises or neither-pleasure-nor-displeasure arises. If he wishes to consider what is repulsive as not repulsive, he can remain considering what is repulsive as not repulsive. If he wishes to consider what is not repulsive as repulsive, he can remain considering what is not repulsive as repulsive. If he wishes to consider what is either repulsive or not repulsive as not repulsive, he can remain considering what is either repulsive or not repulsive as not repulsive. If he wishes to consider what is either not repulsive or repulsive as repulsive, he can remain considering what is either not repulsive or repulsive as repulsive. If he wishes to remain in equanimity, not considering both what is repulsive and not repulsive, being mindful and clear in comprehension, he can remain in equanimity regarding them, being mindful and clear in comprehension.

462. Again, Ānanda, in the bhikkhu who hears a sound with the ear ...p... In the bhikkhu who smells an odour with the nose ...p... In the bhikkhu who tastes a flavour with the tongue ...p... In the bhikkhu who contacts a tangible object with the body ...p... In the bhikkhu who cognizes a mind-object with the mind, pleasure arises or displeasure arises or neither-pleasure--nor-displeasure arises. If he wishes to consider what is repulsive as not repulsive, he can remain considering what is repulsive as not repulsive. If he wishes to consider what is not repulsive as repulsive, he can remain considering what is not repulsive as repulsive. If he wishes to consider what is either repulsive or not repulsive as not repulsive, he can remain considering what is either repulsive or not repulsive as not repulsive. If he wishes to consider what is either not repulsive or repulsive as repulsive, he can remain considering what is either not repulsive or repulsive as repulsive. If he

wishes to remain in equanimity, not considering both what is repulsive and not repulsive, being mindful and clear in comprehension, he can remain in equanimity regarding them, being mindful and clear in comprehension. Ānanda, this is the practice of an ariya who has completed the cultivation of the faculties.

463. Ānanda, in this Teaching of the ariyas, this is how I teach regarding the incomparable cultivation of the faculties, how I teach regarding the practice of a sekha, and how I teach regarding an ariya who has completed the cultivation of the faculties. Ānanda, what a compassionate teacher, who has the welfare of his disciples at heart, should do out of compassion, that I have done for you. Ānanda, there are the places at the foot of trees. There are the secluded places. Ānanda, meditate! Do not be unmindful. Do not be remorseful later! This is our instruction to you all.

Thus spoke the Bhagavā. Delighted, the Venerable Ānanda rejoiced at what the Bhagavā had said.

End of the Indriyabhāvanā Sutta, the tenth in this vagga.

Namo tassa bhagavato arahato sammāsambuddhassa

Index

INDEX

Key to the figures in the Index

Vaggas, subdivisions in this book, are shown in small Roman figures.

Sutta numbers in each vagga are shown in Arabic figures.

Paragraph numbers are also shown in Arabic figures, with a colon after the sutta numbers. .

Footnotes, serially numbered for each sutta, are shown as fn. (Arabic numbering).

Example:

ii:7:140:fn(4) means vagga (ii), sutta 7 in that vagga, paragraph 140 in this Paṇṇāsa, and footnote number (4) for that sutta.

A